H40 562 877 9

'0

D

CE3

# Bubbles, Hammers & Dreams

# Bubbles, Hammers & Dreams

by Brian Belton

The Breedon Books
Publishing Company
Derby

First published in Great Britain by
The Breedon Books Publishing Company Limited
Breedon House, 44 Friar Gate, Derby, DE1 1DA.
1997

ISBN 1 85983 107 9

Printed and bound by Butler & Tanner Ltd., Selwood Printing Works, Caxton Road,
Frome, Somerset.

Colour separations by RPS Ltd, Leicester.

Jackets printing by Lawrence-Allen Colour Printers, Weston-super-Mare, Avon.

# Contents

of West Ham; June 1961: Rudolf Nureyev defects to the West; October 1962: Cuban Missile Crisis; August 1963: The Great Train Robbery; Martin Luther King, "I have a dream" speech; November 1963: US President Kennedy assassinated; April 1964: Bobby Moore voted youngest-ever Footballer of the Year; May 1964: West Ham win FA Cup for the first time; March 1965: Da Nang; May 1965: West Ham win the European Cup-winners' Cup. The first and last team of English players to win a European trophy; March 1966: West Ham reach the League Cup Final; July 1966: England win the World Cup.

## Dreams That Will Not Die 128

Vietnam. April 1975: Saigon falls to North Vietnamese; May 1975: West Ham win the FA Cup. The last team of English players to achieve this; May 1976: West Ham reach the European Cup-winners' Cup Final.

## Nothing To Do But Blow Bubbles 147

April 1978: West Ham relegated; May 1979: Margaret Thatcher becomes the first woman Prime Minister of Britain; 1980: Racism in football; May 1980: West Ham win the FA Cup.

## Heroes and Villains 168

1980: Monetarism, the 'free market' economy and crime; November 1980: Ronald Reagan becomes US President; March/April 1981: West Ham reach League Cup Final

## Relegation, Death and Football 183

April 1902: the Ibrox Disaster; March 1946: the Burden Park Disaster; January 1971: the second Ibrox Disaster; May 1985: the Valley Parade Fire. The Heysel Disaster; April 1989: Hillsborough; May 1989: West Ham relegated from Division One.

## Iron Bars 197

April 1990: Prison riots; West Ham reach the semi-finals of the League Cup.

## 100 years 209

1889: The Great Dock Strike; June 1895: Thames Iron Works formed; September 1895: First game; 1900: The Boer War; March 1911: 60-hour week; 1918: Foreign intervention into the Russian Revolution; February 1929: Vic Watson achieves record for individual goals scored in a single match; 1930: The Depression;
October 1968: Geoff Hurst equals record for individual goals scored in a single match; November 1968: West Ham's biggest-ever win; October 1983: Beirut suicide bombs

kill 500 US/French servicemen; February 1993: Bobby Moore dies; May 1993: West Ham promoted to the Premier League; 1995: Centenary Year.

## 2095 — They Fly So High
Solar System Cup; All 'stander' stadiums; Mixed gender teams; Super Squads (200 players); Two-hour week; Team shirts for every game; No more nations; Total kit sponsorship; Multi-sub system.

Excited and anxious, I await my dream,
To escape, applaud and  embrace my team,
Opening day I can always trust,
It's just for this high that I crazily lust,
Return of our hero does brighten the days,
Just briefly, my troubles get lost in the haze.
The grace from the field arouses the crowd,
Reflects on the days when I was quite proud,
I'm more entranced than the average fan,
I used to play you see, I know I still can,
That time when I drove the ball with such loft,
My exit atop shoulders as they carried me off.
This pass-time and I just fade into one,
Expanded upon from father and son,
My boy is young and awkward for now,
I just need the time and can show him how,
I really am quite close, just a break away,
From straightening things out and being okay.
I can help my team to regain its glory,
With just a little twist to the same old story,
Players say now that they play for themselves,
This causes a burning within me that dwells,
The fan is the one who pays for the game,
He bestows all the riches and welcome fame.
The players will listen, but really don't hear,
All the while hiding behind an invisible tear,
I grow tired now of all this greed,
 and chart a course to set things free.

From *The Fan*, directed by Tony Scott

# Foreword

## by Geoff Hurst MBE

I AM delighted to have been asked to contribute a Foreword to this excellent book on West Ham United.

These are dramatic times for the sport and while not wanting to dwell on the past, it is important sometimes to take time out, and look at the way things were.

Football clubs are changing fast, and sometimes the heartbeat of those clubs — their supporters — can be overlooked.

West Ham, however, have always played a vital part in the local community, from the club's formation in 1895, up to the present day. It is a unique club, as I soon appreciated when I first arrived here as a 15-year-old.

I learned to love the club and its fans, who typified the indomitable spirit of the East End. That spirit survives among the 23,000-hard core Hammers fans who support the club through thick and thin.

Even now, when I'm driving down Boundary Road and approaching the Boleyn on a match day, I still marvel at all the families, mums, dads, kids, even grandmothers, all decked out in claret and blue and on their way to the big game.   West Ham remains an important part of their lives.

I travel quite a bit these days and I am always struck by the affection which many people have for the club. It remains a traditional football club with traditional values.

I hope it remains so for the foreseeable future.

# Foreword

## by Alan Curbishley

LIKE the author, Brian Belton, I was born and raised minutes from Upton Park.

West Ham United stands for much more than just football. No matter where you reside now, or what route your life has taken, you remember your childhood upbringing.

East London — Bobby Moore — midweek night matches — the Chicken Run etc, etc, and pie and mash.

Unlike so many dreams, West Ham United will 'Never Fade and Die' because people care.

# Dedication:

*To the Supporter
and my Support*

# Introduction

IT WAS Muhammed Ali, when asked to speak to graduates at Harvard, who recited the shortest-ever poem in the English language. He held up one finger and, in the soft, thoughtful voice he was sometimes able to call on, uttered, "*Me.*" He then turned his hand into a fist and, in a slightly more determined tone said, "*We.*"

This is what this book is concerned with. It looks at West Ham United Football Club through the lens of history; the eyes of the past. Arthur Hopcroft, in his classic work *The Football Man*, wrote:

> *Football has not been a side-show of this century. What happens on the football field matters, not in the way that food matters, but as poetry does to some people and alcohol does to others; it engages the personality.*

Charles Korr, in his excellent history of West Ham United, states:

> *…it is better to think of football as a product of passion, personalities and mythologies.*

It is the spirit of these perceptions that I have sought to capture, across the decades and generations. The enduring process of support.

Players, managers, directors and now even grounds, come and go, but the supporters are always there. As such, football clubs do not belong to boards, shareholders or chairmen. Football clubs *are* the fans. It is from their point of view, and their moment in time, from the Boxer uprising in China, through the filth of the Somme, War in the Desert, the slump of the 1980s and into the future, the Irons of 2095, the second Centenary Year, that the book looks at the *growth* of the entity, the phenomenon that is *the Irons, the Hammers, West Ham United.*

West Ham was born just before the start of the 20th century, a time when industrialisation and what we know as capitalist society was really kicking in. If you want to know something of what we have become, what the modern world has made of human beings, you could do worse than look to West Ham to give some answers. We and West Ham are products of and have been shaped by modernity, so this is not just a book for West Ham supporters. It is for all students of society and anyone who has an interest in how passion, loyalty and love for an enduring idea or institution are transported over thousands of miles, down the years and across entire communities.

It is not a history book. It does not seek to 'teach' the reader anything. However, it is based on reality. It is an attempt to say something about what football and a football club, can mean to individuals, families and communities, over time and place. Each chapter, like a photograph, portrays a slice of someone's life, a moment in an existence. The characters define the games they see, but to a certain extent they, the personalities, are defined by the matches they watch. Then they disappear back into the crowd. We end up knowing a little about each one of them. Not much more than what we could learn about the person standing (or now sitting) next to us on the terraces during the break for half-time. But that is who these characters are. It is as Ali's *"We"* that they really begin to take some shape. As Emile Durkheim had it: "In the midst of an assembly animated by a common passion, we become susceptible to acts and sentiments of which we are incapable when reduced to our own forces."

## Football Supporting

Football is not a 'better' game than other games, and I don't think it is a more 'beautiful' game than some other games. But, it is football that takes a role in carrying personal and collective emotions, feelings, and sentiments. Generations of people have used the game to help them express themselves. They have integrated it, via a club, as part of their identity; who they are, where they are from.

Football clubs have been a depository of values, common codes, and expectations of behaviour, some quite primitive. These have been set in working class and/or industrial culture and have often been misunderstood as misogynist. But the support of football is to *be* football. That's why teams are called 'clubs'. This is an unconscious acceptance of the corporate nature of the enterprise, premised on the presence of the supporter. Support of a team is not like supporting a garden, a family or a car. There is nothing definite, in a physical sense, that one can do. If one supports a political party or a government you can at least cast a vote, but the fan has no such rights in respect of the board or the manager. The activity of support is confined to expressions of will and collective pressure. Words, shouts and songs carry the message. This is a purely dialogical influence. Support is shrouded in symbols and signs. Mascots, nicknames, scarves, team shirts. The message, within the symbol, is infused with sentiments, feelings, emotions and dreams. Thus to define support one can get into a kind of Jungian project, that goes deep into the human psyche until football itself becomes no more than a symbol. The players and the ground provide a way of expressing what can't be expressed in other ways. However, this relegates the support of football to a kind of repression, the Freudian ambition to shrink the activities of life down to a few constituent drives. But the support of football may be an end in itself. The eco-system of emotions it offers could be, in itself, enough to explain its continued existence and our sustaining need.

A human life is a complicated, contradictory set of experiences. It is influenced by all other lives lived and being lived. The happenings of ten, 20, 50 years ago, hundreds or thousands and, by the end of the 1960s, hundreds of thousands of miles away, shape us. In this way the past, present and the future are all one. No one person is entirely separate from others. Football is slightly different. To some extent each game is only related to a season. Seasons are only tangentially contingent on other seasons. This gives the game an attractiveness in our lives, that are so dependent on what occurs in the wider prospect of time and place. The half, the game, the season have beginnings and endings. The fates of clubs are defined within a certain space: the ground, or pitch. Things happen within a definite period of time: 90 minutes, the season. This book attempts to provide the reader with the restricted, and so telling, view of lives lived within the emotional and temporal context of football.

This, of course, is not life as it is actually lived, but it is something of the way in which the supporter relates their experience of living. The match, the team move between the background and the foreground of life and act as markers in the complicated and confusing stream of existence. Brief moments come to signify particular events and periods. Like the team takes on, or is ascribed, local characteristics, so the highs and the lows of the club are associated with situations and activity. The 'culture' of the club is created and confirmed by society, community and the individual, while at the same time it adds to and complements cultural expression.

*Bubbles, Hammers and Dreams* contradicts the popular belief that is to some extent ratified by the 20 million 'fans' that any Premiership winning side pick up and lose from season to season, (now 'Cockney Reds' who, at the back of a wardrobe, hide those expensive Blackburn shirts from 1995 with 'Shearer' emblazoned on the back), that support is inextricably associated with winning. Just identifying with a consistently successful club may not be support. One could be merely attempting to buy association with success; you purchase your dreams, often pre-packed. It was not hard to support Liverpool, Rangers or Manchester United in the mid-late 1990s. But where were the 'Cockney Reds' in 1974? They were 'Cockney Leeds' supporters. But this is like being in love with a person who has no faults, because they have no faults. When flaws emerge the lover flees. What a fickle and meaningless type of relationship. In fact it is not a relationship at all. It is a peccadillo, a dalliance, an aberration. It is shallow and adolescent. It has no place for tolerance, acceptance and development.

Tony Scott's brilliant 1996 film, of the Peter Abrahams book, *The Fan,* portrayed the lost, disillusioned and unsuccessful fan seeking success, vicariously, through his team. His dream interferes with his life, until the dream and the life become indistinguishable. For *The Fan,* the player was an idol, evoked through team icons. But the player is not a hero or a god. There have been few idols at West Ham. Players are people. The supporter expects no more and certainly no less. If you want Cantona depicted as Christ you are not a supporter, you are a worshipper. Such is not the basis of dreams. Real life is the fuel of dreams. This is illusion. To quote *The Electric Light Orchestra,* 'Hold on tight to your dreams,' they are made up of actuality, do not set them up as alternatives to reality. 'Le Grand Eric' was never more than a person, someone as earthly as Julian Dicks could remove him from a game.

So, support is different from both these models. Support is playing a part in the making of dreams from the raw material of romance, and wishes. This type of support is what makes football. This is what sustains it from generation to generation. If it is destroyed then football will be 'just a game'; 'twenty-two men running round a field chasing a ball'.

This book gives a relatively unusual perspective of the football fan who is often portrayed as a 'hooligan' or yob. There is a whole body of writers who are dependent on the 'vandal mythology' that surrounds the game. One has only to look hard at a section of the coverage of the 1996 European Championship that was held in England to detect the search for incidents. The stokers of moral panic went in for some serious 'social bodice ripping', reporting that 'Hooligan generals' from all over Europe were plotting campaigns. Armies of Dutch and German neo-fascists were said to be ready to disembark at the White Cliffs. Legions of English barbarians, faces painted with the Cross of St George, from Brentford, Brighton and Barnsley, were readying themselves for the blood-bath. In the end the hapless hacks were reduced to reporting a fracas in Trafalgar Square, that, by New Year standards for instance, was petty. Not bad, having attracted hundreds of thousands of fans into close proximity from all over England, Scotland and Europe, including troubled areas like Croatia.

Looked at historically, and in the context of the numbers of people watching matches on any Saturday afternoon, the trouble at games, even when incidents involving violent behaviour were at a high, is insignificant, especially when placed alongside the 'violence' of official neglect, exemplified in recent history at Hillsborough and Bradford. If one analysed aggressive behaviour at any gathering of thousands of people, one is likely to find more violence than at the average football match. If a million people attend Premier and Football League matches every week in England (this leaves out all the hundreds of thousands who watch non-League and amateur matches) this is approximately equivalent to those who might turn up for five hundred local fun-fairs. Who would bet that football would produce more problems for public order than such forms of mass entertainment? The revellers at the end of a night in London's theatreland cause more trouble than a big Cup Final crowd at Wembley, but you never see head-lines saying, 'Bad night in Drury Lane,' or 'Wyndham's management disassociate themselves with upper-circle scum.' The football hooligan, and the scandalmongers, that in effect eulogise and magnify this minuscule part of the game, are part of what Geoffrey Pearson has called "A History of Respectable Fears", that demonises, denigrates and insults supporters. It is part of a tradition; the 'paranoia of the decent', wherein the plebeians constantly threaten the established order. It is related to a fear of the young based on the same social pathology. Hence I have sought not to dwell on this aspect of support. Instead what follows celebrates support as the cherished and critical activity that it is.

## Supporting West Ham

Jet-lagged, I turn on the television in my hotel room in Shanghai early on a Sunday morning. What do I see? The 1,200,000,000 Chinese are watching West Ham slugging it out at 150 miles per hour with Aston Villa. About 15 goals are scored. The game is won in the last four seconds of injury time with a goal struck by every player on the pitch, in a goalmouth scramble that extinguishes the life of at least one goalkeeper and ends the career of three other players. The giant mascots, (one's a hammer, the other, I suppose, is 'a Villa') get in a punch-up. They are both arrested. The game has also had a streaker, a pitch protest against the board, and a pig loose on the park for most of the second half. Or was it the late Dim Sum? And we say the Chinese are inscrutable! But in this lonely room in a dingy, seedy place, thousands of miles from Upton Park, even with Mandarin commentary, I am, just a little bit, at home.

The Irons never quite get there. 'Fortune's always hiding.' The club achieves its 'academic' endeavours, but this is set within a history of near misses, failure and, at times, tragic comedy. A kind of surrealist combination of art and lunacy. For instance, it had to be West Ham who were relegated from Division One to Division One in 1992 (the Premier League was initiated 1992-93). But compared to most English League clubs, the Hammers have consistently had a place in the top flight and have a good record of Cup Finals. However, this just emphasises the 'nearly man' character of the club.

West Ham is the local club that wants to be Ajax or Barcelona. Its ambition, as may be detected in the way its teams attempt to play, is probably above its potential. But its management and its fans disdain the alternative: to adopt the siege tactics which have achieved something for the likes of Leeds, Wimbledon and, in the international arena, Jack Charlton's Anglo-Irish air force. Purest or stupid? Art or pomposity? You could use all these adjectives to describe West Ham. But it is the expectation of excitement, creativity, and drama that keeps West Ham fans turning up to support their team, although what they might end up with is anger, frustration, and disappointment. Many sneer when this is condensed into the noun 'art', but what else constitutes art? The sadness and failure of relegation can give rise to fortitude and pride in loyalty. The joy and camaraderie that create a winning goal have often been seen to invigorate towns, cities and nations. Experiences of the match can be taken into other realms of existence. The game therefore has the potential to be an educational experience.

> ...*individuals cannot satisfy certain of their needs and aspirations by private actions alone, and that there are certain freedoms the pursuit of requires individuals to associate ...Through the interaction of individuals, through them giving of themselves ...and through striving to attain some common purposes enhances the individual both in some specific sense related to the objectives of the voluntary body in question ...and as a person. developing their capacities through running or participating in the work of the group.* (Hirst 1994: p49-50)

An example of this working in the context of football was the West Ham fans' victory over the bond scheme, a plan mooted in the early 1990s to charge fans up to nearly £1,000 for the right to purchase tickets; it was defeated by the activity of the supporters. *When Saturday Comes* summed up the victory of the fans:

> *The West Ham directors were not beaten by the recession ...nor did the events on the field conspire against them. ... They were defeated because of the well-run, vigorous campaign by the people who care most about their club: the fans.* (1993: p7)

This is what the French might call 'Social Animatation', a form of informal education:

> *Animation refers to the purposeful activity on the part of the community itself to bring about change and improvement.* (Berrigan 1976: p3)

Football grounds can thus be seen as gymnasiums for the development of positive social qualities, not just negative forms of rebellion as so often suggested in the popular media and academic literature:

> *Here then we can see a mutual tolerance, accepting and being accepted, knowing and being known, which in itself can be a sources of emotional and social satisfaction.* (Elsdon 1995: p54)

The mass support of football, the history of the game, is to be found in places like Huddersfield, Bradford, Brighton, Leyton, Stockport and Upton Park. These are places that give an opportunity to hope and the chance to develop and express dreams, even if they 'fade and die'. It's not that one's dreams become reality that is important – if it were then they wouldn't be dreams – it's having dreams that makes reality more liveable. The supporters of these types of club far outnumber the fair weather fans of the so-called, 'big clubs', that would dissipate if relegation struck. This is evidenced by the behaviour of some of the 'good time' fans who associate themselves with big clubs as soon as their team fails to win more than two games in a row. In the 1996-97 season, spectators of this ilk at Liverpool were calling for the head of manager Roy Evans, despite narrowly missing a place in the Cup-winners' Cup Final, finishing fourth in the Premiership, and thus gaining entry to the UEFA Cup as a result. In the same season, Harry Redknapp finished up being congratulated for keeping West Ham in the top league. Even when things were really bad, the fans refused to turn on the players or Harry. They went for the relatively faceless board.

This in itself is something of a tradition. Charles Korr detects the same sort of reaction following the statement by director A.C.Davis, quoted in the *Evening News* of 20 April 1936. Davis was alleged to have stated that:

> "*From a monetary point of view it might be better for the club to stay in the Second Division.*" This fuelled an existing "*…feeling among supporters that the board was not much concerned with promotion.*" Korr goes on: "*Versions of the story had been common within the borough for years. They (the* supporters) *attributed the lack of ambition to West Ham's unwillingness to spend money, the inability of the directors to function in the First Division, and*

*the comfort and security felt by directors in the smaller pond of the Second Division" (p34-36).*

These accusations were little different from those that provoked the essentially peaceful protest against the board during the 1996-97 season. This included the directors being shown a red card by nearly all of the 25,000 plus supporters present.

Around 5,000 fans refused to leave the Boleyn Ground long after the final whistle of the match that saw West Ham defeated by Arsenal. When they were finally evicted from the Bobby Moore Stand and out of the stadium, the protesters mounted one of the biggest street demonstrations in East London for years. As in 1997, in 1936, according to Korr: *"The directors were the villains in a drama that ran for 25 years in the East End. Blaming the players would force supporters to undergo the emotionally wrenching act of disowning their alter egos.*

Following the protest of 1997, the board, who up to that time had pleaded poverty, gave Redknapp the better part of nine million pounds to bring Paul Kitson from Newcastle, the Welsh international John Hartson from Arsenal and Manchester City's Northern Ireland midfielder Steve Lomas to Upton Park. They were all young, talented players and Kitson and Hartson netted 13 goals between them in the final 14 games of the season. At the same point, a two million pound offer from Leeds for the promising England Under-23 international, Rio Ferdinand, was turned down, the player signing a lucrative three-year contract. BUBBLE POWER! (now not only referring to the world record for people blowing the round soapy things, achieved in the same season, at the home defeat against Liverpool) the product of support.

Of course, the protest of 1997 was never connected with the transfers in the media. In fact the supporters' actions were pretty much brushed under the carpet by the press and television. The size and vociferousness of the demonstration was only witnessed by the live Radio Five coverage, which was quickly glazed over in subsequent reports.

This demonstrates that these supporters were more than just spectators. This kind of supporter *is* the club. This is why it is hard for the true supporter of West Ham (and all supporters of this nature) to criticise his/her team. There is a connection, made by money, but also faith, fidelity and memory (history/tradition). Human qualities, that turn the game into something more than a sport, and transform the club ('the business') into part of a collective identity. This is what provides clubs, and the game in general, with a 'social meaning' as they might say up at the Centre for Football Studies in Leicester. The player, to the supporter, is his/her representative on the field.

Tony Cottee, following his final home game, for the club, threw most of his kit into the crowd. No one wanted Tony's sweaty sock. But they wanted what Tony represented for them, and that bit of claret and blue helped.

You see, what I have tried to show, and what so often gets missed in plays, books, films and radio programmes about football, is *the fact* of support. Some fans may be depressed or obsessed, violent hooligans or macho bolt heads from the planet Ogg, but most are straight-forward people, living out their lives and building their dreams.

> *Being close for a second of intensity.*
> *Depth without enduring.*
> *No demands other than the mutual recognition of being one in the idea,*
> *The physicality,*
> *The spirit, the being of 'the club'.*
> *But with authenticity.*
> *What the relationship lacks in time it makes up for in reality, truth.*
> *It is brief, powerfully honest.*
> *Human feeling, joy, relief,*
> *Squeezed into what we have,*
> *Together.*
> *For a moment, all are one,*
> *One is all.*
> *Oceanic, encompassing.*
> *A towering tide of passion framed in an instant.*
> *Give and take,*
> *Taken and given.*
> *'We', 'us',*
> *Defined in each other.*
> *Uuuu-nite-'ed.*

# Boxers, Bannermen and a Right-Winger by the name of Reynolds

# Chapter One

I HAD been in China for nearly four years. During this time it had become more and more obvious to foreigners and Chinese alike that China was being strangled by corruption. I have to say the doings of the likes of our own statesmen probably advanced and took advantage of this situation. The system was rotten through and through. Local administrators, Mandarins and area governors were all competing for bribes and back-handers.

I arrived in Peking in April 1896, just one year after China's disastrous war with Japan. I had been assigned to the British Legation as a messenger. Having only entered Government service the previous year, I was quite surprised to be asked to travel to China. At first I flattered myself that it was for my attention to duty and general reliability, but looking back the choice was probably more to do with my comparative youth, lucky good health and capability in respect of the written word, having a good hand and a useful gift of being able to spell most words used in everyday parlance. It was these skills, alongside a good word from my father's employer with his friend, a long standing servant of government, that enabled me to become part of the humble foundations of the Diplomatic Service in the first place. Understanding things as I do now, another consideration that may have gone in my favour was my rather lowly origins. I was, as a working class East Ender, eminently expendable.

The only Chinese people I had seen before my arrival had been those off the ships, or on my rare sorties down to Limehouse. I had no imagination of their way of life. As such, coming to Shanghai, our first port of call in China, was something of an encounter with the unexpected. However, looking back, it is amazing how quickly one got used to the situation. I have even picked up a deal of the local lingo during my posting.

Following the war, the old Dowager blamed all China's problems on everyone except her own administration. The Boxers had taken this on hook, line and sinker. They were ready for it. 'The Fists of Righteous Harmony', as they called themselves, had been condemnatory of the foreign presence for years, including their own — they have a very lively dislike for the ruling Manchus, Chinese Christians and anyone involved with or working for the 'foreign devils' — 'Gwyloes'.

It was strange, but life in the Legation was quite detached from what was going on in the immediate vicinity. At first the Legation area might as well have been in London, especially as far as those of us lower down the pecking order were concerned. Apart from our occasional football matches with local Chinese lads out by the racecourse, news from home was far more important to us than the ins and outs or the goings on amongst those in whose country we found ourselves residing. However, as the crisis came to a head, I was a little more aware of the state of things than most others of my station.

This was entirely due to my discrete liaisons with Chengsei; my beau.

In 1898, the Irons had gone professional and at first this seemed much more interesting to me than Chinese politics (this feels quite improbable now), although serious attacks on missionaries and those they had converted (the Boxers were liable to attack any property in the hands of non-Chinese) did distract me somewhat. These had become fairly common place after the New Year.

Mr Hills, the chairman of Thames Iron Works, had not been one for paying the players, 'sport for sport's sake' and all that. His consent to provide the team with a wage for playing football had been hard won by the committee, but the team were heading for two very competitive new leagues, the Southern League Division Two and the Thames and Medway Combination. The old organisation would have not served our cause, or Mr Hills' pocket.

We, the younger members of the British Legation, had introduced the mystery of Association Football to some of the local youths in order to create competition. We would have whole test series, including French and Italian sides. This activity was kept quite secretive, as our elders and betters would have immediately put a stop to such fraternisation. At first the Peking boys were cannon fodder for the European lads and ourselves, but the last group of matches was close run. They beat the French by the odd goal of three, lost 1-0 to the Italians and held us to a 3-3 draw (or more realistically, we held them). They had a very light style, moving fast off the ball. Not unlike the French, they seemed to pick up team play from us, but there was something quite distinct about them. If I had to put it into one word I would call it ... *insight.*

By the spring the Boxers had control of most of the rural districts surrounding Peking. The Ministers lodged the usual protests with the Tsungi Yamen, the Chinese Foreign Ministry, but most people were convinced that the whole thing would either blow over or be brought under control sooner rather than later.

Chengsei was not so sure. Her family were relatively prosperous Christian, business people. They did not trust the regime and certainly not the Boxers, who, for her, were fanatics. I began to walk out with Chengsei following our meetings on similar missions. I was instructed to take messages to the site of her family business in connection with Legation commerce with her father. She always collected such post from the courtyard of the premises. Likewise, she would be entrusted with communications to Legation staff, which it was my job to collect and distribute appropriately. Her English was excellent, but she was keen to converse, looking to improve her pronunciation and so on. We were close in age and I found her most pleasing. It was not long before I was enquiring of her as to the performance of various words and phrases in Chinese. Seeking more of her company, I devised to suggest that we might make a schedule to stroll and make conversation in order to mutually improve our respective linguistic ambitions. She agreed to consider this and with my subsequent persistence eventually acquiesced.

Of necessity, our meetings needed to be kept quite confidential. Her father would never have approved of our concourse and if my superiors found out it is likely that I would have been dismissed and sent home before my feet touched the ground. For all this, our affection for each other grew apace and we exchanged confirmation of our regard, esteem, respect, admiration and, eventually, tender feelings and concern for each other

However, even with my new amour and the troubles that served as a backdrop to the same, the new faces at the Memorial Grounds did not escape my notice. News of Association Football did not take up much room in the diplomatic bag, and when information did come through, via old newspapers or clerical chit-chat, the Thames Iron Works were hardly ever mentioned. Aston Villa dominated the news that year in the League, winning their fourth championship in six years, and we got wind of the English Cup Final between Sheffield United and Derby very swiftly. United had been taken to three replays by Liverpool in their semi-final and there was a fascinating duel in prospect involving 'Nudger' Needham, the Blades' left-half, and the Rams' inside-right, Bloomer. Needham must have come off best as United won 4-1. Confirmation that England had retained the International championship was also not belated. However, it was surprising how much could be gleaned by word of mouth from people passing through, the informal military grapevine, servants, engineers, business people and artisans from Britain. One was also able to pick up the odd snippet that seeped down between diplomatic communications (the disgrace of professionalism, the working classes paid to play games etc). However, my main source of information was by way of letters from family and friends at home. My mother was my most prolific correspondent and although her coverage of the Irons was not personally informed, she would send regular cuttings from the local press. My father and younger brother were occasional writers, as were my pals George and Albert. Together they provided me with a good idea of what was going on, although inevitably, most of the news was very much behind actual events.

Tommy Moore had been recruited from Millwall to play between the sticks and three big chaps from the 3rd Grenadier Guards, including David Lloyd, who at six-foot-four and 13 stone was to scare the hell out of most of our competitors. Roddy MacEachrane came all the way from Inverness.

Our first home League game of the 1898-99 season was against Brentford. We won a good match 2-1. This followed the fine opening game, a 3-0 win against Shepherd's Bush. Atkinson knocked in a pair. I agreed with my correspondents that this was a jolly good start to our first campaign in the Southern League.

By the end of May things were not getting any better. The Yamen had sent in a few young Bannermen (the local militia, a sort of cross between a constabulary and imperial household guard), but this did not stem the growing insecurity. So, on 31 May in came the troops from ships anchored out in the mouth of the Phe-ho, including 81 British Royal Marines. In total the Legations called in about 450 soldiers, sailors and marines. This was a rather negligible number, especially as the troops really had no cause in common (the various nationalities in the Legation area distrusted each other with some vigour). The mile-square Legation area was basically indefensible anyway. Peking at that time was really a collection of walled cities. Most of these structures were on the Chinese side to the south and the Tarter City in the north. The Tarter City was surrounded by a 40-foot-high wall. The Imperial City was situated within the Tarter City. The Forbidden City, which contained the Emperor's Palace, was inside the Imperial City. The Legation area lay between the southern walls of the Imperial and Tarter Cities. I had no military connections or education, but just looking at the general situation of the Legation Quarter made any option, short of the need to defend it, look attractive.

The Empress was never openly supportive of the Boxers, but at this point she did nothing to discourage their activities. At the same time, the Boxers gave her, and the regime she represented, very little sign of allegiance. The driving force for them seemed to be that we, the foreigners, were devils. The Chinese in our employ were the demon servants of devils and Chinese Christians were possessed by devils. All this did not bode well for Chengsei or her family.

The start of 1899 saw us doing very well in the Southern League. We had only lost two games out of 11, both away. But the Combination had not been a great success and to be fair, that was where the better teams were. A poor win record of three from nine by the New Year showed that we had some way to go before we would trouble the really big boys. However, in the FA Cup, we started off with a home win against the Royal Engineers. Gresham and little Roddy Mac chalked up one apiece. That was a good day according to friend Albert. The Pongos put on an athletics meeting the same day. We turned out against the Engineers three times that year and we beat them each time. It was a pity a few of them could not have been in Peking, they might have been better at fighting Boxers than playing football.

In the next round we were put up against Brighton United from the First Division of the Southern League. It was a hard game and it ended up 0-0. Brother Jim and Dad paid over four bob each to get to that game and, although the family had been for several outings to Gravesend, this was the first sight of the sea proper for young Jim. He thought that there must have been a thousand Irons supporters watching that day, and hundreds more were in Brighton just for the trip. The ground was packed. Moore, Dove and Tranter were towers of strength. It looked like the trip took it out of us though, we got slaughtered in the replay, 4-1.

On 9 June the Boxers burned down the racecourse.

It was common knowledge in the British Legation that the Minister, Sir Claude MacDonald, had telegraphed Vice Admiral Sir Edward Seymour, the senior naval officer with the warships out in the Gulf of Chihli, asking for reinforcements. We understood that a force of around 2,000 had left Tientsin by train on the morning of 10 June. They should have been with us by the next night at the latest. The Japanese Chancellor, having gone to meet the train (that never came), had been hijacked and hacked to death. Come the morning of 12 June there was no sign of the reinforcements. We had no idea of what had happened to the troops, as on 10 June the telegraph had been cut. Unbeknown to us, the troop train had been forced to turn back to Tientsin, 40 miles short of Peking because of damage to the railway lines. We were effectively isolated from the rest of the world.

The Boxers ransacked the Chinese City, paying particular attention to anyone who had dealings with foreigners. It was fortunate that Chengsei and her family had been brought into the Legation Quarter on the orders of our staff. Some of the Allied forces sent to protect us made attempts to save Christians, but it was next to useless. All the time the Imperial Government were very apologetic about the situation, assuring our leaders that action would be taken against the hordes and that very shortly things would be under control. But if anything, things got worse. On 19 June the Ministers of the Legations were handed a note from the Tsungli Yamen, now overseen by the well known nationalist Prince Tuan. The gist of the message was that we could no longer be assured of our safety and that we should be out of Peking by 4pm on 20 June. The Ministers agreed in principle to the demand but asked for a meeting to delay our removal. No reply to this request came. The German Minister decided that he would sort things out on the morning of 20 June, and, although advised against such a course of action, started out on a visit to the Tsungli Yamen. He was shot dead by a Bannerman. It is curious that this incident was reported in the Chinese and European newspapers several days before it took place.

Although the situation was becoming critical, I was heartened that I could now see Chengsei almost every day, and although with the overcrowding it was getting harder to remain discrete about our conduct, we were able to grab some of the sweetest moments together. We were, by now, most surely in love. I had every confidence that the city would be relieved in the near future, but this would not help our general situation. We were now very close and I had a mind to ask for her hand, but this was like asking for the moon. It just was not possible from either of our respective positions.

Mother sent me a couple of cuttings detailing the Irons' final League fixtures, a 10-0 walloping of Maidenhead. Big Davie Lloyd got a hat-trick, and Pat Leonard, formally of Manchester City, went one better. We were on top of the Southern League, Second Division. We didn't drop another point in this competition in all of 1899. We also equipped ourselves well in the Thames and Medway, with just the one loss in the final seven matches.

This took us to the play-off to sort out the championship. We were up against Cowes, winners of the South-Western section. I was told by one of the marines that a friend of his brother-in-law was one of the Cowes team, that the game was held at Millwall (my marine friend, a follower of Cowes, being from the Isle of Wight, made not a little complaint about this venue). They should have been formidable opposition, having knocked in 58 goals in their ten games in the League.

The marine told me that he had never been in a bigger crowd at a football match. He had heard that there had been over 10,000 people there that day. He told me that most of the Irons supporters had set out from Canning Town and West Ham just two hours before the match and walked to the ground. There had been some fear that the Woolwich ferry would capsize at one point, it was that full of Irons supporters.

Pongo Lloyd put us ahead (I don't think the lads from the Isle of Wight could have ever seen anything like him), but Cowes made it 1-1 by half-time. The marine had thought that the second half would have been quite a battle, but in the end Henderson and Leonard made it comfortable for us. The marine had been posted before the final test series that would decide which teams would go into the First Division. He had not made any effort to find out details following the defeat of his team. This did not endear him to me, but I thanked him for what information he had given me, as rivals are prone to false reports, favouring their own side.

The murder of the German Minister was a blessing in disguise. Everyone now knew that the Chinese could not be relied on for anything like safe conduct. The Ministers resolved to defend the Legation Quarter until help arrived. We still expected Seymour at any time, although there was no good reason why this expectation should be fulfilled. At four o'clock in the afternoon the Chinese opened fire.

We did what we could to defend ourselves, constructing barricades made up of carts, barrels and sandbags. European and Chinese Christian refugees had flooded into the Legation Quarter. Over 120 men from their ranks, with military experience, had volunteered to serve with the combined forces of the various Legations. Committees were formed to sort out rations, fuel, water, fire defence and sanitation. The women folk put a hospital service together and produced hundreds of sandbags, often some of the prettiest ever seen I should think, made out of fine dresses and expensive curtains. We had wells, so fresh water was not a problem. Commercial stores and a government grain house made us secure with respect to food.

It was hardly noticed at the time, but the refugee Chinese were treated quite badly. They got no rations, and almost 3,000 of them were obliged to live the best they could off of rats, dogs, rubbish and roots. They were expected to earn what little protection they were given by burying the dead. I could not see Chengsei treated in this way and asked Mr Bennett, my immediate superior, if I could have permission to speak personally to the Ambassador on behalf of her family. Mr Bennett had been with the Colonial Diplomatic Corps for nearly 40 years. He had always been good to me, and while a firm master, he kept an eye out for the younger members of staff. He took me aside and told me that he would see that Mr Wang and his family were well cared for on condition that I kept quiet about my part in the assistance of the family. I agreed.

That afternoon I obtained the use of a hand cart and helped bring Chengsei, her four sisters, her mother and father to the Legation. They were to be housed inside the Legation wall in a disused storage room. About 40 yards from the compound three men came at us from out of the throng that milled about on the outside the British Legation. By their red sashes I knew they were Boxers. I had been given a Shorts revolver by Mr Bennett some time before, to carry with me on my courier duties, although I had never so much as looked down the barrel. Automatically, I pulled the gun from my belt and released the safety catch. I stood like a veteran, one hand on hip, the other extended, aiming at the on-coming target.

I supposed I hoped that this would be enough to ward them off, but it was not. The first man was no more than a couple of yards from me when I fired straight into his face. He fell like a stone. I rounded on the second like a puppet, catching him in the shoulder. He stumbled to his knees. The third was upon me. The force of his rush pushed me back on to the cart and I saw the glint of the sun on his knife as he raised it high to end my days on earth, but his grip slackened and, silently, he fell away to reveal Chengsei holding a bloody kitchen knife. Cripes! As we now dashed for the Legation I looked for the wounded man, but he had scarpered.

The accommodation provided for the Wangs was cramped, but relatively safe. As I left them to sort out the few belongings they had been allowed to bring, I caught Mr Wang's eye. Pausing for a second he gave me a slight nod of recognition.

Mr Bennett told me that I was responsible for providing the Wang family with nourishment the best I could. I called on all my East End background to ensure that my charges were fed adequately. I gained a lot of credit from Mr and Mrs Wang for this.

Although the Chinese were not treated well, nearly 4,000 refugees in the isolated Peit'ang Cathedral were gallantly defended by 43 French and Italian sailors throughout the siege. The Chinese shelled the area intensely and one round had killed 136 people. The young French naval officer who had bravely commanded the seamen, detached from the main Legation Quarter, Ensign Paul Henry, was killed by a sniper on 30 July.

At first Captain von Thomann, the Austrian commander, was put in charge of the military side of things, but having instigated an ill-timed retreat following a Chinese attack on 23 June, Sir Claude MacDonald was given the reigns. We had a lot of confidence in Sir Claude. He was a veteran of Egypt and the Dervish Wars. There was no better man for the job.

The fighting on 23, 24 and 25 June was brutal. Chinese regulars and Boxers (you could tell the Boxers by those red sashes and headbands, they reminded me of Woolwich Arsenal supporters) hit every part of the perimeter. But we mowed them down in the mass attacks. They soon took to more sporadic street fighting. Their artillery was, for the most part, badly off target, much of it shooting over our heads. On 23 June they set the Han-lin Library afire, hoping to destroy the British Legation. Every available hand was put to a bucket chain, and although we were exhausted, we saved the Legation from the flames.

On 24 June our troops counter-attacked along the Tarter Wall, the last thing the Chinese would have expected. The Yanks pushed them back about half-a-mile. The Germans destroyed a whole unit of Bannermen and in the Fu the Japs and the Eye-ties pulled the Boxers into a trap. The Allies, pretending to retreat, had the Boxers running after them straight into a cross-fire. Captain Lewis Halliday with seven other Royal Marines took on the Boxers who were at the western wall of the British Legation. Although shot in the shoulder and lung, Halliday cleared the field of fire from the Legation wall, demolishing a small building from which the Boxers had been firing. Later the good Captain was to be awarded the Victoria Cross.

After the first seven days of fighting, our defence had sustained about 20 fatalities and around as many wounded. It was clear that we would not be able to hold out for long at this rate. Our hopes of Seymour were fading fast. But no one wanted to become a Boxer prisoner. The severed head of a European civilian waved at us on the end of a pole confirmed this attitude. The back-to-the-wall situation seemed to infect every European in the Legation Quarter. We were, despite all adversity, quite defiant and of good morale.

The siege went back and forth, but on the whole, we were getting the better of things. The Germans were forced off of the eastern end of the Tarter Wall by a surprise attack on 1 July. The Americans were also knocked back. But the Yanks, Brits and Russkis fought back and regained the position. At the same time the French were almost forced from their Legation, but bravely counter-attacked to regain the area. The Italians attacked and captured a Chinese field gun. At the western end of the Tarter Wall the Chinese had started to build a wooden tower, to enable them to fire down on the Americans. A combined British and American force captured the construction early on 3 July. We were never without fear, but determination and solidarity was helping us hold the situation.

On 7 July, a gang of Chinese Christians, organised by Mr Wang, while digging defences, unearthed a cannon, a relic from the Opium wars. Mr Wang, a trained engineer, suggested that the gun could be used if ammunition could be adapted. Some Russian shells were duly modified and 'The Dowager Empress', as the gun was dubbed, was turned on the Chinese. Her first round, to our utmost pleasure, landed in the Imperial City. The third round destroyed a Chinese battery.

The Chinese had taken to sniping and tunnelling under our defences, planting explosives. The Americans put sharpshooters up on the Tarter Wall in an attempt to reply to these tactics. One Private Daly caught eight Chinese in his first turn of duty on the night of 12 July. This caused a group of Boxers to fall upon him out of the darkness. He killed three before the rest reached his position. He then felled the first to reach him with his rifle butt and bayoneted two more. After this he shot three more from a distance, and yet another three in a subsequent Boxer assault, using his bayonet on a final assailant. That night he was attacked eight times. Only one of the boxers had carried a firearm. The rest sought to overpower him with swords or knives. Daly was to be awarded a Congressional Medal of Honour.

On 13 July, the French Legation suffered the effects of a Chinese mine. Two sailors were killed and a fire started. Three days later a captain of Royal marines was killed while relieving the Japanese in the Fu. Doubts about our ability to hold out to the end of the month were now in all our minds. Little did we know that *The Times* had printed an account of the last hours of the Legation Quarter, and had printed the obituary of our commander. Then, from out of the blue, a ceasefire was agreed with representatives of General Jung Lu. It transpired that Allied troops had overcome Tientsin and this had caused the Imperial Government reconsider its position.

Things remained tense for some time. The Empress sent in supplies, yet the longer relief failed to arrive, the more contraventions of the cease-fire occurred. We heard that some of the mandarins who had supported the end of attrition had been beheaded. Then, on 4 August, they came at us again. The fighting was fierce around the burnt-out Library and in the Mongol Market. However, by 8 August messengers arrived from the relief force. Four days later large numbers of Chinese troops were fleeing the City, but despite this, they were still throwing themselves against us. However, by 3pm on 14 August the Allies broke through to the Legation Quarter. The first to arrive were 70 men of the 7th Rajputs, who came in via the sewers, with the assistance of our American marines. The Americans and French got to us about an hour later. The Cathedral was relieved on 16 August. Some 64 of our forces had been killed and 156 wounded. Over 1,000 Chinese refugees had died from enemy activity, starvation and disease.

Before leaving Peking we received great piles of correspondence from London. The Civil Service and the Post Office are never far behind the troops. The Isle of Wight marine's commentary had been faultless, but despite the championship game result, both Cowes and the Irons went through to the test series. We had to play Sheppy from the First Division. It was all a bit daft, though, as all four teams to play in the tests ended up in the First Division of the Southern League. The powers that be decided to enlarge the League for 1899-1900 season. They even brought in Bristol Rovers and Queen's Park Rangers from outside the League. One could get quite cynical about official feelings towards the Irons' success. It seems nearly everything was done to lay obstacles in the way of our advancement. It would be easy to draw comparisons between this, the reports of the German Minister's death before it happened and the coverage of the Legation Quarter's supposed defeat. But that would sound as stupid as the test series.

We obtained a new full-back from Chatham, Tommy Dunn, who had played for the Wolves in the Cup Final of 1896. Francis Payne (the Ironworks secretary, there's a whole story to tell about Franny) had nabbed a brace of players from Warmley when they folded early in 1899, including Peter McManus, who, while with Edinburgh St Bernard's, had won a Scottish Cup winners' medal. He had also turned out for West Bromwich Albion. Other interesting acquisitions were George Reid, the former Reading player, and a useful sounding chap called Henderson.

But most intriguing of the new lads came from Gravesend United. He was a right-winger by the name of Reynolds. He had a knack of bending balls from corners and free-kicks. He did well with Alf Hitch, who could really head a ball.

I knew that it would not be long before my stint in China would be over and I could not envisage leaving Chengsei. Mr Bennett gave me no hope of taking her home with me, even if I was able to persuade her father, which was unlikely. For all that, I took it upon myself to ask Mr Wang for her hand. He sat down on the side of a rough table and looked at the floor for some time. He seemed very tired. He brought his head up, his eyes were closed. He opened his eyes and told me that I was a good young man, but that he and his family could not stay in Peking. He said that they were going to start up business in Hong Kong or across the South China Sea and that if I were to marry Cheng-sei, then he would expect me to come with them. I was taken aback. I would have never have dreamt that he would answer in this way.

# Champions
# in War

# Chapter Two

T IS STILL quite cold although it has been an agreeable enough day, more so as the Irons have just done Portsmouth in the final game of the season at the Boleyn. Puddy (as usual) got us two. Casey, McDougall and Danny Shea knocked in the others. We let Pompey have a couple.

The fighting in France continues. From what I can make out from the papers and brother Bill's letters, the Empire seems to have the Bosch on the run. Mum's been worried that we have not heard from Bill for six weeks. Still, I am sure he is quite fine. Before now we have gone two months and more between letters.

We have had a good season. Champions! Although not everyone has agreed with the War League, the London Combination has been spiffing stuff for us, much more so than the ordinary Southern League. We went nine games without defeat at the start of the season (won eight, drew one). Last month we finished the Spurs' 20-match unbeaten run (3-0, Shea, Chedgzoy and Puddefoot). We finished up having played 40 games, winning 30, drawing five and losing five. We scored 110 goals and let in only 45. The last time we got beat it was by the odd one of three against the Arsenal.

I got a letter from Danny today. He was very surprised that we could have beaten the Arsenal in our first game in the competition. He approves of the suspension of contracts. Not just because it gives West Ham a chance to grab a few decent players while they are barracked in London, but because he says, "It is part of the working man's realisation of his labour," whatever that means. I had written to Dan that night after the game. At 2-1 it sounded like a close match, but we had played the Arsenal off the pitch. Mind you, we owed a bit to the Scousers. One of the Everton lads, Chedgzoy, got our first and the Liverpool boy, McDougall, knocked in a corker. But the team changes every with every match, what with the troop movements. Given the situation, I think Mr King is doing a good job. And of course, you've got to remember, our local chaps are playing after all-night shifts. I ask you, how can the likes of Syd Puddefoot be at their best when they turn up after an all-nighter down the munitions?

Dan says that the strikes in Petrograd have led to the end of the Tsar there. "The Committee of State Duma has been formed" along with "the Petrograd Soviet of Workers' Deputies." Danny seems very pleased about that. He's being taught to speak Russian by a princess. Dad reckons he'll be Prime Minister over there. Mum doesn't say much more than he should get himself home, and that she had never understood what he saw in the Communist Party anyway. I believe that Jane Gadley being a member helped in the beginning. I think that Dad might not be far wrong. We saw in the paper that Prince Michael has abdicated and it looks like the Russians will be pulling out of the Kaiser's war.

It seems like a long time since we've all been together. Three years of war and no sign of an end.

### Brothers at arms

**19 November 1917**

The Third Battle of Ypres. They are calling this Passchendaele. It seems that words like courage and sacrifice are not enough. Mix it all in with discipline, mud, sleet, lice, noise and jagged steel, together with the terror stacked on horror, the remains of animals and men smashed and mashed into the dirt, that squirms with the rotting carcasses of sons, fathers and husbands. That's Passchendaele. A terrible confusion. An awful waste to appal the spirit. Martyrdom on a huge scale. And here I am. How did I get here? I've been holding on to a letter from young Charlie. It came at the start of all this. He writes about the Irons. Home. It's like a dream. But it's something to hold on to. Funny that. Amongst the din and the screams, West Ham, the champions, makes a difference. We. Us. To be at Upton Park surrounded by your mates. A drink after the match. It's very simple.

When I joined up we had just finished the 1913-14 season. We started with only one new pro with any experience to speak of. Alf Leafe. I think he was a Lancashire lad. Good soldiers the Lancastrians. I've seen a lot of 'em die. I've seen a lot of everyone die. Young men from the Yorkshire dales, the Scottish slums, Irish farms, and Londoners. Chelsea boys, Arsenal, Tottenham and more than a few Hammers lads. They recruited us by the street you see. You come to war with your mates, and you watch your mates die. Blokes you've known all your life. You know their wives, their kids, their Mums and Dads. Brothers watch brothers butchered. I saw my cousin cut in half by machine gun fire. Back home the chaps who didn't support the Irons, were the enemy. Even if they just came from different parts of London, we used to say they did things differently the other side of the water, or over west. They looked or acted different, because of the width of the roads or the distance they lived from the river. Thing is, they all die pretty much in the same way.

Anyway, I think Leafe had been with the Blades. He was a big bloke. He netted in all of his first four games for us. The game before Bonfire Night old Alf sunk Coventry. A hat-trick against a side who'd held a charm over us for some time. Twenty he scored that season. Leading marksman. Well done Alf! Wherever you come from.

Bleedin' Bonfire Night. Perhaps if old Guy Fawkes hadn't have messed it up we wouldn't be stuck here now. Mum and Dad, our Bill and little Charlie. Ma loved a 'bonny'. I know now that I'd never really seen a fire. We have fires here that come straight out of Hades. What am I saying. This must be Hell. There can't be a worse place than this. On the Somme last year we attacked for four months. They say we had half a million hit. We gained no more than three miles. From the Aldgate Pump to Canning Town, over a 20-mile front. Course, we only pick things up by talk. You get told nothing by the officers. I was speaking to one bloke the other day and he told me that in 1916 he had been put on a ship and told that he was going to Germany to fight the Hun. Not being an educated chap, from out in the sticks somewhere, he had little idea of what this meant at the time, not having a clue what a German was apart from 'the enemy'. He'd been fighting in the streets of Dublin for a week before he realised he was shooting at what he regarded as his fellow countrymen.

It was in early June that all this started. On the first day we advanced two miles or so. The Anzacs went down in their thousands. It was like nothing I'd ever seen before. The first ripple was blotted out. The dead and wounded were piled on each other's backs, and the second wave, coming up behind, were being compelled to cluster like a flock of sheep. They were knocked over in their tracks and lay in heaving mounds.

The world ends here, Charlie. The usual rules just don't apply. Sergeant Joe Soames for instance. He had a reputation for bravery and was a good leader, although only 25. He led forays into no man's land and had been wounded twice in action. On patrol, he was out in front with his commanding officer when they were ambushed. The officer was killed. Joe had no time to get the cover from the breech of his rifle and return fire, so he wedged the weapon across the trench to hamper the Germans who were now after him. His aim was to get back to warn the rest of the patrol, which he did, shouting, "The Hun are upon us." As such, the rest of the lads were able get away. Soames was charged with casting away his arms, while corporals MacTavish and Scrogins were charged with quitting their posts. At the court martial one officer testified that Soames was an enthusiastic and brave soldier and the last man to resort to cowardice. The three of them were shot. I heard it took three shots to kill Soames. Some say that the firing squad aimed wide of him. According to one of his mates, his picture had appeared in their home town newspaper. The accompanying story showed that his mother had been misled as to the cause of his death. What kind of people are in charge of all this? Dan's right to hate them so much. I never understood before, but I do now. They're murderers, bloody mass murderers.

Our job is just to kill and to die. Anything in between is likely to end up in a charge.

How could we know this as we stood watching Syd? An attack meant something was going to happen. Even if it failed, you could see how near or how far it had been from success. Yet he scored his first goal for us in March 1913 and his second didn't come until the end of November that year. I remember it because it was a home game against Gillingham and my cousin, Davey, was up for the match. That side of the family are gypsies, but they had lived outside of Gillingham for as long as anyone can remember. He's an ardent follower of the Gills. Or he was. He was taken at the Somme on the second day. Nothing left of him. Blown into tiny bits. All the lads from his site were wiped out. Gypsy boys dying for the country that treats them like pariahs.

Leafe was good, but Syd was the chap for me in 1913-14. If he hadn't have been injured at Watford (and the game was abandoned anyway!) he would have doubled the nine goals he got that season. He socked in five against Chesterfield in the Cup, three of those inside seven minutes. He got our goal against Liverpool at home in the third round and another in the replay. We lost, but the Scousers did go on to the Final, losing the pot by the odd goal to Burnley.

We were making a noise now. A crowd of 25,000 souls had watched the first home game against Swindon. Our biggest gate of the season at the Boleyn. But that was a different sound. Excitement, fun, a kind of love. Noise for its own sake. At the end of July, two months ago, right in the middle of the night, I experienced another type of noise. Three-thousand guns' worth. One of the artillery boys told me that half a million shells were fired at the Germans and that it had been the loudest man-made noise ever heard on earth. I can believe it too. The ground heaved and the sky was afire. We advanced. Whistles were blowing all around, long screeching notes, like when a foul has been spotted by the ref. But this time there were thousands and thousands of terrible fouls in that awful, darkness.

By the afternoon the rain had turned the Gheluvelt Plateau into a muddy desert. It poured down for two days. God had abandoned us to rain. A watery, soaking, soggy, wet purgatory. We dug our filthy trenches in the wrenching, churning mire. It looked like some mad grave yard from the nightmare of a demon. We sliced the bodies through at each side of the trench, not bothering to dig any more out. The odour was shocking and the more we dug the more dead men's bodies we had to go through. These were sights and smells that no human being should be asked to endure. You had to eat and sleep with the carnage of war.

Charlie told me that Arthur Stallard had been killed over here. We thought he was a prospect. Then we could think about the future. This war has killed the future. We hold on to the past because that's where life is. In this place there is only death. Tragedy becomes mundane. Stallard was killed, good job we didn't let Puddy go to Roker. It's like this is not real and the past is. Then again, at times you wonder if the past is all an illusion and that real life is this bad dream. Here, what is real is made bigger. Even the rats. You've never seen rats until you've seen rats that were born and fed and grow on human flesh.

On 10 August we attacked the Plateau again. It was a quagmire. Dreadful. An unspeakable mix up. No one seemed to get where they were meant to go. When groups got near their objectives they were boxed in by the Bosch artillery and machine guns. We couldn't bring up ammo or reinforcements. You couldn't take too many prisoners as they would have to be marched back through enemy fire. So we shot 'em. There and then. They begged and pleaded, but we killed them. We shot them in the faces that screeched their supplications. What else could we do?

We went to and fro for two weeks. Then the Germans counter attacked and retook most of the ground we had made. An ambulance driver told me that he had heard a medical officer say that we took 25,000 casualties in August. He was from Shepherds Bush. Like our Danny, a communist, he was also a Methodist. Must spend a lot of time arguing with himself, and God. On top of this he was a pacifist. More 'ists' than any man has a right to. He'd just come back from leave. He had seen Puddy get three against his team, Queen's Park Rangers, in a tremendous 3-0 win for the Hammers. We were doing well. Charlie had let me know, in a very detailed report, about the 6-1 opening game. Victory at home to Fulham. Danny Shea, the boy from Wapping, netted four and Roberts came up with a double. I used to think our Charlie copied his reports from the papers, but he also sends me cuttings from time to time and, if anything, Charlie writes better than the official match reporters, if a bit biased towards the Irons.

We fought on all through September. Twenty-thousand casualties at Menin Road Ridge. Over 15,000 Aussies were downed taking Polygon Wood. It is utterly, utterly miserable. How can the condition of the men be des-cribed? I came across some survivors from the Manchesters. Never had I seen men so broken or demoralised. They were huddled up close behind a box in the last stages of exhaustion and fear. The dead and dying lay in piles. The wounded were everywhere, unattended and weak. They groaned and moaned all over the place. Some had been there days. I noticed one chap who I think was being given the last rites by a priest. All of a sudden he sat up on one elbow. He looked at the priest with clear eyes. Sneering slightly through his dirty and bloodstained countenance, he spat bloody sputum straight in the priest's face. The dying soldier watched the other man for a few seconds. Religion had let him down. Perhaps condemned him. The priest started to cry softly. The soldier fell back. Dead.

That night, although I was exhausted, I could not sleep. The sights I had seen would not leave my eyes. I suspect I was not alone as somewhere behind me a man sang, *Maybe it's because I'm a Londoner,* but not in the crass, music hall way. His voice lilted and broke as he slowly paced through the little song, as if his heart would break. It became a pleading prayer, a sobbing of home want that he had no other way of expressing;

*Maa-a-be it's becorse I'm a Lon-don-a*
*Dat I luv Lon-don tarne.*
*Maa-be it's becorse I'm a London-a*
*Dat I finks of 'er, where ever I go-OOH!*
*Eye-I gets a funny feelin' in-side of me,*
*Jus walkin' up and darne,*
*Maaa-be it's be-corse I'm a Lon-don-a,*
*Dat I luv Lon-don tarne.*

I started to weep uncontrollably as the last, piteous note faded into the night. I so wanted to go home.

It was the beginning of October that the rain set in for winter. It is a dead and wringing thing, borne on icy winds. After four wins out of five games, and although Syd scored, we were beaten at Chelsea, 4-3. The battlefield has been peppered by tens of millions of shells. Hundreds of men, mules, horses and guns drowned in the mud. I lie in this sea of muck. My right leg has gone, but I feel no pain. I hold a newspaper cutting in my hand. Oh good God! Charlie's last words to me. It's dated 10 November 1917. It records the Irons' derby win against Clapton Orient, 4-1 at Upton Park. Danny scored his second … and the crowd roars…me, and Dan and little Charlie jumping about …I'm forever …like my *dreams* … United in death.

# What
# White Horse?

# Chapter Three

## Cuts and Changes

FROM the beginning of 1922 dockers' pay had been reduced by three shillings a day. For some this meant that a day's pay could be as low as ten shillings. Most of us were by now members of the new Transport and General Workers' Union. Loads of transport and dock unions came together to make a huge body of workers. The wage cut had not been unexpected. Everybody knew that Ernie Bevin (now in charge of the union) wanted to avoid a dust up in the early days of the T & G.

We had not had a bad season at the Boleyn, though, and this helped the morale of those of us who took an interest in the Hammers, which was practically everybody. Home crowds had been pretty good considering the straitened circumstances many folk found themselves in. We were never out of the top four after Christmas, and for the first two months of 1922 we held on to second place. West Ham had a knack of doing well when things were going badly in the docks. It was in December that Jimmy Ruffell came into the team. He had joined West Ham from Wall End about 18 months before his first appearance. I'd seen him play for East Ham and I rated him highly. At 21 he looked a good prospect. Bill Brown and Billy Williams were other notable youngsters. Williams came out of East Ham and had skippered the English Schools team. It was always good to see a local lad playing for the side.

We dropped 11 points over the last seven games and this put pay to any ideas about promotion. We finished up in fourth place. Just behind Barnsley, just ahead of Hull. Four points adrift of Stoke and a promotion place and eight behind champions Nottingham Forest.

Before the start of the 1922-23 season, captain Billy Cope went to Wrexham. He had been with the club since 1914. We would miss Bill, he had a kick like a mule, which was effective in more ways than one. A few visiting forwards had scars to prove it. Crossley had been brought in from Everton, the former Wolves man Dick Richards had arrived along with Billy Moore from Sunderland. Moore was an England amateur international. A small, slight inside-left, he looked a bit lightweight. But he was to contribute much to the club and gained a full professional cap at the end of the season. George Kay took over the captaincy from Cope.

Just when it looked as though Syd King meant business that season, he went and sold Syd Puddefoot to . . . Falkirk. This left me flabbergasted. One of our top goalscorers, 107 in 194 appearances, gone. Puddy was a local chap, he had been with the club for ten years, he was an international player, and very much a favourite with the supporters. This did not make Mr King the most popular man in the East End for a while.

Work in the docks had been scarce for some time. The pay cut made a bad situation worse. But other unions continued to take further wage cuts, so no one was surprised when, in September 1922, Ernie surrendered yet another bob. He promised that a proposed further shilling cut wouldn't happen until June of '23, and then only if the cost of living fell. At the same time, things were not looking good for the Hammers. At the end of September we had lost two games on the trot to Stockport, 2-1 at their place and 1-0 at the Boleyn, although new boy Billy Moore scored his fourth goal for us at Edgeley Park. This left us with a record of only two wins in eight games.

We were not happy with all this. Many dock branches were so disgusted that they didn't even bother to take a vote when the settlement was proposed. At the time we were lucky to be getting two or three days' work a week. This meant trying to live on half wages, around 30 bob a week.

Bevin pointed out that the employers had been trying to lengthen the working day, but we had held on to existing hours. This 'victory' tipped the balance in the branch vote. The settlement was accepted by a branch vote of 26 to 21. However, 29 branches failed to cast a vote.

Most of the work in the docks was casual. Waiting on the cobbles was always part of a docker's life, but now the pursuit had turned into a mad scramble. The natural answer to less pay was to seek work more vigorously. You'd wait by a gate where it was known (or rumoured) a ship had berthed during the night. Some men were regular, but many relied on ships coming in and were paid by the day. The foreman would eventually emerge and, like on the day of judgement, point to the men he wanted. It wasn't unusual for a bung or two to be expected for this favour. The chaps who were left standing made a frenzied dash for the next gate in the hope of employment there. Competition for work was always fierce, but now it became a vicious rivalry. Friends and relations, bearing the marks of hunger, rake thin men, literally fought and tore at each other for jobs. The employers were whittling away at our unity with this 'all against all' strategy.

Although things were hard, they were nowhere near as hard as they were going to get. We knew we were in for a dust up with the employers, but that September we could never have dreamt how the Hammers would provide us with an example of courage. It helped us face up to the hardship that dragged on all through the 1922-23 season. It steeled us for the fight that would come before the start of the 1923-24 season.

In July the employers tried to enforce a further cut of a shilling a day. Hull came out on 2 July and the action spread like wild-fire.

## Looking back at a season of glory from a strike against hunger

The nature of the strike, being unofficial, prevented us from getting strike pay. In our neck of the woods we had the advantage of the Poplar, Bermondsey and West Ham Guardians. Over in East Ham you had to produce a doctor's certificate to say that you were starving before you'd get a penny. Towards the end of the strike I bumped into Johnny Ald. I've known John all my life. He had moved over to Woolwich when he got married. He had three kids to support, all just tots. Most dockers had been burning up more energy than they were taking in for years by now, so it was not unusual to notice that someone you hadn't seen for some time looked a bit scrawny, but he was so thin I hardly recognised him. The last time I had seen him had been at the Upton Park replay against Brighton. This was the second round of the FA Cup. We had beaten Hull up north in the first round. Billy Moore chalked up his tenth goal for the club at Anlaby Road while Vic Watson, the lad brought in to replace Puddy, put two away.

We were drawn away again in the second round. Brighton were doing well in the Third Division South, having lost just two times at home that season. We held them to 1-1 at the Goldstone. Jack Tresadern (at left-half-back) played a blinder in the replay. John had looked full of life that Wednesday. We were standing on the terraces together, giving it all we'd got. We went potty when Moore finally drove home the only goal of the game from a cannon ball cross by Ruffell. John was a big strapping bloke, but the strike, the wage cuts before this, and the callousness of the Woolwich Guardians had made a shadow of him.

Most of the Poplar lads didn't apply for relief, but many of those who would have been quickly forced back to work were helped. So where the Guardians were on our side, they held the action together at the seams. In Poplar we were treated as if we were simply unemployed. This was, of course, illegal and the Guardians got in no end of strife for helping us out. It was called 'the Strike on the Rates' by the Tory newspapers.

The Poplar Guardians included Councillor Davie Adams, a T & G official. Adams was one of us. He was born in Poplar, although he moved to Wales at the age of 12 to become a miner. Later he'd gone to sea, before serving three years with the Welch Regiment in India. Then he went into the docks. He became secretary of the Export Branch, Dock, Wharf, and Riverside Workers' Union, serving from 1911 to 1920. He'd been a Guardian since 1913 and a Councillor since 1919. Every week old Dave was interviewing around 400 of us; one week it was said that he got close to 1,000. However, Councillors 'Irish' Julia Scurr and Helen McKay had a better average overall. Both these ladies had a campaigning past. Julia had been brought up in Limehouse and had a pedigree as a Suffragette. Helen and her old man (a baker's van man) had been arrested together supporting Sylvia Pankhurst. All three had been sent to jail in '21 for their part in the 'equal pay for equal work' policy in support of municipal workers.

In the third round of the Cup we were drawn at the Boleyn against old foes from the Southern League, Plymouth. The official attendance for the game was over 30,000, but I would say that there was nearer 40,000. It's surprising where people find a few bob in hard times for something like a football match. But it's something, like the grog, that keeps you going. It's an escape and a place where everyone wants the same thing. But some credit has to be given to the men on the turnstiles, who often let in an unemployed lad for every two paying spectators.

By now our League record didn't look quite as bad. We bagged four against Wolves at Molineux just before Christmas, Billy Brown hit the back of the net twice and was unlucky not to make a hat-trick. Watson got a hat-trick against Coventry at Highfield Road before the new year, we put three past Port Vale, again away from home, and we belted Leicester for six with no reply at Filbert Street nine days before the third-round game. Billy Henderson and Jack Young had shored up the defence and we had gained 30 points from a possible 52. As such, the match against the Pilgrims went to form. We had a comfortable 2-0 win. Taff Richards and Moore did the honours.

Our next opponents were Southampton at the Dell, where we had lost in the League in October. This was a really drawn out affair. A dour struggle produced a 1-1 score-line that brought the Saints to Upton Park. This was another battle. We managed another 1-1 draw, but only after Southampton had taken the lead. This meant a showdown at Villa Park. I wasn't able to go to too many away games outside London, but I did make it to Birmingham for this one. I managed to arrange a lift from a lorry driver who was taking some timber from the docks up to Solihull. Villa Park was quite a stadium, the best I'd seen apart from Highbury. The last time we went there we had been slaughtered 5-0, but that was in 1913, also in the Cup. Dad was at that game. However, on this occasion we managed the game well, and won quite easily, if just by the only goal of the game. A Dick Richards free-kick was put away by Bill Brown. Lock, the Saints 'keeper, didn't stand a chance. This set us up for a clash with Derby County at Stamford Bridge.

Our scoring performance in the Cup was beginning to look impressive. Watson had got both our goals in the draws against Southampton, taking his Cup tally to five. Billy Moore had notched up three, Richards and Brown had grabbed one each. By the time we got to Stamford Bridge our League record showed that we, having played 31 matches, had won 14, drawn nine, and lost only eight. Our goals 'for' had reached 44 at a cost of 29 goals conceded. We had gone nine games without defeat. We had lost one game out of 18, winning 11 of these.

The crowd at the Chelsea game was impressive. I read in the paper later the following week that almost 51,000 people had attended that game. This was an all-Second Division tie and it was a real cracker. Derby had taken three points out of four from us in the League, but that had been at the start of the season when we were going through our bad patch, or settling down period as it had become known on the terraces. County had knocked out Bristol City, the Wednesday and First Division Tottenham on their way to the semi-final, no mean feat. But more than this, they had kept a clean sheet in the process. As such, we couldn't believe our eyes when just seven minutes into the game we were two goals to the good. We ended up taking the game 5-2. A truly splendid performance. The two Billys, Moore and Brown, scored twice each and Richards got the other. Another Moore (Jimmy) scored for Derby and their other goal came from our very own Billy Henderson, who put the ball into his own net. We were only the third Cockney club to reach the FA Cup Final.

I suppose I was one of the lucky ones really. Like everyone else, I was feeling the pinch, but as a young man, with no family obligations, apart from 'keep' to mother, I was not as hard put as those who had to put toke into the mouths of wives and six or seven kids. Before the strike, there were days when if I had got some work the day before I wouldn't bother going on the stand. I can read you see, and am good with figures. When there was work, the fore-man knew that I could be on the pencil with no fear of problems.

I wasn't work-shy though. On Saturday's (when the Irons were away) Dad and I became Thames Borley men. He had worked on the shrimp boats down at Barking as a boy, and he knew a bit about what life there was in the river. Whilst he took our catch home to boil up, I'd go down to Covent Garden on the bus and buy a bag of celery. You could get quite a bit for a tanner. The whiter the celery, the better it sells. So I would spend the rest of the day polishing the stuff with a clean white tea-towel. On the evening we'd push an old barrow around the pubs with mum's home-made bread. We'd make nearly as much as a day's work on the ships. This was the money I'd spend going to

West Ham. It would provide more than enough for the tram fare to and from the ground, a portion of fish and chips before the game, entrance, a programme, and a drink for me and a mate after the match. Often I'd still have a sprasey left for a bite to eat on Monday morning.

I do not come from a big family. My older brother Bill had been killed at Passchendaele. My other brother, Danny, went off to Russia just before the Revolution. We hear from him occasionally, he's quite a big cheese over there, up to all sorts. He speaks fluent Russian, but still with a Cockney accent by all accounts. Now, I'm the only one left at home. I knew a lot of blokes not much older than me, like John, were out, married and producing sprogs like there's no tomorrow, but at that time, the strike notwithstanding, I was happy with my lot. Besides, It was no bad thing to be helping a bit at home. Dad was in the docks for over 20 years, all the time as a casual. That's how he lost his leg. He got knocked down in a scramble for work on the cobbles. He hit his knee on a railway line. Eventually he had to have the leg off. There's a lot of blokes who, in one way or another, have lost bits of their bodies due to the hazards of dock work. But that's the least of it. I saw one chap literally sliced in two when a mooring rope snapped off a mushroom and whiplashed back on him. So Dad counts himself lucky. Apart from the fish barrow, he makes a few bob mending watches for a shop in Crisp Street and he helps Mum with the washing she takes in. Most of the time they get by, but like everyone else, the strike takes its toll on them.

## The Cup Final

It was Bolton Wanderers, a good First Division side, in the Final at the new Empire Stadium at Wembley. There had been parades, rallies and celebrations all over the East End since we got through to the semi-final. Everywhere houses, shops and streets were decorated in claret and blue. There was a great feeling of expectation and congratulation just for reaching the Final.

Like us, the Trotters had not got to the Final by an easy route. Norwich, Leeds, two games against Huddersfield, and a quarter-final at Charlton was some campaign. They had beaten Sheffield United in the semi-final at Old Trafford, when a Davie Jack goal put paid to the Blades' hopes.

The Wanderers had some masterful players. Ted Vizard, the long-time Welsh international, outside-left David Jack, the smart and dangerous inside-forward Joe Smith, and in goal the stone wall himself, R.H.Pym. They scored nine goals on their way to the Final and only let in two. On form, they looked better in defence than us. We had conceded seven goals on the way to the Cup Final, but we looked stronger on the offensive, having netted 15 times in Cup games that season. I reasoned that this indicated that we would win the Final by three goals to two. It's a good job that this prophesy did not get back to a few of the dock foremen. They may not have been so trusting of my aptitude.

I had been a useful scholar as a kid. Dad didn't have any proper schooling, mother had taught him to read and write. She was always a stickler for education. It was her influence that caused me to take an interest in reading. Many of my days off work were spent at the library, or the local reading room. I read everything I could get my hands on. But the month before the Final was devoted to Tom Paine's *The Rights of Man*. I must have read it six times at least, not counting dipping in and out of it. I had bought the book for tuppence (the price of a programme) at a shop near to Covent Garden. I picked it up quite by chance. It was in a 'bargain box' outside the shop, which meant that it was falling apart. It was a toss-up between Tom and *The Nooks of Kent* by the Reverend Festimus Binstock. I think I made the right choice. I discussed it avidly with any one who would put up with me. I got into a big argument with a chap at the working men's club who was reading Adam Smith. He was at least three times my size, but I had him on the ropes from the start. I think he was about ready to clock me, which would certainly have knocked my head clean off my shoulders, before my mate Joe Gray pulled me away as I 'was urgently needed at home'.

I took Tom with me everywhere. During a terrible 0-0 draw at home to Bury, I tortured poor Joe (and everyone else in the vicinity, and that was quite a few, there being a 30,000 gate) that day with a reading just before half-time:

*What is government more than the management of the affairs of a Nation? It is not, and from its nature cannot be, the property of any particular man or family, but of the whole community, at whose expense it is supported; and though by force and contrivance it has been usurped into an inheritance, the usurpation cannot alter the right of things. Sovereignty, as a matter of right, appertains to the Nation only, and not to any individual; and a Nation has at all times*

*an inherent, indefeasible right to abolish any form of Government it*
*finds inconvenient, and to establish such as accords with its*
*interest, disposition, and happiness. The romantic and barbarous*
*distinction of men into Kings and subjects though it may suit the*
*condition of courtiers, cannot that of citizens; and is exploded by the*
*principle upon which Governments are now founded. Every citizen*
*is a member of the sovereignty, and, as such, can acknowledge no*
*personal subjection: and his obedience can only be to the laws.*

I paused at the end of this to find the surrounding throng looking at me as
if I had just fell out of the sky. It was one of those moments when less than
nothing was happening on the pitch. Jack Young was standing over the Bury
centre-forward. Our visitor looked lifeless. The referee seemed to be admin-
istering the last rites. The linesman on the left was talking to a bloke in the
Chicken Run, scratching his back-side with his flag. Someone shouted from
the back, "Oi, Garibaldi, give it a rest!" Joe looked at me and said, "Tell it to Syd
King."

We had 11 games to play in the six weeks prior to the Final. Something of
a tall order. The Hammers had gone 15 games without defeat before we lost at
Barnsley, game number 38 of the season. For some reason, King played his
strongest team for all the remaining games, giving no one a rest. This seemed
really daft to me. Come the week of the Final there were doubts about the
fitness of Ruffell, Watson, Young and Hufton. But they were all in the starting
line-up.

The day of the match I decided to walk to Wembley. I could have taken
public transport, but most of my mates didn't have the fare. I wasn't exactly
flush that week, having spent five bob on a ticket to the match, so I decided to
go along with them. About a dozen of us started out, but we soon joined the
throng walking from the East. It was like a pilgrimage. We spoke to farm boys
who had already tramped from Romford and Dagenham. I chatted for a while
with a group of fishermen from Southend, who had moored at Barking and
had marched from there. As we walked through the East End, hordes joined
us from Whitechapel, Limehouse and Bethnal Green. Tens of thousands of
shoes and boots already worn and holed, trudged towards the Empire
Stadium. Veterans from the Great War on crutches, small boys pushing and

pulling each other on every species of cart (two had a wheelbarrow). A sea of claret and blue rising towards Wembley. A cacophony of hooters, horns, klaxons and rattles filled the air. Everywhere hammers were waved, some purloined from fire-places, others six-foot creations of wood, papier maché and cardboard. Facsimiles of the Cup were hoisted on high from every quarter, painted white, silver and gold. The Irons were on the march.

We got to Wembley at around one o'clock. It was a fantastic structure, finished off just four days before we got there. At that point there seemed to be plenty of room. I guess we just took it for granted that everyone who wanted to see the game would be able to do so. After all, this was meant to be the Biggest and Best Stadium on Earth. The official programme said that it was "incontestably the finest sports ground in the world" and that it was "the largest in the world, the most comfortable, the best equipped." It went on to claim that it could hold "more than 125,000 people, and will accommodate 1,000 athletes. In area it equals the Biblical City Jericho. The circuit of its walls is half a mile in length …" Who would have thought they wouldn't get in? Pretty quickly the place was packed. People were coming in from everywhere, through gates, climbing over walls. Most of us had paid the dollar for our tickets, but the three or four that hadn't managed to get hold of one just clambered over a broken turnstile. It seemed that paying customers were in the minority. It was chaos and a bit frightening. We passed a rather posh couple of blokes offering some bemused attendants money to get them out, but the officials were as helpless as everyone else.

We found ourselves a place for a while. Kids were being rolled down over the heads of the crowd like a water-fall, being placed over the barriers at the foot of the terraces. Not long afterwards the whole crowd followed, firstly on to the cinder track, and then on the pitch itself. A solid mass now formed right across the field. By three o'clock, when the match was due to kick-off, the whole place was chocker-block. The pitch was covered with a seething mass of humanity. Being early birds, we had been pushed right to the centre of the pitch, face to face with the Grenadier and Irish Guards bands. The King must have arrived, because they started bashing out *God Save the King*. They got through this pretty sharp, in fact I can't recall hearing it being played at such a pace. It was like a gallop. Before the last note died away they were making a swift retreat. Joe thought that they were probably Arsenal supporters. Still, everyone stood motionless and quiet while the anthem was playing, so it had the effect of calming things a little.

After around three-quarters of an hour the playing area started to clear. At first this seemed to be simply because people had got fed up with milling about on the field, then I noticed the horses. Soon everybody was at least behind the touch lines, but only just. The pitch looked as if it was carved out of people. I read about the White Horse the next day. My first reaction was, "What white horse?" We had noticed a kind of dirty grey creature out on its own at one point, but it was one of many actually clearing the pitch. But I assumed it must be me, because people (most of whom hadn't been at the match) had seen it in the papers. It had been a nice day up to about half-past two and had clouded over about three o'clock, when His Majesty arrived. I took this as a sign that God was on the side of the working man. It then started to drizzle a bit. I reckon this must have had an effect on the photographs. Still, there you are. You can't always believe what you see.

Well, the match finally started. I think the authorities would have called the game off, but had been frightened that it might cause a mass protest. I mean, the stadium had already been effectively stormed. It wouldn't have looked good either with the King up in the royal box and all. We were in about six deep just by the goal facing west, so our view of the pitch was relatively good.

The playing area was cordoned with people. This gave the initial moments an intensity such as I have never experienced before. The pitch was darkened by the surrounding crowd and you could quite tangibly feel the collective gaze of the throng. Every individual movement seemed to threaten an incursion on to the field of play as we were packed so tightly together. Kay lost the toss so, of course, the Bolton skipper, Joe Smith, had us play the first half against the wind and into the sun. The players seemed quite understandably intimidated by the heavy presence of the crowd. At first, both teams huddled around the middle of the pitch, keeping well away from the shifting, undulating parameter. I could hear our goalie, Hufton, talking to supporters about his concern for his family in the stand. So when Davie Jack (their inside- right) broke away after only three minutes, his way to goal was more or less clear. No one seemed to have much heart to chase him. It was as if the players had agreed that the game wouldn't go to full-time and decided to make a show, at least for the time they were on the field. 1-0 to Bolton. While all this was going on, West Ham had only ten players on the pitch. Tresadern, a key defensive player, had been stuck in the crowd after going in to retrieve the ball.

After a short while, the game was stopped for around ten minutes while the crowd were pushed from the edges of the pitch. The situation was now suffocating. Every time the ball was making the touch line below head height it was bouncing back into play off of the spectators. At the restart, things were not really much better, but King (Syd not George) must have said something to the team. They slung everything at Wanderers. The pace was frantic. Then West Ham won a corner. As with all the corners Ruffell had to make a human alleyway, with the help of the peelers, to make his run at the ball. It was a beauty. Vic Watson closed in like a cobra, hitting an ironclad shot just over the bar. Hopes rose again as Richards bore down on the Bolton goal from the right wing. He teased past Jennings and then, in close, feigned and twisted to avoid Finney. Wanderers (and everybody else) expected him to centre the ball, but Dickie boy smacked in a low, rising shot, that tore through the concentrated atmosphere. The Bolton goalie, Pym, stuck out his right peg in desperation and he just about prevented the ball from entering the goal.

Just as we were bemoaning our luck at not being 2-1 up within 40 minutes, Butler, Bolton's outside-right, sent in a torturous cross that John Smith (their inside-left), who had come haring towards the Hammers' goal, managed to connect with. He barely got a toe to the ball. Hufton touched it, but could not stop the ball going into the net. The relief amongst the Irons supporters when the ref, Mr Asson, gave offside could be felt right through the vast host. We kind of reacted as a single unit. This was not the usual comfortable feeling of being in a crowd. There was some menace here. You felt as if, at any time, the quiet, lava-flow, insurgence that had taken part before the mass had settled was liable to reoccur. This had no connection to individual will. It was down to the instinct of the Leviathan crowd. The great, brainless, grunting beast that sagged around the touchline.

Half-time was a strange affair. The players decided to stay on the pitch. I say 'decided' but they were prisoners. There was no where for them to go. The stare of the multitude was oppressive and seemed to cause them to cower. It was less than ten minutes before they decided that they might as well get on with things.

The second half started with everything to play for. And the situation looked good for West Ham early on. However, with less than ten minutes gone, Jack Smith, their centre-forward, the only Jock on the park, picked up a lovely, drifting pass from Vizard on his left. Smith anchored his leg to a thunderbolt and shot past Hufton. The ball rebounded off the people standing behind the net, as reticent as any of the players to dwell too long near the swarm. As it darted back to the relative safety of the field, it very nearly bonked Smith in the back of his napper as he trotted back. Scottish footballers! They are a breed apart. The poetry of their movement is different, something …fluent and hopeful. The goal was met with a kind of muffled ripple of cheering and applause, which heightened the macabre, slightly unreal feeling the whole event had taken on. It all happened so fast that not many spectators realised that a second goal had been scored. After this the game petered out and Bolton won at a stroll. We never really showed the ability we'd demonstrated all season.

Charlie Paynter (the West Ham trainer) said afterwards that the pitch had been torn up badly by the crowd (and the horses) wandering over it. He was of the opinion that wingers Ruffell and Richards were impeded by holes and ruts. Billy Moore agreed. He saw the wings as an important consideration for the Hammers, that had been effectively cut off. But Captain Kay conceded that the better team had won and that West Ham had not been on form.

Being so far into the stadium, we were some of the last to get out. Wembley looked like a battlefield. Entrances and turnstiles had been smashed down, the whole outer ring of the stadium was damaged in some way or another. It was quite shocking. This was the site of an attack; mass destruction. Nowhere was it stated after the game, but what had taken place was a slow, insidious, magmatic, riot.

The walk back to East London was a long drag. I got home not much before midnight. The folks from up north were still celebrating in Piccadilly Circus. There were also celebrations in Canning Town that night as the team came home, but of course, I missed all that. To tell the truth I never expected that we would be celebrating defeat. But the next day I followed the second parade through the streets. Hundreds of thousands of people lined the roads to see the team being carried along in a tram covered in electric light bulbs, blazing out the crossed irons and the motto, "Well Done Hammers." We didn't quite make it, but we made it that far.

## Fortune's always hiding

Now it was back to the League. That was all a bit of anti-climax at first, but it was an intense run-in that went to the last game of the season. The team had to drag themselves up from the Cup on Saturday and the Sunday celebrations, for a game against the Wednesday, at Hillsborough, on Monday. Brown and Watson made it 2-0 to us. We were top of the table on goal average from Notts County and Leicester. We were all on 51 points.

The final day of the season could have thrown up anything. County were at Upton Park, Leicester took on Bury, who had a good season behind them, but nothing to play for now. If we lost and Leicester won, we would stay in Division Two. If everyone drew, or if we won, as long as Leicester didn't win by as many as us, then we would go up as champions. What a sweat! We lost to the County by the only goal of the game. This meant that Bury gained 26,000 temporary supporters. The Shakers did Leicester. We just got the runners-up spot from champions, Notts County. Leicester finished just behind us (quite rightly after putting eight by them and taking three points out of four). Into Division One for the very first time. It was our away form that had seen us through. We scored half as many at home (we got 42 away). We won over half of our games outside of Upton Park. Eleven victories on hostile territory. Looking back, the 6-0 win at Filbert Street during February had been crucial.

### 27 August 1923

Almost a year on from the last Stockport game. Our first home game of the 1923-24 season, Upton Park's baptism in the top division. I am provided with a bit of consolation. A decent enough win over the Arsenal. Bertie Fletcher got the only goal. Last Friday it was all over. We managed a month of unofficial action. The boys from the East End would have struggled on, it was the ports outside London that let us down, although Hull held out to the end of July. In the Smoke we had 60,000 out at the peak of the action.

It's strange, but the Cup performance looked a much bigger achievement as we battled it out for promotion. Later, during the strike, it seemed to mean even more. The Final itself was an historical moment. It got much more publicity than our strike, which is also peculiar. There was a quarter of a million people at Wembley and most came away, at worst disappointed. But, taking families into consideration, probably just as many people in London alone suffered from malnutrition, sickness and poverty as a direct result of the squeeze on wages and the unofficial action it provoked. History will remember the "White Horse Final", but will it remember us?

I suppose many of us chaps in the London docks thought we were unbeatable after the season we'd been through with the Irons. We'd won promotion, finishing as runners-up in the Second Division. Our number nine, Vic (Sergeant) Watson knocked in 22 League goals. I'll always say that he was the best 25 quids' worth that Syd King ever brought to the club. He finished the season off playing for England. His first cap and his inaugural international goal came against Wales. Oh how kind fate can be! Ted Hufton and Jimmy Ruffell also did well in the same team. Watson went on to bang in two against the Jocks. Then there was the Cup.

I wonder how it all happened. We put up with a lot while we had West Ham to think about. The results helped us take what the employers were doing to us. Perhaps it was just coincidence that they chose to make their final move in the close season.

But things come and go. I can't see West Ham winning the First Division, no matter how much I want it. And I know that our condition will force us to confront the employers again, probably the government too, before much time has passed. Perhaps a year or two. These things are, to some extent out of our control. Tom Paine understood this:

> ...it is impossible to control nature in her distribution of mental powers. She gives them as she pleases. Whatever is the rule by which she, apparently to us, scatters them among mankind, that rule remains secret to man ...There is always sufficiency, somewhere in the general mass of society for all purposes; but with respect to the parts of society, it is continually changing its place.

Our time will come again. Down here in the docks and at Upton Park. Our job is to be ready.

# Homage to
# Len Goulden

# Chapter Four

*Feathers —*
*That perches in the soul —*
*And sings the tune without words —*
*And never stops — At all —*
      Emily Dickinson

## Letter 29 August 1936

Dear Danny,

Well this brings back memories. You off on another crusade and me writing to you about what's happening back here. Everyone's pleased that you got where you were going though. I think some of us had visions of you ending up back in Russia.

I've just got back from the match. I went with Joe and it was pretty good. It's always nice to do Tottenham. Len Goulden got both our goals. It ended up 2-1. With Charlie Walker at the back and Reggie Weare between the sticks we look strong defensively again this season and with Len up front I'd say we are a fair bet for promotion.

There's been quite a lot about Spain in the papers, it's hard to say where the government is likely to come down on it. Baldwin and Eden have kept their cards close to their chests, but on the whole the spirit is to go along with the non-intervention agreement.

Mum sends her love. She doesn't say much, but I know she's concerned about you. Take care of yourself Dan, if only for her sake. After losing Dad in the winter, I think it would kill her if anything happened to you.

Work is just the same really, swings and roundabouts. Oscillation from the hard to the downright intolerable. We had a few deep sea traders in last week, on a job and finish so it was fairly busy. But I'm still happy to be a single man as far as dock work is concerned, but you know all that anyway. I suppose it's the same in your case. Blow being spliced to you! You would have sent any right thinking woman round the bend by now. I spoke to old Jed Crother the other day during a muggo and he said that even though he doesn't agree with your politics, you being "something of a 'Philadelphia lawyer' when it comes to matters political". There was always a huffling job for you as far as he was concerned. If that's not enough to keep you in Spain I don't know what is. How that man hasn't been topped by someone over the years. Many a time I have thought of whacking him on the noggin with a portion of dunnage. Still, enough of these happy thoughts.

I don't know why you're doing what you're doing Dan, but stay safe and the very best of luck to you.

Well, I'll close now. I hope this gets to you.

Best wishes.

Charlie.


## Letter 21 November 1936

Dear Charlie,

It was good to hear from you. I hope Ma is doing a bit better now. Tell her I am fine and will be back as soon as we've sorted the fascists out, which I don't think will be very long.

It was heartening to know that Goulden is still knocking 'em in for us. I hear that he got his first cap against the Irish. First of many I suspect. I'm sure you're right, it's a promotion season for the Irons. It'll be interesting to see how Ted Fenton's brother Benny will work out. I saw him play for West Ham schoolboys and he's played for London and Essex schools as well. He comes from a good breed, but at 18 perhaps he's a bit young. If we hadn't have taken so long to warm up last season, we'd have been in the First Division this year. Look who finished in front of us. Manchester United, Charlton and Sheffield United. We scored more goals than any of them. Fifteen from Len, 22 from Mangall, 90 goals in all. With them out of the way, who's to stop us? It was close in the end anyway. We goes and beats the eventual champions up at Old Trafford, what an opening goal that Fenton effort was, then we get ourselves beaten by them by the odd goal at home, with 6,000 more supporters than they could muster. I remember going.

It all hung on that game at the Boleyn against Charlton. A 43,000 gate. What a crush! How did we lose that one? Still, the Haddicks have done well. From Division Three South to the First Division in two years, that's good going.

It's a difficult story to tell you why I'm here and to be honest Charlie, I don't really know myself. There are a number of chaps out here in their late 30s, but I am one of the oldest at 41. I should know better I suppose, but I'm still fit and unattached. I think the blokes who are married, some with kids at home, are really much more committed than me. I mean, where else would I be? I recall coming back from Russia. The first match I saw was when the Hammers entertained the Duke and Duchess of York in March 1924. It was the game against Spurs, in aid of the Dockland Settlement. I remember then thinking that their kind had won. Then there was the General Strike and all the problems following that. I suppose this is doing something.

It's not just chaps here. There's a lot of women too, many involved in the fighting. Most of us came with the idea of simply 'Fighting against Fascism'. In that way it's a bit like the reason I took myself off to Russia 20 years ago. You go with a simple moral reason in mind and it all gets complicated from there on.

The history of this war goes way back to 1931, when the Spanish Republic first started. The government had problems with the right-wing in the army and the church. At the same time it had trouble with its own more militant supporters, who had it in for the clerics in particular. To add to the difficulties there were strong Nationalist movements in Catalonia and the Basque country (sort of equivalents in Britain would be Wales and Scotland). It didn't get too much attention in Britain, but there was a right-wing attempt to take power in 1932, one of the armies involved being led by Franco. General Sanjurjo was in charge of the whole thing. This was put down, it has to be said, with a heavy hand. Just a couple of years later there was a communist revolt in a coal-mining district. This was again crushed.

In the elections in February of this year the parties on the left won a resounding victory and established a socialist government, with Azana in charge. With the memory of what occurred in 1932 still fresh in their minds, groups on the right were frightened that Azana would be like Kerensky was in Russia (he was the chap who succeeded Lenin). Out of this anxiety came what happened in July, a nationwide, right-wing, counter-revolution against a democratically-elected government. Franco, who had been banished to the Canary Islands, came back to Spain with contingents of the Spanish Army in Africa, which has linked up with the right wing here. With Franco at the helm the fascists have now taken much of the north-west and have a foot hold around Sevella in the south. It's really important for the Republic to hold on to Barcelona and Madrid if Spain is to maintain its democratically elected Republic. Otherwise, like Italy and Germany, it will become part of a Fascist Europe that will threaten first France, then Russia and finally Britain and America. We have to stop it here, Charlie.

You can tell that old goat Crother where he can stick his oar. I can't see me coming back to the river, Charlie. This war is going to change the lives of every working person in Europe. It's just part of the same thing that happened in Russia. Franco first, then Mussolini, and if 1935 was anything to go by, 154 seats Charlie – that number stays with me – the Labour Party will do the job in Britain sooner rather than later.

Our training was carried out at Albacete and La Rada over a month. We English did badly. There were few of us involved, and we found it hard to blend in. We were moved around a lot between stations. As soon as we had started work on one type of weapon, it was taken away from us. We were obliged to take part in manoeuvres. Not having much command of French made it difficult for us. We finally started working with the machine gunners, but the training was cut short and we were sent to the front. We were pulled out of training because of the big Nationalist offensive on Madrid. That was in October. We were put in the general reserve. We thought this meant a rest, but we were soon under bombardment. Our section leader was away, so I took command and was able to get our guns into position. We had five in all. But, thankfully, the artillery fire was not followed up by an attack.

We've been at the front the last ten days, a bit outside Madrid. We still haven't seen any fascists yet, but since that first day we've had to regularly put up with pretty heavy artillery fire from German and Italian batteries.

The worst thing, though, is the cold. You'd think Spain was hot wouldn't you? It freezes up at night, and sleeping in the open you really feel it. One or two chaps have literally fainted with the cold. But no one complains. Even though sleep is hard to come by and exhaustion is seemingly always just a moment away. We don't have the proper equipment either. For all that, the moral of the brigade is good.

The Republic has had big losses in continuous fighting. However, we've been successful in the main.

The fascist first wave got fairly near to Madrid, but they are not thick on the ground. This means that they can't drive any attack home. They can only concentrate on one place at a time. We've given them a bit of a hammering I can tell you. Whatever the papers say over there Charlie, we're not going to lose Madrid. We just need a bit of time to organise and get hold of and become conversant with our equipment.

We've taken some unfortunate casualties. Fred Jones was killed in one of the last bombardments. What a waste. Fred was our section leader. He was a posh bloke, but tough. He'd been kicked out of Dulwich College and had worked in the oil industry in South America. He had three years in the Guards behind him. Fred was a sincere communist and an organiser of the unemployed. It was a great loss to us. One of our best Lewis gunners, a former British Army man, was shot twice in the belly on reconnaissance. Another comrade is missing, probably dead. A good pal of mine over the last few weeks, Maclaurin was found dead. A sniper got him. He was always happy that chap. A real morale booster, no matter how dire the conditions. You can't help but be a bit shook up by such losses. This war is full of heroes. They risk and give their lives for democracy and stand against those who would force their rule on the people. I just hope most of them make it out alive. If only we could get to grips with the fascists. This kind of killing is closer to murder than war.

My Russian has been helpful. I've been doing a lot of work as liaison man and political delegate. None of us really know what's going to happen next, it's clear that things are going to get tougher.

Take care of Mum, Charlie. Like you say, it may be just as well we're both confirmed bachelors. But you should be looking for a wife now. Someone has got to carry on the line, how will the docks be worked otherwise? And who's going to go over Upton Park unless you get breeding? Let's face it, West Ham have to get 'em from birth.

All the best.

Dan.

## Letter 2 January 1937

Dear Dan,

I hope everything is going well for you and the cause. A collection was taken up the other day. I was told it was going round all the workers in the docks, it was for the International Brigade in Spain. Even though things are not good here, and people are just getting over Christmas and the New Year, I was informed that nearly £10,000 was raised from the dockers' pockets. It looks as if the pubs are going to be a bit quiet this weekend.

Mum is still pretty weak. But considering the weather, I think she is doing quite well. She reads everything there is to read about Spain and searches the wireless for reports and talks. She's becoming quite an authority on the subject. She tells me that she has tried to write to you more often, but can't help herself but implore you to come home. She ends up tearing the letters up. But she reads your letters over and over again, so do keep letting her know how you are.

You will be pleased to know that I have started walking out with Daisy Leggett, and have, for the moment, given up 'the floosies' as Mum calls my usual escorts. We have been to the cinema twice since you last wrote and went for an overly healthy stroll around Greenwich Park last Sunday. The films were really first class. *Anna Karenina* starred Greta Garbo as Anna, and Fredric March as Vronsky . The cast also included Basil Rathbone, Freddie Bartholomew and Maureen O'Sullivan. It was not entirely faithful to Tolstoy's great classic, but it was a very well crafted work. Rathbone was marvellous as the jilted husband, and Garbo seethed as the unfaithful wife, moved to forbidden love with the handsome Captain Vronsky. The final scenes are so dramatic as Anna does for herself under Vronsky's train.

*The Barretts of Wimpole Street* was also very good, with Freddie March again. This time he teamed up with Norma Shearer and Charlie Laughton, as Edward Moulton Barrett. I believe Laughton to be the best British screen actor of our time. He was masterly in his role, and had both of us resenting his character, the overbearing and dictatorial father. Maureen O'Sullivan was also particularly good as Elizabeth's younger sister Henrietta. Daisy and I were deeply moved by the plight of poor Elizabeth (Norma Shearer) and pleased at the final outcome achieved through her relationship with Robert Browning (March).

We also frequented the West Ham United ground to take in a friendly match against foreign opposition. It was most enjoyable.

I tell you all this ahead of Mother to cut-short any aspirations or aspersions you might have in respect of this acquaintance. Before you ask, we have no long-term plans, but are very comfortable in each other's company. I remain as confirmed as ever in my status as a single gentleman, with thoughts on intellectual and career developments rather than ambitions in the matrimonial stakes. As you know, I have long respected Daisy, both as a woman and as a member of the debating society, so watch what you scribble in response to this news my good brother.

Now that's out of the way, more news from the Hammers. Well, we've started the New Year on a positive note. We trounced Blackpool at home by three goals to nil. Stan Foxall opened the scoring followed by Simpson's first goal this season. Blackpool obliged with an own-goal to round off the match.

Some interesting newcomers have joined the ranks of the Irons since our last correspondence. We've got David Corbett, formerly of Hearts, a tough-tackling Caledonian right-half, and Fred Dell from Dartford. The Kentish man is six-foot plus, with a good history. We now also have Tudor Martin (yes, Tudor as in Henry VIII). He's a Welsh miner. He scored a hat-trick during the game up at St James's in September, unfortunately the rest of the team conspired to chuck the match 5-3. This was the second game for Jim Holmes (formally of Sheffield United). His first game saw us lose 1-0 away to Blackpool. I think we can hope for much from Martin, having scored 45 times in 116 outings for his previous club, Swansea Town. Another Welsh import, this time coming to us via Ireland (Newry Town), is Bill Roberts. I watched him when we entertained Olympique de Marseille (the friendly Daisy and I attended together) at Upton Park in October. He played well alongside his former team-mate, Paddy Peters, whom we acquired at the same time as Roberts. So, as you can see, Mr Paynter has been working hard. I think he wants to start up an International Brigade of his own.

I think the board had to do something after that outburst from old Davis last year. Remember? Better off in the Second Division!? With Charlie Walker at the back and goalie Reg Weare coming down from the Wolves, the defence looks more secure. Sam Small from Birmingham has replaced Mangnall and looks a useful signing. What with bringing in Martin, Fred 'the new Charlie Buchan', and Corbett, the directors have had to pay for Davis' bloomer. Still, at least he was honest enough to show up what everyone had been saying for years. It's voting with the feet that does it Dan. By my reckoning at this stage last season, the first ten home games, 30,000 more people had turned up. That means that gates are down by about 3,000 for each home game. Yes, old Davis has certainly cost the club a few bob. Solidarity, that's the word Dan. If the people stick together they can get what they want, never mind what the big-wigs think.

Incidentally, Len has now got three caps bestowed against Northern Ireland, Wales and the Czechs. All good wins. Not bad for a chap from the Second Division I'd say.

That, I think, concludes my news. Take care of yourself Daniel. We are all thinking of you.

Every good wish.

Charles

PS — Joe Gray got himself wed just before Christmas — Stratford registry office. I was a witness and found him guilty as charged. Now for the surprise. Mary Simkins. That's right, the barmaid at the Green Gate. A whirlwind romance with a woman of experience and ample proportions, just 12 years older than him (I was surprised the age gap was not wider). The happy couple have set up the matrimonial home in Mary's Plaistow residence (nice and close to the Boleyn, so he can hear the cheers at least). No one has seen Joe since, we hope for the best but fear the worst.

**Letter 24 February 1937**

Dear "Charles",

Thanks for your last letter. Call me an old, superstitious, socialist, but did I detect Daisy's fair hand in parts? If you ever see Joe again, tell him good luck. It seems a man is safer in the throes of a foreign civil war than he is at some of the watering holes back home. As you will know, I write quite a lot to Mum, and will do my best to keep doing so, although for most of the time this war is pretty mundane for long periods. It's crushingly boring at times. This moroseness is interspersed with very short periods of frantic activity. It's hard to write anything that does not relate to tedium, discomfort or news of someone's wound or death.

I heard about our Cup exit the other day. A chap from Lancashire was gloating about Bolton's performance. How is it that we can get double their crowd at home and still can't produce a team to beat them? But then Bolton are a bit different to Olympique de Marseille. Before you know where you are old Charlie P. will be pitting the Irons against the Follie Begiare. I'm not sure Daisy would approve of that fixture, she being an ardent attendee at the Tabernacle. How did she consent to be seen arm in arm with a Godless heathen such as yourself? Kin to a dammed socialist atheist. It must be Mother's Methodism that gives her hope of your conversion. Such faith is moving.

I've been with a small English group in the Machine Gun Company of the French Battalion of the First International Brigade. It is considered to be quite fortunate to be in a machine gun company. The section I am with is Franco-Belgium and is one of the best of the machine gun companies.

There's some good fellers in amongst the English blokes. Most a lot younger than me, but my experience as an organiser is helpful I think. David is the political delegate. He has taken my place in this job because his French is better than mine. He has not been well, and reacting badly to the cold, but he bears up bravely, and is now much better as the climate warms up. Guy Thomas is a hardy sort. He has no military training, but is now a good soldier and an even better scrounger, which is quite an asset in an army as ill equipped as ours. John McCormick, a Scottish teacher, he's just 24, is a fine hand on the machine gun as well as a sharp-shooter. He is also a bit of a poet. Then there is Harry Nation, a journalist, ex-actor. He's one of the few about my age. He strikes you as a bit of drip at first, always misplacing bits and pieces, but Harry has a way with things mechanical.

At the moment we are holding a vantage point in a country district, some way outside Madrid. I guess the fascists have about the same numbers as us in the area, but we don't see much of them. I was on watch a few days ago and I caught a glimpse of some movement on the stony chine about half a mile away. We have no binoculars so I pushed my body in close to the side of the trench to give myself some time to identify the figure. It moved in and out of view, all the time in a sort of rapid, crouching walk. It couldn't have been one of our group so far out. We knew that the fascists had been moving about a bit lately, probably looking to set up some better positions. After a while I was certain that this shadow was a member of a group maybe placing themselves in a position to take pot shots at us. I raised my rifle slowly over the rim of the trench, sideways on, trying to minimise the profile I was offering. If I could see him, then it was possible that he could see me. I looked down the sight. The figure was like a tiny, black beetle rummaging on the end of the barrel. He disappeared. I raised my head slightly, widening my focus to take in a wider area of the hogback my target was occupying. He emerged again and I quickly returned to my aim. I followed his course, as he popped in and out of view. Pretty soon I would have to commit myself. I have not killed anyone before, not in any direct sense. Although I had seen my share of atrocities in Russia, I had never had to watch as I cut another person down. I was losing my nerve. Was it just a peasant? But why would a peasant be up here and jigging about in such a way? The figure had started to retrace its steps. I had drifted up from my stance. My grip lightened. I stared at the tiny dot, that had now been exposed for sometime. I guessed that whoever it was could not have much fighting experience, given the time he had been presenting himself as a target. Swiftly I returned to the firing position, took aim, squeezed the trigger and fired. The figure froze for a split second and vanished. Had I hit him? If I had, was he dead or wounded? Had he taken cover? Was he ever there in the first place? I feel terribly guilty or perhaps it's resentment. I don't think I would feel this way if I just knew that I killed the man. But the whole thing is so detached. You kill, or try to kill another person, who is no more than a spot on the landscape. The person, the act, is so distant that you have no knowledge of who this human being is, what does he look like? Were my intentions realised? How do I take the responsibility/consequences of my actions if I do not know the outcome of what I do?

You'll probably be interested to know that we have been playing the noble game here. The Spanish love their footy.

I couldn't get a West Ham team together, but we had a London v Glasgow match, which the Jocks just took 13-8. An all-British side beat a combined American/Irish team, but lost to a French XI 5-3. The Spanish, who have the home, not to mention the numerical advantage, beat the French by eight goals to four. All this was pretty suspect as the 'tournament' was organised by a Japanese barber who speaks no known European language. All the games, calling for a neutral official, were refereed by a Flemish-speaking Arab engineer who revelled in the name of Ahmen O'Harah (he claims no heritage from the Emerald Isle). He had no idea about the rules of Association Football at the outset, but having received 40 minutes coaching from the Tokyo sniper, proceeded to act just like an English referee at Upton Park. Yes, that bad!

I suspect something decisive will happen quite soon and that it will not be too long now before I'm back home. Love to everyone Charlie.

Take care.

Danny


### Letter 1 May 1937

Dear Daniel,

We are all thinking of you and hope that you are keeping well, despite the inclement conditions that prevail within the theatre of war.

I am pleased to tell you that Daisy and I are now officially engaged. We have set the date for the nuptials a year hence. We both very much hope that you will be able to make this happy event, and will do us the honour of acting as best man. Joe has agreed to be a witness while Mary will be maid of honour.

It's been a while since we heard from you last Dan. Please write soon as we are all quite worried about you. I know that it may be that you are writing and the letters are just not getting through and that we sometimes went months without hearing from you when you were in Russia, but that was not a war, well at least we didn't know about how dangerous it actually was at the time. So please contact Mum as soon as you can.

End of season Dan and all our hopes are dashed. Sixth! Seven points behind the champions. Leicester, who go up with Blackpool. They are replaced with Manchester United and Sheffield Wednesday. That's four seasons in the top seven. It drives you crazy don't it? But what can you do? You lose 12 matches, what can you expect? We scored 73 goals. We let in 55. It takes us so long to warm up. We didn't lose a game in the last nine, and lost only two over 22 games in the second half of the season. But we were defeated in nine matches out of the first 18, we won only six games in that lot. Additions like Dr James Marshall from the Arsenal (a quack playing for the Hammers, Paynter must know we are sick) and Charlie Bicknall from Bradford at the back, have made all the difference. Since Bicknall arrived we've conceded nine goals in 12 games, one and one third goals a game. In the previous 30 League games we let in 46. Over a goal and a half per game! Likewise after Dr Jim started his career at Upton Park, at inside-right, we scored 22 goals. That's almost two goals a game. We scored something less than one and three quarter goals a game before we signed him. That's an overall improvement of over a third of a goal a game. Over a 42-game season that's around 14 goals to the good. On the 73 goals scored in the League this season this would represent more than a one-fifth improvement overall!

Len scored just 15 again, but as usual he made many more. East End boy does good, eh Dan?. He's a cert for England over the next few years.

I feel better now I've got that off my chest. Don't forget, write soon.

Charlie.

### Letter 15 May 1937

Dear Charlie,

I send this, like my last letter to you, via an English comrade who is going home. Mum's letters I send through the usual channels. So while our exchanges take a little longer, they are uncensored, as you might notice if you compare Mum's letters to this and the last one I sent you. All written material is molested without mercy. Even the most harmless of details are scoured out for the most obscure reasons.

I'm glad to hear about you and Daisy. She's a lovely girl Charlie. I'd be glad and proud to be your best man. Mary as MAID of honour? Modern times! Thanks for all the stuff on West Ham's performance. I've got no idea what you mean, but I do see more and more what you and Daisy have in common. You're either brilliant or unhealthily obsessed. Maybe all that tally work is doing it. Perhaps you need to have a word with the man on the beach, some time on the block, just to rest your brain, might be a good idea.

I'm in hospital at the moment. I've been here for nearly two months. I've been wounded, and although it is not life threatening, I have been pretty poorly and am still quite weak. It is certain that I won't be much good as a soldier from now on. I was knocked unconscious by sniper fire. At the same time I got a round in the chest and I then sustained another wound in the knee while I was down. Never be a sitting duck when there are fascists around Charlie.

We were in reserve in the Casa del Campo, that's a big forest, a bit like Epping, but it is behind a big mountain range. Snow capped peaks and all. It's called the Guadarama. McCormick and three other Lewis gunners were sent up to the front with a French infantry company. They were ambushed by Moors. The gunners covered the retreat. The young teacher was found dead at his gun.

Then it was back to the front for the rest of us. We were now plagued by the cold. We were obliged to sleep out in the open with no blankets, they had been left behind in favour of more ammunition. We advanced into position at the worst possible moment, dusk, moving into some abandoned trenches. The fascists had the precise range and did for us.

We were sent back into reserve. We had to make a night march back. There was a truck full of wounded following us. The driver must have taken us for fascists because he flew past us, a rifleman in the passenger seat of the cab shot Dave, catching him in the side. Most of the group went on, but Guy, Harry and me waited with Dave in the hope of picking up transport. We knew vehicles would pass, but it could mean a wait of minutes, hours or all night. Anyway, carrying Dave would have killed him pretty quickly, so we thought we had no choice. As dawn broke, we stopped another lorry. We loaded Dave on the back. As we climbed in, I was stunned by a bullet that skimmed the side of my head, just above my right ear. The next thing I knew I was waking up here. It seems I was hit in the left knee as my comrades were dragging me into the cover of the lorry. Guy had tried to return fire to cover me and was hit twice himself. First he was caught in the shoulder, which stopped him firing, then straight between the eyes. The lorry sped off leaving him dead in the road. As we left the scene Harry discovered that he had also been wounded, but in the panic he hadn't noticed it. He was at my bedside when I woke up. He'd caught a round in his right shin, not a bad break, but he died yesterday of blood poisoning.

It's quite wonderful to be in this place in many ways. The commitment you see in the wounded is amazing. What they have done for people they did not, do not and will not know, is beyond belief. If anyone is doubtful of humanity and people's concern for others, they should come to Spain. The nurses too are above words. They tend to us tirelessly, sometimes working around the clock. They come from everywhere. I have adopted Carla, a black American girl from New York. She is a marvel Charlie. Her care is awesome and she is quite the most beautiful woman I have ever seen. She has a massive intellect, and has read everything. She reads me poetry when I can't sleep and we discuss all the facets of life, even football. I will convert her Charlie, her charity would make her a natural for West Ham. I've asked her to marry me more than once, but I'm not the only one. She pats my hand and tells me that I'm beautiful, laughing slightly. But I am, for the first time in my life, smitten. She is an ebony light. My love for her humanity has rooted. I dream of her relaxed smile, half-closed eyes and the tone of her voice reading Walt Witman, Emily Dickinson and Robert Frost envelops my mind:

*I loafe and invite my soul. (Walt Witman)*

Well, it's all over bar the shouting for me Charlie. I don't know where this war is going, but it's an awful type of attrition; a kind of deadness. The spirit is willing, but it gets no nourishment. This is what drives you mad about it. At least in Russia, in the first place, there was a belief, a sense of getting somewhere. But like Russia after the revolution, the worst type of human ineptitude takes over.

The Republicans must win this war Charlie, but it doesn't look promising. Like all civil wars, the fighting is bitter. It's probably the most traumatic event in Spanish history. The war is important for Europe. It has become a focus for the struggle between left and right. An ideological battleground on a continental scale. Irish Catholics are fighting on the Nationalist side, Welsh coal miners have signed up with the Republicans. Almost every European nation is represented in the war as well as people from South America, the USA, Asia and Africa. Hitler and Mussolini want a Nationalist victory. They are using it as a testing ground for their new weapons and military tactics. The Soviet Union supports the Republicans as they hope to install a communist government.

The French Popular Front government under Blum is naturally sympathetic to the Republic but afraid to rub the right wing in France up the wrong way by being over supportive. I know that there's a lot of support in Britain for the Republic, but the likes of First Sea Lord Chatfield see Franco as 'a good Spanish patriot'.

The non-interventionism has overwhelmingly favoured the Nationalists. France, America and Britain have given no aid to either side, sticking by the international agreement. But the Germans and Italians have provided the Nationalists with masses of equipment and tens of thousands of troops. Italian submarines attack merchant ships. Guernica was bombed in April by German planes. True, the Soviets have also broken the agreement in favour of the Republicans, but they have not been able to match the German and Italian contribution.

Now Britain has agreed with Mussolini to accept the status quo in Med, under 'A Gentleman's Agreement', and have made it illegal for British subjects to fight in Spain. Strange that our lot should accept Mussolini as 'a gentleman'.

If the Republicans lose this war it will be a defeat for France and Britain. A legitimate government would have been overthrown by force. What would Tom Paine have to say about that Charlie? It will put the Soviet Union into a defensive posture against the nations to its west as a whole. This will leave Europe open to the combined forces of fascism.

Do you know, the nearest I got to a fascist was a dot in the sights of my rifle. I don't even know if I so much as bruised him. The nature of war has changed since Billy's day. Now wars have become remote from the people fighting them. The enemy is anonymous. As in Guernica, death comes suddenly from the sky or from over a ridge.

I'll need to stay here until I'm completely fit as I will have to smuggle myself out of Spain, so you might not hear from me for some time. Tell Mum not to worry. I'll be home for the wedding.

What a waste if the Republic fails. We will be paying for it for a hundred years. I'm probably very down, but we started out so full of optimism and within the space of less than a year the whole thing has turned sour. Just like our dreams, eh Charlie?

Dan

*14 May 1938 — Berlin. The England football team were obliged to give the Nazi salute against their wishes, following a request by the British Ambassador. The side that opposed England was selected after months of trials. They came to the Olympic Stadium in Berlin fresh from ten days' intensive preparation in the Black Forest. Goering, Goebbels and 110,000 Germans watched Stanley Matthews, who had torn the German defence apart throughout the game, glide, yet again, through their lines. He sent a perfect cross to the feet of a Jewish boy from the East End of London. Len Goulden struck the left-foot volley from 25 yards out . It screamed into the back of the net. It was England's sixth goal of the game. The representatives of 'the master race' had scored three. First Jesse Owens, now Golden Len.*

*Goulden went on to play 14 times for his country. He was on the losing side just twice (both away games). England scored 42 goals in those games (excluding the match against the Rest of Europe), more than three goals a game.*

# From Water Rat to Desert Rat

# Chapter Five

**T**WO DAYS after West Ham's appearance in the Cup Final at Wembley, Italy declares war on France and Britain. 10 June 1940. Not unexpected. The declaration of war that is. The War Cup Final would have been a surprising prospect at the start of this strange season. I had very little idea quite what these events would mean for me.

The Hammers had reached the Final with some smashing form. It was the time of the Phoney War, of course. Mind you, we had almost blown it at Stamford Bridge in the semi-final. 4-0 up and we let the Cottagers put three past us. I was praying for the final whistle. This is when football is agony and you really ask yourself why you put yourself through such trials. You try to rationalise it. You say to yourself that it doesn't exactly matter very much. You tell yourself that in the scheme of things, what with the war and all, a football match, a whole football season, the bloody game in general, doesn't amount to a great deal in comparison to history, world events, your own bleedin' life. But it just does not work. Every minute is a lifetime and your guts twist and turn. You want to leave but you must stay. You hate every one of the team for throwing the security of a four-goal lead away, but you are blindly, stupidly, angrily loyal, as you rain curses down on everyone from the directors of the club to the tea lady.

As the last ten minutes of the game crawled by, more and more I convinced myself that the referee 'looked like a West Londoner'. I could see him going home to his old ma somewhere off of the Fulham Palace Road (the last she heard of his old man was when he was going to check if his bike was all right, that was in 1895). As soon as the final whistle goes, all this just disappears into thin air. West Ham have won. You are going to Wembley and everyone of the lads out there on the pitch is a great bloke, who has given his all for you, the club and the East End of London. That's what keeps you going until the next time and it is why you pay at the gate. Nearly 33,000 of us had done just that for this game, and those of us who made our way home to the East felt we had got value for money. It's always good to beat another London side. You can whack the FA Cup winners or the champions of the First Division (not that we do that very often), but it still does not compare to coming away from another London ground having just plundered three points or bundled them out of the Cup, preferably in the early rounds.

I volunteered for service late in 1940. Being in the docks, I didn't need to go to war, and Daisy was not totally taken with the idea, what with little Jenny being so young, but I thought I should really. Joe had joined up right from the start, and a lot of my mates had followed suit. Besides, in the end it was a fight against fascism. By the end of March 1941 I found myself in North Africa facing a massive advance by General Erwin Rommel and the Afrika Korps.

Our Cup Final team looked quite strong. Herman Conway in goal, at the back Charlie Bicknell, Charlie Walker, and Ted Fenton. Dick Walker played inside-forward. At wing-half we had Joe Cockcroft. Sam Small, Alec Foreman Archie Macaulay, Len Goulden, and Joe Foxall made up a strong attacking line-up. Wembley was the culmination of what had been an interesting season, that had taken place in an odd and frightening time.

The proper season had only gone three matches when we declared war on Germany. I can't believe that I saw the stopping of football as a bit of a tragedy at the time. We'd opened the season with a 3-1 win at Plymouth, Hubbard had got two and Wood the other. Two days later we beat Fulham at Upton Park. Wood and Ted Fenton got one apiece in a good 2-1 victory. Although we lost 2-0 to Leicester at home, in what proved to be the final game in the English Second Division until August 1946, I was disappointed that we would not get a chance to build on our early form. It just goes to show by how much you can be out in your priorities. Football had just carried on in 1914, but now there was the fear of air raids, so it seemed to make sense, alongside all the other restrictions on crowds at the pictures, the races and the like. But time went by with not much happening and after a few friendlies, leagues were put together within a regional framework.

I was sent up to Scotland to disembark. Before we left I managed to go to Ibrox Park. I had heard there was a game, but until I got to the ground I had no idea who was playing. It was an 'old firm' game. It was an eventful match that almost ended in a riot. Delaney, a Celtic forward, was floored by the Rangers' goalkeeper. Mounted police were brought in as the rival supporters went potty. So not a bad introduction to the battlefield. The next day we boarded the very fine looking *Stratheden* and zig-zagged down to the Med, arriving in Egypt after about a week. It was only when we reached dry land that we found out that our sister ship, the *Strathaden* had been torpedoed.

I suppose the war in the desert had begun when Italy had invaded Egypt in September 1940. It looked like it hadn't lasted long. The whole advance came to a halt after about 50 miles and just three days, at Sidi Barrani. Early in December we started our offensive in the Western Desert. The Eye-ties fell back in total disorder. The Aussies captured Bardia, just inside Italian Libya and took 40,000 prisoners at the start of the New Year. By the end of January, Tobruk (about 60 miles up the coast from Bardia) was taken by a combined British and Empire force. Not long after this the main body of the Italian Army had been cut off by British armour at Beda Fomm. By mid-February 130,000 of the enemy were prisoners of war. It looked all over before half-time. Then in March the Axis decided to play big Erwin up front.

Our first game in the Football League War Cup was against Chelsea. The last time we had played the Blues had been the spring of 1932, our last game in the First Division (we finished rock bottom that year). They had beaten us 3-2 at Upton Park (Tommy Yews and Stratford lad Jim Barrett did their best for us). In the winter of the same year they had knocked us out of the Cup in the first round. We lost 3-1 at their place. This time we were drawn at the Boleyn. It was an exciting game that we just took 3-2, courtesy of an own-goal. Fenton and Archie Macaulay got the others. I liked Macaulay a lot. We'd signed him from Glasgow Rangers before the start of the 1937-38 season. Archie could make and get goals. He scored 16 times during 1938-39, including a tremendous hat-trick in our 6-1 win over Tranmere Rovers at Upton Park. We had an easy 2-0 win in the second leg at Stamford Bridge, Foreman and Sam Small doing the business. 'Revenge is a dish best served cold' and I had two helpings over this tie with custard on the pudding.

On 24 March the Afrika Korps struck. We fell back in disarray. By the end of April we had, at one point, been forced all the way back into Egypt. Wavell was replaced by Auchinleck as commander-in-chief in June, but things really didn't go any better. A string of reversals and outright defeats followed. In November, Operation Crusader got no where. The 5th South African Brigade was destroyed. Rommel took Benghazi in January. By mid-June the British Operation Cauldron was defeated and by the end of the month we had lost Tobruk. In July, Auchinleck drew a line in the sand. We made our stand at Alamein and managed to repulse a series of German attacks. This was to be the first Battle of Alamein. Churchill came to Egypt at the start of August. He couldn't have been too keen on what he saw because first Auchinleck got the big elbow in favour of Alexander and on 13 April, Bernie Montgomery assumed command of the Eighth Army.

At about this time that I went out of the line back to Cairo. For me this was one of the most marvellous places in the world. It is a huge rambling city, packed with people. It gives off a terrible stink. The open sewer of the Nile mixes with the constant smoke of cooking fires and the strong tobacco that most people are killing themselves with. This mingles with the clanging of the trams, the shouting that literally everybody seems to be involved with, and the clatter of backgammon that gets played in every corner and nook.

The city is a mixture of old and new, west and east, military and civilian. The tall buildings with their flashing adverts and the stately white houses, bedecked in red peppers put out to dry, create a kind of contradiction that can make you a bit dizzy at first, coming from the monotony of the desert and the khaki-clad world of war.

Of course, most of the chaps wanted to make for the Berka, the area of the city given over to brothels. If you didn't pay a visit there you would be seen as a bit peculiar to say the least. But it was a real dump. We went into one of the huge houses and were shown up a stone staircase. The place reeked of disinfectant and urine, like a poorly attended public toilet. There was a queue at every door. As one chap came out another went in, to demands from the girls, "Be quick. Very busy." The women really did not appeal to me. They were dressed in rags that were soaked through with sweat. I saw a couple of the girls fighting over one bloke, really slamming into one another. An Aussie at the front of one row was looking through a keyhole giving a blow-by-blow account of a comrade's activity to the others waiting their turn. Two others behind him were shouting at the door telling 'Reg', the performer, to 'get on with it'.

It turned me right off, I can tell you. My group got lost in the various lines for service, so I gradually doubled back and waited outside. They all turned up fairly soon after, bragging about the action they had seen. I smiled and jeered along with them, not having the courage to tell them that I had sloped out without doing the business. This wasn't out of any strong feelings of guilt about Daisy, although she'd have killed me if I'd have brought anything more than a souvenir pyramid back. This would have probably been a much more painful death than any dose of 'syph'. The thing that had really done it for me was the little girls of about eight or nine who went in and out of the rooms with towels and disinfectant, occasionally telling the prossies that the Madame said that they were taking too long. Soon they would be taking up their place in the rooms. When you looked hard at the whores, they weren't much older than these little lasses. Take away the fag that they had cadged from a soldier, the runny make up, the stained hair, they were just kids. But to most of the chaps these girls were not really women. I don't know if they regarded them as even being human. They were 'bint', part of this life in this place, that, in some sense, bore no relation to reality. Reality was at home. For many of the boys, being out of the line was like being on holiday from hell in hell. The law was that you made the best of it. If it was good or bad it was better than the front and the desert. Even the questionable comforts of a squalid brothel and a harrying whore were better than a slit trench facing the Afrika corps. They dehumanised these girls, but at the same time they were dehumanised. In war everyone involved is the victim. The only victor in war is war itself. Bits of young men died in those knocking shops. The search for warmth and sanctuary in human contact was brutalised, raped, but it all gets dismissed by 'Marleesh'. In the end the soldier learns to value little more than the survival of himself and his mates

Now the lads were determined to get drunk. I had a few in a dingy dance hall, but didn't fancy this for rest of the day and night, so I wandered off and managed to get a lift in an Aussie lorry to Mena to take a peek at the Pyramids. It was the Sphinx that took my breath away though. I gazed at it in awe, but was puzzled why it had no nose. I'd been nabbed by a guide, who told me that Napoleon had knocked off the nose because the face was Negroid. I didn't really grasp what this meant, but didn't push the point. The Great Pyramid was quite something from the outside, but it was a bit of an anti-climax inside. The smell was not unlike the brothel, so I didn't stay long.

The next day I jumped on a tram from the barracks. Cairo was about a 40-minute journey, a bit longer than the lorry drive of the day before, but much more interesting. People were hanging on to every bit of the tram. One bloke, who I think had a nail hold in the paint work, fell off while trying to pay the conductor who had been bawling at him for at least 15 minutes.

I got into the city and went into a cafe after running the gauntlet of the nagging street traders. Worse than Petticoat Lane ever knew how to be. I sat down at a table in the street and ordered a coffee. What I got was nothing like I'd had before. At first I thought I'd been done. The cup was not much bigger than an egg-cup. The stuff in the cup – to call it 'liquid' would not be accurate, it was more like half-set tar – was a pungent brown-black morass, something to chew rather than drink. For all that, I thought 'when in Rome...' The sweet-ness of my first cautious sip was overpowering. I would have spat it out but my mouth would not open, I was compelled to swallow. The brew wound its way down my neck and into my guts, seemingly taking most of the inner lining of my throat with it. I then noticed that something was touching my foot. I looked down and there was a little lad. He'd cleaned one of my boots, which was shining like freshly polished glass. The other boot looked disgusting next to it. He had his hand out. This was blackmail; piastres or it would seem to the rest of the world that you'd stolen a dead man's boot for the next 24 hours. I gave him his ransom and he pointed to my coffee and then made a motion as if to eat. I took this as advice and asked to see a menu.

I had no idea what I was ordering, but I was brought something that resembled a clutch of large shell fish, a bit like whelks, but with a deep orange-red hue. There was something brooding about them. They were accompanied by something that looked akin to my coffee, but had the smell of old socks. I carefully dipped the very tip of my little finger in this to taste. I placed the drip on the end of my tongue. At first it was similar to the taste of vinegar, but then a kind of shock went up into my eyeballs and the front of my mouth was on fire. I gulped the rest of the coffee down in one go in an attempt to extinguish the fireball that had spontaneously combusted in my head, but this made it worse. Now my neck was ignited as well, and an instant cramp ensued in the pit of my stomach. The boy was still furiously polishing my boot, following it around as it lashed about in response to my torture. Somehow I remembered the boy's advice and rammed one of whelk look-a-likes into my blazing mouth. I chomped at it in desperation, watery eyes bolting, searching what was left of my taste buds for any sign of relief. I jammed in another, although my furious mastication was having little effect on the first evil mollusc. The boy was now on his feet holding the little platter with the remaining whelk things on it up for me. I pushed in another, although I could not properly close my mouth now. I grinded away at the creatures. Then I became aware that most of the people sitting around me on the crowded pavement were staring hard at the performance. So, almost without thinking I sat back down, shoo'd the lad away and crossed my legs in a nonchalant manner, continuing to slowly chew my rubbery burden. The eye-splitting shine of my boots made me look even more ridiculous. After a while I rose out of my seat with all the aplomb I could muster. I laid a few notes down and sauntered away, looking about me like a student of anthropology, still champing deliberately although my jaws ached. As soon as I was away from the cafe I turned into an alley and unloaded the obstinate crustaceans. Not a mark on any of them! If Rommel had found out about these things and stuck them around his panzers there wouldn't have been a weapon in the British Army that could have stopped them.

My mouth was sore for the next two days, but I did my best to take my mind off it. The next day I went and had a look at Farouk's palace and the Gezira oasis. The following afternoon I went to the Citadel and the three famous mosques. I had to put overshoes on to enter the mosques. I didn't want to take my boots off at the door; if I had I am sure I would have had to have gone back to the camp in my socks. You saw a few soldiers in these places, but mostly officers and older men. It seemed a shame to me. Most of the lads spent their entire time, when they got to either Cairo of Alexandria, in brothels and boozing. For most Egypt meant the four S's — Sun, Sand, Sin and Syphilis. This was the philosophy of the desert war when out of line; 'alakeefic'.

In the second round we were drawn away to Leicester. We held them 1-1 up at their place (Archie) and punished them 3-0 in the home leg. Foreman got the first two and Stan 'the Lincolnshire Poacher' Foxall knocked in the third. Next it was Huddersfield away. A hard-fought six-goal draw meant a replay just three days later. Foreman, Foxall and Macaulay (the same trio who scored in the first leg, in the same order) ensured a resounding 3-1 victory at the Boleyn Ground. We did Birmingham at Upton Park in the fourth round, Foreman and Macaulay netting yet again, Goulden and Small getting one each in an entertaining 4-2 win in front of our biggest crowd of the competition, nearly 19,000. So we told Goring to go and Luft his waffer as far up the Sudeten as he liked that day. Off we went to Stamford Bridge to take on the Cottagers. Always sounds so silly that. The 'Cottagers' from Craven Cottage. I looked up the word 'craven' just out of interest. It means 'cowardly'. A 'cottage' is 'a small, simple house, especially in a rural area'. It might be thought, by someone who didn't know better, that the mighty Hammers were going to play a band of cowardly rustics, from a home for simple midgets! Strangely, I remember thinking that maybe this was, in a way, a kind of ironic truth, although it was a peculiar time for me, having just finished Swift's *Gulliver's Travels*.

Monty hadn't been around much longer than a couple of weeks when the Afrika Korps came at us again. We found ourselves facing them at Alam Halfa ridge. Their advance was dogged by RAF bombers and we held out determinedly to bring their offensive to a halt. Within a week they had to withdraw. It was after this that Montgomery set off a big training stint. He came out to see us all the time. Although some of us found him a bit of a pompous old sod, I liked his style. At least he acknowledged our part in it all. The attention to training was indicative of this. You see we had never really been trained for the job we were doing. You were kind of meant to pick it up as you went along, by word of mouth I suppose. Monty also seemed to be telling us, as much as he could, about what was happening. I admit that some of his efforts to 'be one of us', 'knocking Jewwe fwar six' and all that, were a bit sickening, but he was having a go, and he got a deal of credit for this.

The information sharing bit also filtered down to the lower officer ranks. They would regularly come round with the fighting maps and explain the current position. This made a difference to the morale. I wouldn't say it created an interest in what we were doing, but now we had an idea of what it was we were doing and why. I supposed you felt more involved.

The training went on and on. Part of this were small patrols and probing operations which also had an intelligence gathering role. These nightly outings into No Man's Land, and now and then beyond enemy lines, got some useful results. We inflicted damages and gained information. We also captured stores and weapons. Engineers would use information not only to lay mines but to steal dumps of mines. Soon Jerry started to wire themselves in. Machine guns, mines and booby traps all over the place. At the same time the moon was getting brighter by the night, but we carried on. This activity tied them up, made them less mobile.

I went out on one patrol with an officer, two NCOs and about nine other enlisted men. We made our way to the German wire. We were challenged but continued to move, covering about 200 more yards before we were challenged for a second time. By now we realised that we were surrounded by the enemy who were well dug-in. We went to ground, and placed Brens on each flank. I heard the click of a rifle bolt a little way in front. It seemed to trigger something off in us and we bunged grenades in all directions and charged. One bloke near me was killed as he stood up, and someone else got caught in the foot as the rest of us stormed in. I passed a machine gun post and saw that the German manning it was playing dead. Me and the captain dragged him to his feet. The skipper was covering him, so for some reason I just galloped on. I ran straight into three Germans in a pit. They looked up startled. For a split second I saw Bill's face, I saw him dying in the dirt of Passchendaele. I blew one's head off and, almost in the same movement, plunged my bayonet through the throat of another. The third one had turned to run. I shot him in the back and, as he fell, I dived into the hole and ran him through. I fell back. I stared at what I had done, my eyes were bolting out of my head. My chest was straining. I was gasping for breath. There was a trickle of blood coming from the side of my head. I felt dizzy. Now Jerry was firing all around me. I lurched against the side of the pit, in time to see Captain Bridger wounded. He swerved round and shot his prisoner in the chest. I leapt out of the ditch and took off towards Bridger. I saw Bill off to my left. He was on one knee, aiming his rifle, covering me. I ran harder. The crowd bellowed, *Guu-Ron-U-I-ons!* Danny was to my rear, he was wearing his International Brigade bandanna 'of deepest red', spraying his Thompson at the fascist fire. '*Char-lie, Char-lie, Char-lie, Char-lie*'. Before I got to Bridger he had taken another bullet and was out cold. I couldn't see the NCOs so I threw my rifle over my back and tried to lift him. It was no good, I was covered in blood and exhausted. But a big, burly docker hauled the captain up and draped him over my shoulders. I stood there for a moment looking into the ice blue eyes of my father. "Hold on to him son, remember where yer from." Then I just took off back to our lines. I saw a German rifleman to my right, I knew I was in his sights. He was so near he could not miss. I heard the crack of a pistol, the German slumped forward. I saw a thin, pale man. He seemed to be wearing a neat black suit. Like a marksman, he stood left fist high on his hip, his right arm out straight, still holding his aim.

One of the corporals had organised some cover and we made good our retreat. I suppose I had carried Bridger about a quarter of a mile when he came round. It was just as well because I'd had it. He was able to walk back to headquarters. Small bloke Bridger, and a posh git, but a tough little runt. He called me 'docker' from then on. I didn't know how to take this. It was a bit like being called 'mule' or 'serf'. But I thought it might be an attempt at flattery. I had taken a slight head wound. Shrapnel, probably ours. I was a bit concussed for a few days, but I don't believe that it was this that brought my family and the thin, pale man to me.

Me and Joe went to Wembley for the second time. This time we bought a return ticket. We still had bunions from 17 years previous. Only 43,000 this time, mostly East Enders judging by the tribal choruses of *Bubbles, Mother Brown* and the *Hokey Cokey*. I wonder what Swift would say about the hokey cokey or even Bertrand Russell? *You do the hokey cokey and you turn around, and **that's** what **it's all** about*. I put this to Joe and he thought Canning Town WEA had a lot to answer for.

Mr Dutton, the referee, looked a rather dapper sort of chap. The programme said he was from Warwick; that I associated with Warwickshire, so Stratford-upon-Avon, thus Shakespeare. I toyed with him as Prospero but settled on Polonius, as he had an air of authority, but also a strong streak of pomposity. Barron, the Rovers 'keeper, on the other hand was definitely a Caliban; a moon-calf if ever there was one. I was deeply affected by the sight of the blokes from the British Expeditionary Force, who had their own seating area. They received a great ovation. Many of them still carried their wounds. Dressed in their hospital uniforms, blue jackets, white shirts and blood red ties, I had to ask myself why I was standing in Wembley when the fascists were knocking at our door. *Abide With Me* was very special on this occasion. Britain, needed all the help we could get.

Monty's plan was to make the most of his resources. As the Jerry lines went from the Med to the impassable Qattara Depression, he could not be outflanked. This being the case, we were to come at them from the front, in the north. This played to our strength in numbers bringing down the advantage of the mobility of the Panzers.

The Eighth Army would be divided into three. The 9th Australian, the 51st New Zealand and the 1st South African would be the main strike force. This group would break through the enemy front. A couple of routes through the German minefields would then be made. Armoured divisions would move along these and take up defensive positions. The initial strike force would await the counter attack from the enemy armoured divisions. In the south, two supporting attacks would be undertaken. The point of this was to tie up the Axis forces down there during the critical first part of the battle.

Our huge artillery barrage was breathtaking. It was certainly the biggest bang the desert had heard. It became very quiet after dark. Then a searchlight broke the northern sky. It pointed straight up. Then all hell broke loose. For a second the sky lit up without a sound, but this was succeeded, as lightning is followed by thunder, by an almighty, shuddering cluster of smashing noise. The sound hit you in waves.

The Irish Guards played the *National Anthem* and followed up with the *Marsalles*. Alexander, the First Lord of the Admiralty, shook hands with both teams. By now the guilt of every non-enlisted man in the ground could be felt. They were doing a grand job on us.

In the first minute Rovers got a corner. Was this the shape of things to come? For a little while it seemed as though we wouldn't be getting a look in, but we soon warmed up. Foxall went so near and Foreman brought the very best out of the Barron, the Blackburn 'keeper, who was playing as if he was old Blighty's last line of defence against the Hun. For all this, the down-the-middle tactic was being muted by Blackburn's devilish use of the offside rule. This is where our flexible attack line-up paid off. West Ham were able, like a well-oiled machine, to switch to wing offensives. It was this that provided us with the only goal of the game in the 34th minute. Foxall ignited the move. Goulden and Foreman, with great finesse, and a deal of guile, moved the play into Rovers' box before they could respond. Barron was half mesmerised by the cut and thrust of the West Ham attack. Foxall hung over the ball. He looked coldly towards goal for a fraction of a second that took an executioner's hour to pass. The shot came in like a spirit freshly arrived at Valhalla. Barron parried bravely, but it fell to Small and Sammy put the ball away with a flourish of ease that spread around Wembley like the wafting scent of a thousand spring roses.

Although it went backwards and forwards in the second half, the game was always ours. Coming away from Wembley I had made my mind up to enlist. I was getting on. Thirty-four was not young for a soldier. I had a wife and young daughter. But everything in me said I should play a fighting part in this war. Not really for King and Country, but against the evil that had hatched in Europe and now sat menacingly just across the Channel. I wasn't properly sure what the Nazis were. I couldn't fully form what the threat of fascism was to us – me, Daisy and Jenny, the place where we lived, the people we knew – but, like so many others, I was aware that this war was a people's war. The first lot had been a war of dynasties, a struggle for Empire and world hegemony. Hitler's war was different.

A dark side of humanity had stirred. Tyranny and domination were the goals. A world ruled by fear would be our future if we were complacent. Hundreds of millions of people would perish unless this force was resisted by what was best in the world, those who held consensus and liberty dear. Tom Paine and Jonathan Swift would have fought in this war. All those labelled as 'non-Aryan', Arabs, Jews, Gypsies, Poles, Slavs and probably the black and yellow peoples too, if Mussolini's antics in Ethiopia were any thing to go by, would be exploited, enslaved and exterminated. I did not believe that this was just Communist Party rhetoric. Danny had seen what the fascists would do and his friends in the East had told him of what the Nazis had been up to since the middle of the 1930s. No. This was a war like no war before. It was truly a struggle between good and bad. All things in between had melted away. Those who would not face the foe colluded with them. I could go, so I would go.

On the morning of 24 October the infantry had done their job, but Jerry was holding out. We were brought up from the south. The diversionary activity had not really worked out. Before I knew where I was, I was facing a fierce German offensive. It was mid-afternoon and about 30 or so tanks turned up, one or two German Mark IIIs and the rest were Eye-tie M-13-s. At that moment we took a heavy bombardment, this was supported by mortar and machine gun fire. We made for our slit trenches as the tanks closed in. Our six-pound guns opened up on the tanks, the nearest one to us being about 150 feet away. As more tanks were taken out, the crews tried to escape. One of the Italians struggled to free himself from a turret. Suddenly he flared up like a firework, then gradually his body was consumed by flickering flame, in the fashion of fat burning. As the barrage let up a bit, the platoon commander thought a bayonet charge would be in order, but was persuaded otherwise.

As it got dark, one of the Highland Divisions attacked under the light of the moon. The skirl of the pipes filled the air as Jerry laid down a field of fire and the Jocks were driven back. In the morning we discovered that the Germans had placed snipers in the dead tanks. A couple of blokes were badly shell-shocked. We had to have one taken off strapped to the stretcher.

When another Highland Division relieved us, mortar fire and snipers had knocked out half the platoon. We made our way to the trucks that were left and were taken to the rear. In four days I hadn't slept at all. The dirt and the cordite made me look as if I'd escaped from Gehenna.

We held the German counter-attacks, but we couldn't make much progress. It was obvious to anyone involved that we were taking a lot of casualties. Monty had us regroup. We came out again early on 2 November (Operation Supercharge). We started to walk silently through the minefields at about 1am. About five minutes later it started with another big bang.

The shells screeched over our heads. At the front the shells were exploding in a blood-red sea, that loomed over the dark horizon. The din was terrible. The bombardment was accompanied by mortar and rifle fire. Occasionally the drone of aircraft could be heard. Flares hung over the desert like avenging angels and illuminated it in a kind of deathly white hue; it reminded me of looking at photographic negatives. It was a cold light, that never the less burnt everything it touched. Tracer fire from Bofars guns criss-crossed the atmosphere. At one point it went relatively silent, although you could still hear a distant rumbling of guns further away. I remember thinking that it might be an echo. We were walking through smoke, mist and sand. Bird song? An insect chirping? Nature signalling a late alarm. Strange, incongruous sounds. This was the final battle. A battle of gods was about to be waged, and we had been taken out of the world and placed in a hideous limbo to fight it.

The armour moved up. Tank engines burst into life and complained as they moved forward, sending up great clouds of oily dust that more or less obscured them in the dark. Great avenging burning bushes, ploughing death through the desert.

The company commander shouted, "Up Brigade! Charge!" He got lost in a storm of tracer bullets. I followed with enemy fire whistling past my ears. I was amazed that I was not hit. I saw figures with their arms in the air appear through the murk. The enemy surrendering. But about half a mile out we started to take machine gun fire on both flanks. Then came the flares and mortar bombs. The leading platoon were badly hit. Men were falling to the ground all about. I dashed forward to get a Bren to aim at the enemy fire, but I only got a couple of bursts off before it jammed. The flares and explosions lit up the desert like noon. One of the sergeants had made directly for a German machine gun. By the time I got to him he was hit all over. Just before he died he asked me to place him facing the enemy.

I went forward in rushes, firing my rifle at the hip. Suddenly I was behind the enemy positions. Germans shouted and started to fire in my direction so I threw myself into a hollow. I could see a German position about 150 feet away. I made my mind up to rush it. I must have been out of my nut! I went screaming at it, bayonet first, tracer from a Jerry machine gun making a kind of path around me. I reached the gun, and found that I had been joined by a small group of other lunatics during my charge. We took a couple of German prisoners.

We received orders to withdraw. We ran back, dodging German fire all the way. A chap next to me got hit in the side and his left arm was shattered. Me and another lad dragged him into a divot where he had cover. When we got back, just after day-break, roll-call was taken. The company had 13 men left. Of my platoon there was just me and two others left. One of them had not taken part in the attack due to an infection.

4 November saw Rommel give way after a real beating from two Indian divisions. Three divisions of New Zealanders went after him. Four days later

the Allies landed in Morocco and Algeria. Rommel was now looking at attacks from two directions. The Germans fought all the way back, but by the end of January 1943 we were in Tripoli. We had been making for this destination from the start. Although Rommel is still in the Tunisian mountains, for the Eighth Army the war in the desert is over.

I am going home now. It will be well into spring when I get back to London. During my two years in North Africa I have received all the news from home and have a string of photos of Jenny, who is an ardent Hammers supporter. We have to get them from birth. No one would follow West Ham as a mature choice.

During 1941 the Hammers had been able to hang on to most of their players. Three of four of the lads, like Charlie Bicknall, were specials and others, who were in the forces, were based in the Norwich area. Some sides weren't so well off. Dan told me that Bill Voisey had turned out for Millwall against us. He's their trainer and is 50 if he's a day.

We had high hopes of retaining the War Cup, we beat Norwich in the first round and Southend in the second. But in the third round we were beaten by Arsenal, losing both legs (1-0 at Upton Park and 2-1 at White Hart, where Arsenal played because Highbury was closed to football for the duration). 1941 saw our inclusion in the London War Cup 'B' Division. We beat Spurs away and at home, 2-1 and 3-2 respectively. We won six games out of ten, walloping Clapton 8-1 at the Boleyn in April (Chalkley, Corbett, Foxall and Goulden got one each while Small and Foreman scored two apiece). But we lost three games making it a good, but less than an outstanding season. We did well in the London War Cup. We won five out of our six games. The only loss was to Arsenal, 4-0 at Upton Park. It's weird because we slaughtered them at Spurs, 4-1, Len Goulden put two away. Good old Len!

I'm looking forward to our first game in the Football League (South) Cup. We've got Watford at home. I have every confidence that the lads will do it for a docker back from the wilderness. A water rat who went to the desert. A real corker I bet. It's unlikely to be a big crowd, but for me it will be part of being home. Home is making love with Daisy as the sun rises over the river. It's Jenny giggling. Home is real tea drank sitting in an arm chair and listening to the muted toots and bellows of the ships hooters dancing across the evening sky. Home is spring rain and the smell of the pitch. It is the crowd waiting for the kick-off. Len and Sam slotting them away. Home is claret and blue and full of bubbles.

# Ted Fenton — the Last Hope for Humanity

# Chapter Six

*If sailor tales to sailor tunes.*
*Storm and adventure, heat and cold,*
*If schooners, islands, and maroons,*
*And Buccaneers and buried Gold,*
*And all the old romance, retold*
*Exactly in the ancient way,*
*Can please, as me they pleased of old,*
*The wiser youngsters of to-day.*
*- So be it, and fall on! If not,*
*If studious youth no longer crave,*
*His ancient appetites forgot,*
*Kingston, or Ballantyne the brave,*
*Or Cooper of the wood and wave:*
*So be it, also! And may I*
*And all my pirates share the grave*
*Where these and their creations lie!*

## West Ham United 2 Lincoln 2. Attendance: 19,900

THE LAST GAME of last season we lost 1-0 at Anfield. Eighteen days later we let off a hydrogen bomb, like the Russians and the Americans. On Christmas Island it was. I dreamt that it had blown up Father Christmas, all the reindeers and the elves. I don't believe in Father Christmas any more, but it was frightening all the same.

The 1957-58 season started with a draw against Lincoln at Upton Park. Billy Dare got our first ... *Billy Dare here, Billy Dare there, Billy Dare every blinkin' where, la,la,la,lar,la,la,lar,la,lar.* Malcolm Allison got the other. He's a good bloke Allison. Most people say he's arrogant. I say he's confident. Mum says he's handsome. It was a relief that we didn't lose. I said that if we lost we would get blown up by the bomb. If we won we wouldn't. I didn't think about the draw. Come to think of it, this must mean that we might get blown up and we might not. I'm no better off!

Mum sometimes takes me to games, but mostly I go with Dad and Uncle Dan. Uncle Dan says that West Ham United *is* the area, that without West Ham local people wouldn't be who they are. Dad tells him to leave it alone.

You see, Captain Smollett, out of *Treasure Island,* could organise people. He don't stand out so much as Long John Silver, you like him in a way, although he's a bad sort. Squire Trelawney was a good bloke too, but none of it would have worked without Jim Hawkins. He tells the story, he watches it all, but he's involved as well. He sees what goes on better than anyone in the end. Ted Fenton is like Smollett. Uncle Dan says he was born in Forest Gate about the same time as Dad so he can't be a captain like Smollett was, and that a captain of a ship is different to being the manager of a football team, because ships' captains are posh and Fenton ain't posh. But I'm not saying that he is a ship's captain. I'm saying he is like Smollett. He knows what people are like. He saw straight through Silver didn't he, when no one else did, and Fenton knows what to do with Allison. Allison likes to take over the team and he does a good job. Fenton can see this and gives Malcolm his head. Clever. Dad agrees. He says a good manager is able to take a backseat and use the talent he has, and that Fenton doesn't let his own ego get in the way. I've got to ask him what an 'ego' is.

I've been listening to the radio about nuclear disarmament. If something isn't done soon we are going to blow the Russians up, and they will blow us and the Americans up, and that will be the end of the world. But if we get rid of our bombs the Russians won't, and we won't be able to blow them up when they blow us up. So we've got to keep 'em to blow them up and that's what's called a deterrent. Uncle Dan reckons this is all eye-wash and that the only way the Russians could get a bomb to America is through the post. But Dad says that they've got rockets that can blow up the whole world. Mum reckons that the only answer is a world government like the United Nations and that would mean an end to bombs and wars.

> *"Well, gentlemen" said the captain, "the best that I can say is not much. We must lay to, if you please, and keep a bright look-out. It's trying on a man, I know. It would be pleasanter to come to blows. But there's no help for it till we know our men. Lay to, and whistle for a wind, that's my view."*

Ted Fenton was in the war. He was a PT instructor. Dad says he was with him in North Africa. He brought young players along with the youth scheme. He got us to the Youth Cup Final. He's bought good players too. Ted Fenton could be Prime Minister of the World. Uncle Dan thinks he would be better than someone like Macmillan, who's an upper-class twit, and that why shouldn't a lad from Oddessa Road School not get a chance. Dad thinks that anyone who could have worked with Syd King and Charlie Paynter, and still have got on, must be a pretty good diplomat. He could deal with Eisenhower, Macmillan and Khrushchev. I have nightmares about the end of the world.

> *...and the worse dreams that ever I have are when I hear the surf booming about its coasts, or start upright in bed, with the sharp voice of Captain Flint still ringing in my ears: "Pieces of eight! pieces of eight!"*

### West Ham 3 Fulham 2. Attendance: 24,000

Dare got two. Noel Cantwell got his second goal of the season. Mum and Uncle Dan took me to the game. Billy Dare is now into double figures (ten).

What I don't understand about the bomb is how it can destroy the world. How big is it? Dad says that it's about the size of a rowing boat or a big sofa. It works by splitting an atom and that's a very tiny thing that you can't see. But if you can't see it, how can you split it? What do you split it with? Perhaps it's all what Uncle Dan calls 'propaganda'. That's like lies that make people think things are going on that are not really going on. Perhaps no one has got a bomb and what happened in Japan was really lots of smaller bombs. But that wouldn't make any difference. Mum says that Dresden, that was a German city blown up by ordinary bombs, was just as bad as what happened in Japan. So it doesn't matter if there's one bomb or hundreds of bombs, it still means the end of the world. But if the Martians invade we might be able to bomb them, so perhaps it's just as well ... What if the Martians have a bomb?

**West Ham 5 Stoke City 0 Attendance: 11,878**
Vic Keeble got a hat-trick, John Dick, Billy Dare scored one each.

*Hopping is all over,*
*Money is all spent,*
*I'll go no more down hopping,*
*Hopping down in Kent .*
*With an ee-i-o, tee-i-o,*
*e-i-e-i-o.*

This is the first game I've seen since we came back from hopping. I hate hopping. The hops are all wet and when the vines get pulled down it all goes down your neck. Everything stinks of smoke, the palliasses are always damp, creepy crawlies everywhere and the toilets are horrible. You can keep hopping. I want to go to Brighton like Bob Wastell at school. But everyone else likes hopping. Singing round the flippin' fire and that. Sitting outside the 'Pig and Whistle' or 'The Woolpack' or the 'Hop-Pole' ...**IT'S BORING!** The Russians should bomb hopping, but when there are no pickers there.

Ted Fenton signed Keeble just last month from Newcastle. We've won nine, drawn three and lost five. Mid-table.

The Russians have sent a dog up in a rocket. Her name is Laika. Uncle Dan says they are sending her to the Dog Star. I asked Mum what he meant and she said he was round the bend, and that the fascist bullet in his knee must have travelled to his brain. I didn't know that could happen. I'm glad Mum got that splinter out of my thumb the other day.

I think politics is boring, but it seems to take up a lot of time in our family. Uncle Dan is a communist and Dad, Mum and Jenny are in the Labour Party. Uncle Dan doesn't believe in God. "Man made God, not the other way round," he says. I don't know. I prayed that everyone won't bomb each other and that we won't be invaded by Martians, and so far these things haven't happened.

Mum says we are God and that God is us. She's a Methodist. I sometimes go to Sunday school. Jenny's done a bit of teaching there. I'm not anything yet. Mum and Dad wanted to wait till I make up my own mind. Uncle Dan knows a Muslim, Ali. He says he's a good bloke. Muslims believe in Islam. That means submission. Like on the wrestling. He knows a Hindu too. Another communist. Dad asked him how a man can be a Hindu and a communist, being as communists don't believe in God. Dan said his mate thinks he is God and that all people are God, so this doesn't interfere with his communism because that's what Marx thought anyway. I don't think anyone knows what Uncle Dan is talking about sometimes.

## West Ham 2 Fulham 3 Attendance: 37,500

Grice, Bond – FA Cup, 5th round.

We'd beaten Blackpool and Stockport, and me and Dad fancied our chances against Fulham. A couple of weeks ago we got a draw at Craven Cottage and the last time we had played them at home we had won 3-2. Fulham are called the Cottagers and Dad thinks that's stupid. I think the Hammers is better. Northampton are called 'the Cobblers'!

West Ham marked Johnny Haynes really closely — Andy Malcolm kicked lumps out of him. But the two had a superb battle. Every tackle ended with one of them on the ground. I'd say Haynes just had the edge. He was all over the place egging the Fulham team on. We scored after only 90 seconds. Mike Grice moved in after a mistake by Langley. Fulham drew level after 12 minutes when, from the inside-left position, Stevens sent Dwight down the middle and he lifted the ball over Ernie Gregory. Twenty-four minutes later they took the lead. Jimmy Hill drove the ball home. Hill had collected the ball from Chamberlain and sent it to Haynes who passed to Dwight. Dwight looked up and seemed to think for a moment before lobbing the ball over for Hill to finish.

Just after the hour, Langley again slipped up, missing a tackle. Grice crashed to the ground and the penalty was awarded. John Bond socked in the conversion. With just over a quarter of an hour left, Langley picked out Haynes. Haynes got it back following his pass to Chamberlain. He skipped over Bond's lunge to put us out of the Cup.

Johnny Haynes has got a fantastic amount of energy. Fulham are now London's last hope in the last eight. They've got some decent players. Roy

Bentley, Hill and Macedo. They are good in defence. Although Langley made a couple of rickets, giving away a goal and conceding a penalty, he made a couple of smart clearances. He also made the pass from which the winning goal was scored. Their attack, with Haynes doing the prompting, can be terrific. Dad says that they are better against teams who play good football. We must play good football.

## West Ham 1 Barnsley 1 Attendance: 27,000

Lewis.

Two days ago the Manchester United team crashed in an aeroplane in Germany. Seven players died. Nine others were hurt and the manager. I asked Mum if I could go to the Mission with her, because they are going to have a special service.

## Leyton Orient 1 West Ham 4 Attendance: 25,284

John Smith, Dare, Keeble and Dick.

My first away match and biggest crowd I've been in. I went with Dad and Jenny. Mum had a win on the premium bonds. She's been buying three a month since they started and now she's got around 30 numbers. But I mustn't tell anyone. Dad and Uncle Dan would make Mum's life a misery she says. I hope Mr Busby and Bobby Charlton and all the others will be made better. I will pray to God for them. Uncle Dan said that Ali had prayed to Allah for them. I asked if he would pray for them and he told me he had, but that I should keep it a secret. I asked him who he had prayed to and he told me, "The spirit of humanity." I think that's God.

> "Then, Hawk-eye, we were one people, and we were happy. The salt lake gave us its fish, the wood its deer, and the air its birds. We took wives who bore us children; we worshipped the Great Spirit ...My tribe is the grandfather of nations ... The blood of the chiefs is in my veins, where it must stay forever."

I asked my teacher if the little Russian dog was all right. She said she died because there wasn't enough air in the rocket for her to live. I went to the toilet and cried.

Jenny went up the city to a meeting of the 'Campaign for Nuclear Disarmament'. Dad said it was a 'socialist knees-up' with Bertrand Russell, J.B.Priestley and Michael Foot being there. Are they singers?

I like our house. It's very quiet when Jenny's not around. We've got loads of clocks. It's nice in the cold weather, as it gets dark, to just sit with Mum and listen to them ticking, staring into the fire. Sometimes Mum reads to me. She's been reading *The Last of the Mohicans* recently, by J.Fenimore Cooper. Tonight I pretended to be Hawk-eye, smoking a peace pipe with Chingachgook (Dad). He gave me a puff of his briar and my eyes popped out of my head. Mum gave me three glasses of squash to get rid of the taste and called Dad a silly old fool. He said, "White-man speak with fork-lift truck," and demanded the return of his ancestral lands. He picked up the book and read:

> *Listen, Hawk-eye, and your ear shall drink no lie. 'Tis what my fathers have said, and what the Mohicans have done ... Does not this stream* [pointing to the tap that was diluting my second glass of squash] *run towards the summer, until its waters grow salt, and the current flows upward ... The fathers of Chingachgook have not lied ... We came from the place where the sun is hid at night, over the great plains where the buffaloes live, until we reached the big river.*

Mum hit him with the tea-cosy at this point, saying, "Eat hessian, redskin." I think Mum and Dad really love each other. Mum is a big Hammers supporter. She gets really excited. Once, last season, against Bury I think, Billy Dare scored the only goal of the game and she nearly knocked Dad's glasses off as she picked me up and swung me round. The man in front lost his hat. Good job it wasn't a big crowd that day. She'd have probably killed half-a-dozen with me as the deadly weapon. 'Tomahawk Billy'!

Jenny took me to see *Moby Dick*. It was great! *Call me Ishmael.* On the way home me and Jenny were back in 1840. We made out that the trolley bus was the *Pequod*. A man in the seat in front of us started limping up and down the aisle, saying he was Captain Ahab. "This will be no routine whaling expedition," he said, "but a mission of vengeance against the Great White Whale, Moby Dick. He's still got me blasted leg." I leapt up on the seat and cried, "Thar' she blows." We fired the harpoons, but it was no good, the big old sod got away. The conductor came up for our fares and the man paid for us all, saying, "Blast yer Starbuck, you ruined our aim." The conductor said he was sorry, but he had missed his tea. I kept a lookout for Moby the rest of the way home. Jenny chatted and laughed a lot with Captain Ahab. He had a big smile and was very dark. He had a funny way of talking too, like us, but sort of like a cowboy as well. His name was Ronnie. I made my mind up that I would get hold of the book.

### West Ham 0 Charlton 0 Attendance: 30,500.

What a boring game. The worst I've ever seen. This was the first goalless game at Upton Park for more than two years according to Dad. Loads of people were leaving before the end, but me and Uncle Dan stayed to the final whistle. He always does. I suppose Malcolm Pyke did all right at number six. We've had a few problems there this year. Allison and Lansdowne have had a go. Still, I think that it is more or less certain that we are going up to the First Division, probably as champions. We've got 52 points with four games left. Uncle Dan said the last time he had seen West Ham play in Division One was 26 years ago, before he went to Spain, not very long after he got back from Russia. The last time we had won a league was in 1917, and Uncle Dan said that it didn't really count as it was in wartime. It had been over 60 years since we won the Southern League, but that was Thames Iron Works, so, according to Uncle Dan that didn't count either. I don't think he likes the idea of West Ham winning anything. He's not much like Dad. You wouldn't think they were brothers sometimes. Uncle Dan is always so serious. He doesn't smile a lot and never seems to look at anyone, although sometimes, when he is making a point, he stares straight at you. It's not really frightening, but it seems to like, freeze you.

The crowd coming out was pretty thick, so we decided to walk at least to the Green Gate. I asked him why he was not married. He said he sort of had been, in Spain. He told me that I had a cousin, his son, in America. "Why is he in America?" I asked. "That's where he lives Bill. It's where his Mum's from." I was thinking about my next question when Uncle Dan stopped and lifted me to sit on a wall so that we were now face to face. He looked into my eyes. "Sometimes people fall in love Bill, like your Ma and your Dad did. But life does things and it doesn't always work out exactly as you might want it to. I loved, and I still love your cousin's Mum. I have never, and will never love another woman like I loved her." I went to say something, but he slowly blinked his eyes to quieten me. "Can you understand Bill?" I didn't but I nodded all the same. "Good," he said, "Now let's see if we can find a bus, that fascist bullet is making my knee play up again."

> *Chingachgook became once more the object of common attention ... "My race has gone from the shores of the salt lake and the hills of the Delawares ... I am alone,". "No, no," cried Hawk-eye "... no, Sagamore, not alone. The gifts of our colours may be different, but God has so placed us as to journey in the same path ... He was your son, and a redskin by nature, and it may be that your blood was nearer ... but, Sagamore, you are not alone." Chingachgook grasped the hand that, in the warmth of feeling the scout had stretched across the fresh earth ... "The palefaces are masters of the earth, and the time of the red men has not yet come again. My day has been too long ... before the night has come, I have lived to see the last warrior of the wise race of the Mohicans."*

Me, Ronnie and Jenny have joined the 'Campaign for Nuclear Disarmament'. On Good Friday we went to Trafalgar Square to a big rally with Mum and Dad as well. It was pouring with rain and freezing cold. Jenny and Ronnie went on a march for three days. I was going to go as well, but I dozed off and Mum and Dad took me home. Ronnie came round on Monday. He had got terrible blisters and had to hitch a lift home. A man on a motor bike brought him back in his sidecar. He had been very ill, and said it was worse than anything he had experienced on the ship coming over from Australia. Jenny was back on Wednesday. She'd finished the march and had got buses and trains home. I asked her why she had done it. She said, "For you, peace and in memory of a good lady, Christabel Pankhurst who had died on my birthday."

## Middlesbrough 1 West Ham 3

(Musgrove, Dick, Keeble) Attendance: 30,000 — champions!
This has probably been the best ever season a West Ham team has had. Ted Fenton has done us proud. He's a brilliant bloke, and a real leader of men.

Ronnie agrees with me. 'Dinkum,' he says. He reckons that if Fenton was an Australian, he'd be up for Prime Minister. So I think that my notions about Ted Fenton being in charge of the United Nations or something ain't such a bad idea.

Fulham got to the semi-final of the Cup. They took Manchester United to a replay. I decided that I don't like Jimmy Hill. I was glad United got to the Final. I wanted them to beat Bolton, for all the lads still getting over the crash and those that died. They lost.

Ron borrowed a car and took me and Jenny to Gnats Valley in Kent. The woods were full of bluebells, millions and millions of them; seas of blue that come almost up to your knee. The blue is soft, like the blue in the Hammers shirts. It is cool but not cold. It kind of fills your eyes and the smell makes you feel as if you've come into another, fresher world. A hidden place. I see that blue before I go to sleep. Moby Dick rises out of it and we follow him through the forest, winding between the green shadows and the shafts of sunlight. But he is gentle and Ahab does not want to kill him. He wants to find something out from Moby; knowledge, a secret that lives in the heart of everything. The blue holds me, covers me, and that kind blue makes me feel safe and yet away from where I am. Distant but close. The inside of me is blue and it whispers noises that are more than words. Red, dark red noises of home and someone, far away, who cares about me and touches me so lightly, so that I sleep without the nightmares.

I went with Mum and Dad to see *The Day the Earth Stood Still*. A bloke from outer space, Rennie, comes to earth with a robot called Gort. They want to stop everyone from blowing up bombs and destroying the Earth. So the Yank army shot Rennie, and Gort is about to blow-up the world anyway, but Rennie tells him to stop ...'*Klaatu barada nikto*'. Well then Rennie goes to hospital, gets out and shows everyone what will happen if they don't stop blowing up bombs. I think that's about right, because, as Dad says, why would the Martians want to blow the world up? Ted could talk to the likes of Rennie and get everyone to do away with their bombs and stuff.

Ronnie wants Jenny to go back to Australia with him. I'd like to go, but I'd miss Dad and Mum and Uncle Dan. Of course, we couldn't go and see West Ham. I don't think Jenny would like that, not now we're in Division One as well ...Up the Irons!

"My lads," said Captain Smollet, "I've a word to say to you. This land that we have sighted is the place we have been sailing to. Mr Trelawney...has just asked me a word or two, and I was able to tell him that every man on board had done his duty, alow and aloft, as I never ask to see it done better, why, he and I and the doctor are going below to the cabin and drink your health and luck, and you'll have grog served out for you to drink our health and luck. I'll tell you what I think of this: I think it handsome.." ... "One more cheer for Cap't Smollett," cried Long John.

# Preston, Munich and all the way to Wembley

# Chapter Seven

*There are times when football steps out of the flow of history and becomes history itself. This does not happen often but disasters like the Munich air crash and the tragedy at Bolton in 1946 or great games, the 1953 Stanley Matthews Cup Final, and the wonderful 1954 Hungarian victory at Wembley, cause the game to emerge. It takes on the identity of a seminal moment in time; a symbolic milestone offering meaning to the sum total of our existence. No other game has this potential. The most successful period in the history of West Ham started at Upton Park on Boxing Day 1963 and reached its zenith at Wembley in the summer of 1966. This was a time when the modern game came of age and West Ham was at its centre. These were the high days of the 1960s in London. A legendary time, more talked about than any decade in modern history, but mostly by people who were not around at the time. It has become a kind of golden age, but being in it, at the middle of it, in London, was quite different from the mythology.*

*The one thing that most people who were compos mentis in the 1960s agree about is that it (what ever 'it' was) didn't start until about 1965 and it ended in the winter of 1968. It also went very fast.*

I'd been working in London since '57, having come from Sydney, Australia, looking to make my fortune in the Mother Country. Fat chance! I wanted to be a writer, but writers were low on the wanted list in Britain at that time. I'd done some work back home on a local paper and I took up where I left off in West Ham. I'd never seen such a grey place. But it was a start I thought. The people looked tired and pasty, dragging round a still war-ravished world. No one had any money and people seemed to be determined to remain holed up in dinge and damp.

After about a year I'd all but given up. I was getting like the people around me. Lodging in the dock area of East London with a bulbous, bearded mad woman. She had hardly any hair on her head and must have been a thousand years old. Her language, apart from the obscenities, was an incomprehensible blend of some obscure East European dialect and a sort of 'pidgin Cockney'. Not that I had much occasion to speak to her. The house was a derelict drum hanging precariously to the edge of a bomb-site. My room was damp, draughty and without a source of heat. It was too damp for cockroaches, but a community of toads lived under the floorboards. I was often lulled off to sleep by their croaking. I would get up in the morning and shiver my way to the office to huddle over the hot pipes until everyone else came in at nine. I'd stay in work until the caretaker threw me out and then nurse half of bitter in the pub for most of the evening or else sit through the same picture show two or three times at one of the local flea pits. All I got from the crone was something like, "Fishmar-reekin' morting," as I left in the morning and, if she should be out of the sack when I got back, "Grantlet furk te'necht." Except on Fridays when the rent was due, then she would greet me as I descended the creaking wreck that was the staircase with a screeching, "RENTA!"

The woman, Mrs Voleska, was never seen outside the house. I swear this was because she was too fat to get out the door. At a quick glance she looked like three drunken Sumo wrestlers, rolling along supporting each other in a wobbly stagger back to barracks. I never saw the husband. I guess she'd eaten him years ago and now kept her weight up by devouring former lodgers that she stored in the cellar. When I was a kid I didn't think anywhere could be worse than the institution I was brought up in, but 'Voleska Towers' made Barnado's look like the Waldorf.

I'd watched *Moby Dick* three times one evening in February 1958. Gregory Peck was terrible in that. It was tipping it down, so I decided to treat myself to a bus ride back to the swamp. That's when I met Jenny and her brother Bill.

He was doing his nut about the flick. She was pretty and he needed an 'oppo', so I did my Ahab impression, which by that time was impeccable, in-Gregory-Peckable in fact. That was it. I started seeing her. At first I hoped that she'd come back to Oz with me straight away, but she held out. She wanted to sort her life out. So I stayed. Jenny, Bill and the rest of the family went to West Ham like some people go to church. The whole family were adherents. Dad Charlie, Mum Daisy, crazy old Uncle Dan. All devout supporters of the claret and blue. 'Hammerites' I called 'em.

At first I just went along to be with Jenny, but soon I was going with Billy, Dan and Charlie in various permutations. Back in Sydney I was always a doer. Cricket, the footy, I wasn't the spectator sort, that was for soapos and okcas. Even playing soccer was for nancys. But like on the road to Damascus, my conversion was sudden. It was inexplicable. I suppose I had gone to about half-a-dozen matches during the 58-59 season. Football was hardly the cen-tre of my world. Buddy Holly was dead, race riots in London, two Soviet and one American monkey had orbited the earth and got back to tell the tale, there had been a revolution in Cuba and then Castro invaded Panama. But all the same, West Ham predicated almost every conversation.

As far as I could judge it was a mediocre season by general standards. But every goal scored was celebrated and every defeat mourned. West Ham were a fantastic group of blokes one week and a bunch of inadequates the next. The team finished sixth in the First Division and, while I saw this as failure – in Oz you either win or you're nowhere – Jenny and her family, and most other supporters I came across thought this quite an achievement.

The following year was worse. By this time I was spending a lot of time with Jen and Bill. I'd got myself a furnished flat in Stratford, but was hardly ever there. Whilst people were not generally pleased with 14th place, 'we still steered clear of relegation', which seemed to be a kind of equivalent to pur-gatory. But by now I was becoming quite important to West Ham's finances. I'd attended around a dozen home matches and had taken Bill to Highbury in the spring.

The first full season of the new decade was more of the same. A final position of 16th brought similar condemnations, commiserations and 'at leastisms'. It was in April 1961 that my perspective began to change. I'd been covering all the usual stuff locally for the paper, more than weddings and funerals, but not much more, when the editor asked me to write a pen picture of the new manager at West Ham. He saw it as something more than a sports story, a local interest thing, and thought that it would do no harm for me to do the job. Not the interview with Yuri Gagarin I'd been hoping for, but I saw it as progress.

Ron Greenwood was a novel choice as West Ham manager. He was not quite 40, born in Burnley. He had no connections with the club, the first West Ham manager not to have had previous involvement. He had played centre-half for Bradford, Brentford, Chelsea (he was in their championship side in 1955) and Fulham.

Greenwood was also unusual in that he had become a coach while still a player. So when he packed in playing he quickly got involved in management. He did some coaching for Oxford University and got his first job as a manager with Eastbourne United. Around the same time he took charge of the English Youth team. He had done well at both these jobs. The prize was the role of Arsenal's chief coach and working with the England Under-23 side.

The article went down well and it led to an occasional series of similar pieces concerning West Ham 'personalities'. I found myself scribbling about players, sponge-men, directors and the like. I was a bit sceptical about this until I interviewed Lawrie Leslie. Thick set and crew cut, here was an ordinary, yet exceptional man. He was one of the most popular goalkeepers ever to turn out for a West Ham side. As a small boy, Lawrie was knocked down by a lorry. He was told that he would be fortunate to walk again, but during his time in the army he had played alongside the likes of Duncan Edwards and Bobby Charlton. On leaving the forces he entered big-time football with his local club, Hibernian, in 1958. He was in the Hibs side that lost to Clyde in the Scottish FA Cup Final. He went on to skipper Airdrie, winning five caps for Scotland and playing three times for the Scottish League while he was with the Lanarkshire club. Leslie was an outstandingly brave goalie, seen as something of are dare-devil by the supporters. By the time he arrived at Upton Park, for a fee of £14,000 in 1961, around the same time that Rudolf Nureyev defected to the West, (not that these two had much in common, but from then on I could not think of the one without bringing the other to mind), he had broken practically every bone in his body. His worst injury was sustained at Upton Park against Bolton in the winter of

1962. He broke a leg badly, but got back into reckoning for the first team before the end of the season. I was struck by the courage, dedication and focus of the man. He set something off inside me, a curiosity about the interesting mixture of people that made up West Ham United. So, by the start of the 1962-63 season, I was something of an authority on the team. For all this, I still did not regard myself as a supporter, even though I had been present at most home games and gone with Bill to White Hart Lane, Stamford Bridge and Craven Cottage. I was also surprised to find that I was quite pleased with the position of eighth achieved that season. The metamorphosis was kicking in. I was also talking about the weather more.

All this made me appreciate something of what was going on at West Ham. Greenwood inherited a team that had been dominated by the personality of Malcolm Allison. As a player, Allison had given good service to the club and was a fair enough player. But his influence over people like John Bond, Noel Cantwell, Ken Brown and Frank O'Farrell was tremendous. The player meetings at a local cafe, led by Allison, were the start of the 'Academy' and the basis of West Ham's Second Division championship team. Allison was also largely responsible for the development of players like the young Bobby Moore. He brought continental ideas about tactics, boots and strip to West Ham, long before any British club departed from the traditions laid down by Herbert Chapman in the 1930s. Greenwood, already a disciple of one of the most informed of English coaches, Walter Winerbottom, used the results of Allison's work to build on his own ideas. He was an intelligent, thinking manager, but he had come to a club bristling with intelligent, thinking players.

When Allison finished playing, losing a lung to TB, Greenwood had wanted him to stay at the club in a coaching capacity. Although both Spurs and Ajax of Amsterdam were also after Allison, the West Ham board, in their infinite wisdom, wanted Allison out of the club. He had always been a thorn in their side, questioning contracts and rebelling against the system in general. But Greenwood was never to get over the value and respect West Ham players had for Allison, particularly Bobby Moore. This was something he would find difficult to emulate.

The mixture of Allison's inventiveness and Greenwood's association with the likes of Alf Ramsey, Helmut Schoen and Otto Gloria through the England connections, made West Ham United into a kind of football laboratory. This couldn't last forever, given the departure of the 'Allison ingredient', but it was obvious that the results would have a lasting effect on English football. You only had to watch the West Ham game throughout the early 1960s to notice how different it was from what everyone else was doing. Whilst the players were not the best, they were much more aware, and so organised, than other teams. Thus they achieved results way above their individual potential. It was also pretty to look at. The likes of Tottenham, Chelsea, Arsenal, Liverpool and Manchester United learnt from this. Whatever England or other clubs might achieve in the future, the seed of their development was sown in Cassetari's cafe, Upton Park.

I got a job with one of the Fleet Street nationals in the summer of 1962. Nothing great, just writing up copy, but it was a steep learning curve and I got rather preoccupied. I followed the Eichmann trials and the Sino/Indian war. But the Cuban missile crisis was the biggest thing. Young Bill, always a worrier about the nuclear threat, almost lost it at this time. He had ages off school and watched the news like a hawk. This often caused him to vomit violently afterwards. He had terrible nightmares. In October things got really hot. Kennedy had photographs that demonstrated that the Soviets were building offensive missile bases in Cuba. If completed, this would have doubled the number of US cities and bases threatened by Soviet attack. After passing up an immediate military intervention, the President ordered a naval blockade on Soviet ships heading towards Cuba. He also promised retaliation if the blockade was broken. The situation looked as if it might come to a super-power confrontation. However, six days after the US ships moved in, Khrushchev called his ships home and agreed to dismantle the bases in Cuba.

I didn't see any games in 1962-63. But as far as I could see at the time, I hadn't missed much. Twelfth place in the League, out of the League Cup in the first round, and the quarter-final place in the FA Cup, left me with few regrets about my lapsed ways.

I went to a couple of games with Billy at the start of the 63-64 season, but the Great Train Robbery at the front end of August, Martin Luther King's "I have a dream," speech at the end of the month and the assassination of President Kennedy at the end of November meant that work was uppermost in my mind.

Strangely, my final conversion from interested spectator/student to supporter happened during a defeat. It was the first game I'd been to with the whole family, Bill, Jenny, Charlie, Daisy, Dan and Dan junior, who was over on his second visit from the States. The big marine was by now an avid fan, having abandoned his native grid iron for his paternal inheritance.

It was Boxing Day 1963. We (this is when 'West Ham' became 'We') were up against Blackburn Rovers, who had come to the West Ham ground on top of Division One and without defeat in ten games. Bryan Douglas, the England winger, was at peak form, and bamboozled the West Ham defence. The game was no more than five minutes old when one Fred Pickering hit the ball from around 20 yards, sending it sailing passed Standen. It was such a stunning goal that I found myself applauding, much to the consternation of my party. Within ten minutes the equaliser was scored by Johnny Byrne, Greenwood's record £65,000 signing from Crystal Palace in March 1962. This, too, was a terrific goal. 'Budgie' twisted and connived passed three Blackburn defenders and 'passed' the ball beyond the Rovers goalkeeper, Fred Else. As the ball went in something just took me and I shouted, "TAKE THAT, YER UMPING GREAT GALLAR!" I got a few funny looks, but the most surprised person was me. What was the matter? Where did that come from?

The goal seemed to invigorate West Ham, because pretty soon afterwards Byrne made a sweet connection. The ball seemed to stick to his boot momentarily as he hit it. It smacked against the bar. Hurst was on the rebound like the predator he was, but in the rush he wasted the chance. However, Douglas had started to cause mayhem. He pulled three defenders in his wake all through the first half with magnetic consistency. He put the 'blue and whites' back in front on the half-hour, made McEvoy's goal about five minutes later, and laid on the ball that allowed Ferguson to score after 40 minutes.

At the break 'we' were 4-1 down. It was Bovril all round, except for Dan junior. He may have been converted to 'soccer', but he had not given up coffee, although the stuff the Hammers catering called 'coffee' didn't really impress young Danny. It might as well have been Bovril as far as he was concerned. For me it was a dirty brown colour so there was every chance that it was a close relative to Vegemite. We lived on that stuff in the home. Drank it, ate it on stale bread, used it to block up mouse holes and even shine shoes. It was also the source of the great Vegemite wars waged between houses, which involved the slinging of the used jars, that had a dreadnought quality, at rival inmates. I hit that drongo Godfrey Pullman right on the nut with one once. He was a spotty giant, with a propensity to pick his nose and bully everyone. He was out for a good hour.

Jenny decided that she would not let the current state of play get us down, and started a beautiful rendition of *I Want to Hold Your Hand*. It was slower and more determined than the Beatles melody. Daisy joined in and young Danny, and soon a whole section of the crowd had turned a Liverpool pop ditty into an East End love song. I looked at her. Her bright blue eyes, watery with the cold, gazing into the middle distance. She sang with a dream-like smile: "*Oh you, got that something, I think you'll understand . . .*" Her powerful, yet sweet voice rang out over the rest of us. "*When I, say that something, I wanna hold your hand.*" Her eyes closed. "*I wanna hold your haaand, I wanna hold your hand.*" She savoured the words, raising and shaking her head ever so slightly. "*And when I touch you I feel happy, inside, it's such a feeling that my love . . . I can't hide, I can't hide, **I can't hide!***" She was holding my hand tightly, Billy held her other hand. "*I wanna hold your haa, aaa and...*" Daisy held Charlie's right hand, Dan grasped the fingers of her right hand. "*I wanna hold your hand.*" Dan motioned to his son for his hand, Billy reached out for the marine and we were a circle. "***I wanna hold your han aan aan aa a and!***" She came round to the applause of the whole ground.

Douglas didn't lose any of his venom in the second half. He was instrumental in McEvoy's second goal and then helped Pickering complete his hat-trick. McEvoy finished off the Rovers barrage with his third. Byrne did get a consolation goal just after the hour. 8-2. A record defeat. Now, before this experience, I would have thought a defeat of this magnitude, in any sport, for any group of supporters, would initiate a hurricane of recrimination and admonishment. But, as Mr Osborne blew the final whistle, the stadium became a sea of claret and blue as, it seemed, every one of the 20,000 crowd 'upped scarves' and let out the melancholy, yet gently defiant, Hammers anthem. And I was letting rip with the rest. "I'm forever blowing bubbles, pretty bubbles in the air." . . . Here was I, a dyed-in-the-wool Aussie, standing with a great big Yank, three ancient Cockneys, an East End teacher, her little brother and a choir of tens of thousands, on a freezing Boxing Day, celebrating . . . defeat!

"They fly so high, nearly reach the sky …" Take that, world! Everything and everyone that ever did these people down. All those who think that working people can be cowed by poverty and war …"And like my dreams, they fade and die …" You will never beat 'us'. 'We' cannot be beaten, we will always be here, we will always come back, no matter how terrible the bashing you give us …"Fortune's always hiding, I've looked everywhere, I'm forever blowing bubbles …" Yes forever and ever and ever … "Pretty bubbles in the air." **U-nite-ed, U-nite-ed**.

But these Hammers could learn. Two days later, at Ewood Park, the very lair of the Rovers, the Irons won 3-1. 'We' would soon be on our way to Wembley, and I had found a family.

On the way to the FA Cup Final that season, West Ham scored three goals against every team they came up against, Charlton, Orient (following a draw at Brisbane Road), Swindon and Burnley. Hurst got a goal in every round apart from the sixth. Two Second Division teams reached the semi-finals. Preston and Swansea were drawn against each other, leaving the Hammers to face Manchester United, the Cup holders and the eventual runners-up in Division One that season. United came to Upton Park a week before our semi-final. George Best played in that game and we were soundly beaten 2-0. The Irons' chances in the Final were completely written off by the press. No one gave us a hope at Hillsborough, as the likes of Law, Charlton and Crerand were returning to the United side for the match.

The game, being played in Sheffield, gave the advantage to the Northern side, but the pre-match entertainment was provided by the Dagenham Girl Pipers, so this more or less seemed to even things up as far as some of our supporters were concerned. West Ham competed above themselves, depriving the opposition of the ball. Jim Standen played ripper in goal, showing why he was also a first-class wicketkeeper with Worcestershire, while Byrne and Hurst worked well up front, adapting to the muddy conditions much better than their counterparts in the Manchester team. Bobby Moore was dominant that day, marshalling Bond, Burkett, Bovington and Brown to generate a resilient defence. 'Ticker' Boyce got two of West Ham's three goals, one was lofted in from just inside the United half. Ronnie didn't score many, he seemed to save them for the big occasion. Our final goal came from a Bobby Moore pass which Hurst picked up and put away from the edge of the penalty area. Beating Manchester United is a big event in the history of any team, but to knock them out of the Cup at the semi-final stage is a rare achievement for an English club. Any United team are good, but this was one of their great sides. That semi-final will always stand as one of West Ham's finest 90 minutes.

Jenny and I got hitched (West Ham registry office) after the FA Cup semi-final win and just before the League Cup semi-final second leg against Leicester. (Leicester made the Final, 6-3 over the two legs. They took the pot in the Final against Stoke). Billy was my best man. I had my first-ever suit made, lashing out £9. We thought about a honeymoon, but as Jenny had just paid nearly £500 for a new car, we decided that a decent holiday later in the year might be a better idea. Jenny and me went up West and had a slap-up meal, it came to nearly eight quid. I was earning 16 quid a week now, so we got ourselves a mortgage on a three-bedroomed house in East Ham. I had known Jenny for over six years. A long courtship, but Jenny had wanted to complete her training and probationary year before getting spliced. We never lived together before we were married. Although I knew of a number of people 'living in sin', this was not a popular mode of cohabitation in Canning Town. It wasn't Charlie and Daisy though, they were both quite modern in their outlook and seemed determined to enjoy life. They had seen *Beyond the Fringe* in 1961 and cheered on *That Was The Week That Was,* from the edge of their sofa . They were both self-educated people, who made me, a product of the repressed and prudish colonies, and embarrassed, single-sex institutionalisation, feel like a Victorian spinster aunt in their presence. *Lady Chatterley's Lover* and *Fanny Hill* had been on their shelf for years, but perhaps more tellingly, *The Outsider, A Taste of Honey, The Golden Ass, Eros,* and *Decameron* were also well read. The two of them were disciples of Swift, Voltaire, de Maupassant and Richard Hoggart. They had seen *Room at the Top,* twice, agreeing that these 'contemporary foci of moral indignation' were only the honest portrayal of what had gone on secretly for years. Daisy told me that she saw no reason for marriage other than the release from the stupid gossip of others. She recalled walking on Hampstead Heath as a girl with a friend. They had spent the day sitting together by the pond, reading and chatting. They left it late before making their way home, wanting to watch the sun set up on 'Kite Hill'. She told me that their way back over the Heath was an

117

obstacle course of copulating lovers of every possible sexual pairing. She saw the prevalent moral outrage in any specific case as a bore and, in general, she dismissed it as hypocrisy. For her, Professor Carstairs in his BBC Reith Lectures was right when he said, "The popular morality is now a wasteland …It is littered with the debris of broken convictions. A new concept is emerging, of sexual relationships as a source of pleasure." For Daisy, "About time too."

Not everyone could go to Wembley. Between us we got four tickets. Billy had to go, of course, but who would go with him? At first it seemed to make sense for Jenny, Charlie and Daisy to go, but Daisy thought that I should go instead of her. That led to Charlie thinking that he could stay at home with Daisy and watch the game on the tele and this would allow Dan to go. Dan, of course, would not hear of this, as Charlie had got three out of the four tickets (I had got hold of the other through the paper). In the end Jenny said that she would rather I go with Billy and she would watch the game on the TV with her Mum. Charlie said that as Dan did not have a television that he should go with Billy, Jenny and me. Dan said he chose not to have a tele and that he didn't want any charity. It was finally settled by the drawing of names out of Charlie's hat. Billy would have one ticket, the other three would be decided from a draw between Dan, Charlie, Jenny, Daisy and myself. Danny's name came out first, then mine and Charlie's. Dan protested, saying that the whole thing should be decided by consensus and that he would stand-down anyway. Charlie got angry and told him that he was making too much of it and that everyone was happy with the result and that he should accept that with magnanimity. He reluctantly took Charlie's point, and then a whole new argument started about him insisting that he should pay for the ticket. Daisy muttered to me as she went out to make the tea that sometimes she cursed that fascist sniper for his poor aim.

For once West Ham were favourites. The fine 3-1 defeat of Manchester United at Hillsborough, Bobby Moore being voted Footballer of the Year (Johnny Byrne came fourth), and both Byrne and Moore being picked for England's match against the Scots at Hampden (the last time two Hammers had played together for England at Hampden was in 1923 according to Dan, Jack Tresadern and Vic Watson… apparently), seemed to make the Final a formality. On the other hand Preston, although they had barely missed promotion to the First Division, were really a Second Division side. They had also suspended their left-half, Ian Davidson, basically for being a naughty boy.

For all this, Preston had done well to get to the Final, taking the First Division scalps of Nottingham Forest, and Bolton on the way. Their main weapon would be Alex Dawson, a centre-forward of the English tradition. A big, mighty man with the aerial presence of a Lancaster bomber. West Ham started the game with Moore in a sweeper role. I had my doubts about this given Dawson's ability in the air and Moore's weakness off the ground. But Bovington was playing deep, so this gave us an extra defensive option.

A big worry for West Ham supporters was Ron Greenwood's decision to stage John Lyall's testimonial the Monday before the Final. It was quite a game against a London XI. It attracted a big crowd and pride was at stake. John Lyall was a decent player, cut down in his prime by injury, but this was a poor decision on the part of Greenwood. It would have been better to have played the game after Wembley. The players went for it, providing a terrific spectacle, but it would have taken a toll on the team, especially if the Wembley Final should go to extra-time.

The youngest player on the pitch, the youngest ever to start a Cup Final I was later to find out, the 17-year-old Howard Kendall, started the move that led to Doug Holden putting Preston in front. Jim Standen fumbled Alex Dawson's shot and Holden, who had been to Wembley with Bolton on a couple of previous occasions, followed up.

In response, West Ham came forward in numbers and soon Johnny Sissons capitalised on a pass generated from Moore's move up field. Having stolen the ball from the Preston attack, Bobby picked out Byrne. 'Budgie' put the 18-year-old through for his run and Johnny levelled things up with a shot from an acute angle. Sissons became the youngest player ever to score in a Wembley Final.

Byrne came close to putting the Irons ahead about midway through the half, but it was Preston who went in one up at half-time following a well-timed run and strong headed goal, from Dawson, courtesy of a Kendall corner.

But worse than this, the Ashworth-Dawson combination looked to have the more potential up front than Hammers' efforts. Something had to be done. They had acres of room in midfield and Preston's forward play was by-passing Moore. West Ham switched to four accross the back at the start of the second half. Brown and Moore moved in to mark the Preston strikers. Bovington was pushed into the open spaces of the midfield. This had the effect of stepping up the pace of the game. Before ten minutes of the second half had been played, we won a corner. From this Geoff Hurst sent a header on to the underside of the bar. It spun in the air for what seemed like ages before twisting off of Kelly to the ground and twirling, slowly, over the goal-line.

The speed of the game became frantic, the match going backwards and forwards with chances at both ends. It was anybody's game, although overall, the Lancastrians had made the most chances. The 100,000 crowd ooohed and ahhed in agony and cut-off ecstasy. With five minutes left to play, extra-time was on the cards. Tired West Ham legs were now feeling the cost of Lyall's testimonial and the echoes of Cockney rivalry threatened to rob the Hammers of victory. In the last moments of the game Hurst burst forward. Smashing through a minefield of tackles, he forced the ball to Brabrook, who swiftly slung it into the centre. Ronnie Boyce had started to rise just as the ball was struck. The last minute of the match, the second minute of injury time, was now ticking by. The Preston defence looked on as Boyce connected close to the goal-line. The ball flew just wide of Kelly, Preston's beaten 'keeper. It was the 22-year-old's third goal in the Cup, his 11th of the season, and the 17th of his professional career. Billy and I were ecstatic. I turned to Dan to shake his hand or something. He was motionless. He started out at the pitch. "West Ham have won the Cup...Dinkum!" I shouted. "For the first time," replied Dan softly, not looking at me at all. His eyes were full of tears.

Billy went up to Anfield for the Charity Shield game and this time Daisy, Jenny and Charlie went along. I stayed at home with Dan. Apparently it was a good match, 2-2 on the home turf of the League champions, a fine Liverpool side. Hurst and Byrne scored for the Hammers.

1963-64 had been a good year for me and West Ham. It was the happiest I'd been in my life. The Hammers had been all the way to the Cup Final and won it. We had finished 14th in the League, but this had been of secondary interest. Much the same could be said of the 1964-65 season, but this time it was the romance of Europe that dominated attention.

In September, Jenny and I went to Belgium for the holiday that we had promised ourselves. It was no coincidence of course that this coincided with West Ham's first round, first leg European Cup-winners' Cup match with La Gantoise. Ronnie Boyce scored the only goal of the game. This was the first time either of us had been to the continent, and the first time abroad for Jenny. We felt very sophisticated, travelling around the country by train, eating in unusual restaurants and small hotels. Jenny spoke a deal of French, which improved during our stay. I could cough a bit of German, which proved to be less than useful, but all in all we got on quite well, and we liked the Belgians who were a gentle and friendly people.

We drew with La Gantoise at home. Sparta Sokolova of Prague were the next to come out of the hat. Sparta were leading their league at the time. We scored twice against them at the Boleyn. Moore couldn't make the second leg, so Boyce was brought in as sweeper. He did well, moving quickly around the defence. Sissons and Byrne held the ball up front to good effect. We lost the game 2-1 but went through 3-2 over the two legs.

Round three pitted us against Lausanne of Switzerland, managed by the legendary Karl Rappan. Forty years in the game at top level. We did well to beat them 2-1 away in something of a chess game for possession. The second leg was played with much more abandon. It ended in a 4-3 victory for the Hammers. At this time, much of the family attention was following the war in Vietnam. Young Dan was involved in Da Nang and a great deal of silent worry tinged the other events in our lives.

In the semi-final we were drawn to face a Spanish club, Real Zaragoza. They were, by far, the best team we had come up against in the competition. A draw against a Spanish side was always going to be problematic with Danny around. We were on a loser whatever happened. If we had drawn a 'Republican' side, the division of loyalties would have been unbearable. As it was we had to play a 'Nationalist' team, that we really should not have anything to do with. It turned out that Dan decided that we must beat 'the fascists' at all costs (Zaragoza had been in a Nationalist area during the Civil War in Spain). As such, the game at Upton Park was a tense affair, involving all the clan. We were vociferous, inspired by Danny's partisan incantations. Thankfully we won 2-1. A packed ground saw local boy Brian 'Stag' Dear and 'Budgie' Byrne give us some kind of chance for the second leg. Dan, and not a few other old boys, hung around in the ground after the game. We sat on the terraces waiting for him. They spoke for a while, then turning to the pitch, raised clenched fists and sang the *Internationale* in Spanish. The last stragglers stood and watched them in silence as the old men's voices echoed around the shadowy ground. A few clapped hands at the end, one or two odd cheers were heard, but mostly it was quiet.

We listened to the away leg on the radio. The crowd were going mad from beginning to end and you had to work hard to make out what the commentator was saying. Greenwood had decided not to play with a centre-forward. Sissons was on the left, Sealey on the right. Hurst and Dear went deep. This seemed profoundly conservative and chancy. We fell behind quickly. For over an hour, the Spanish dominated the game. Standen and Moore fought an heroic rearguard, thwarting one attack after another. Bobby cut out and tackled, sometimes fencing with two raiders at once. Standen defended his goal like a mythical hero, diving and leaping as if given wings. Then, from nowhere, out of the airwaves, as quicksilver, flew the golden-haired Ariel of the side, Johnny Sissons. He sent the Hammers into the Final. Dan nodded slowly at the wireless. He mumbled something that sounded like, 'Viva Republic'.

Things only die if you let them. For Dan, a seemingly cynical old boomer, there is always hope. Football can be a college of attitudes. I'd never been aware that sentiments, emotions and dreams could be so ...tractable, so enduring.

Back to Wembley! I had bought tickets for Billy and me as soon as I knew the Final would be held in England. Whether West Ham had got to the Final or not, it would have been good for Billy. Charlie and Dan got two tickets each from West Ham and I got one from the paper. Daisy having not been very well for a time, decided that she would watch the game with neighbours on the television, so a party of five went to Wembley. Jenny and Charlie were in one part of the West Ham section of the stadium, Billy and Dan in another. I was with the German fans. We'd got 'em surrounded! I thought that there might be similar difficulties about our opponents, TSV Munich 1860, to those experienced with the Spanish, although this time centring around Charlie. But he didn't say a word. I did ask him about this, and I should have known his answer: "I fought fascism in the desert Ron, not Italians or Germans. Most of those fellers on the other side were victims. They had as little to do with Hitler as we did with Churchill. It just so happened that we had the potential for a better moral position. And we've not lived up to that potential either."

I hired a doormobile to take us all to Wembley. Charlie's mate Joe and his grandson came with us. Joe looks a bit of an okca, but he is in fact a real nice guy and a regular card. He had us in stitches most of the way. The traffic through the City and outside the stadium was awful. Dan said that it would have been quicker to walk. Charlie counted that he had done that once and could tell him that his hypothesis was mistaken. Joe whipped his socks and shoes off to show us the scars. We managed to pick up a programme while looking for a parking space and fed it to the old boy in the hope of keeping him quiet. It did. But his one utterance was enough to bring a cloud of pessimism over the group: "I.Zolt An **Hungarian** referee?!" Joe related an old Polish saying that he had picked up during the war: "If you see a Hungarian in the street, hit him. He will know why!"

The game had one of the biggest audiences ever for a football match. About 30 million people watched it on the tele all over Europe. It was a warm evening that generated the kind of atmosphere that can only be experienced under the floodlights of Wembley in a late English spring.

Byrne had been crocked in the England-Scotland game. Brian Dear had been brought in. This was a worry, even though Dear had done all right in Spain. Again, Hurst was going to play behind the main attack of Sealey and Sissons. The team looked very different from the FA Cup winning side. The right flank had been transformed. John Bond had made way for Joe Kirkup at right-back, Martin Peters had come into Eddie Bovington's right-half position and the right-wing place had been transferred from Peter Brabrook to Alan Sealey. From the first kick we went at the Germans full throttle. It was really a cracking first half. There was some immaculate football displayed and although no one managed to score, it could have been 3-3. Before a quarter of an hour had been played, Sissons had put a shot wide from only about ten feet out. Radenkovic, the Munich goalie, pulled off a string of magnificent saves, foiling Dear more than once. Both Dear and Sealey failed to connect with a Sissons cross, that if diverted would have almost certainly have put us one up. Kuppers, maybe the best Munich forward, also had his chance at our end.

The second 45 minutes started where the last period had left off. Dear again went close, and Sissons pounded the ball against a post. Brunnenmeier, whose pace was blinding, Grosser and Kuppers were only denied by the fortitude and inspiration of Standen.

With only about 20 minutes of the match remaining, Boyce placed a perfect ball between two Munich defenders, Sealey picked it up and the former Orient lad sent a rocket of a drive beyond Radenkovic from what looked like an impossible angle. Sealey somersaulted with delight. Before a critical goal there is a period of time, something less than a second, when all the noise that is to come is condensed into a silence, not a complete quietness, but sound goes out as the ebb of a wave on a sea shore. The sand is still wet, but the flood has retreated for a moment. In this small time is huddled expectation for something that is about to be born and respect for that which is going to die. This was quite tangible where I was standing. The Munich fans stared in disbelief at the ball as it bounced, all jolly and round, inside of the goal. The roar of the West Ham crowd dug a hollow into the darkening skies. The Germans looked up as one towards the Irons, the source of the tumult. The tidal wave crashed solidly into every crevice of the great, old stadium. I felt my ear-drums compress. The Munich supporters around me instinctively flinched, just slightly. We were drenched in sound.

We had caught the Germans on the ropes. Just two minutes later the knock-out blow was delivered. Dear, having got past the 1860 defence with a late run, was pole-axed by a desperate German defender. A free-kick was awarded. Hurst ran over the ball, leaving Moore to lift it to Peters, who had moved in to the middle from a characteristically late run. Peters connected perfectly. Radenkovic made an attempt to intercept but missed, leaving Sealey to seal the game (so to speak).

It was a classic match. One of the great Wembley Finals. Both sides had played with flair and determination. This, alongside the FA Cup Final, would be a crossroads for English football. Nothing would be the same again. West Ham had carried in the future with its dreams. The past was now a dream.

Jack Burkett had been stoic at left-back, playing just behind Moore. Jim Standen had yet another good day. An intuitive save, with his legs, from the Munich skipper Brunnen, may well have been crucial to the final result.

The 1965-66 season had not been under way long when West Ham wrote a another little bit of history into their own record book. At Upton Park on 28

August, Peter Bennett became the club's first-ever substitute in a League game, the Football League having condescended to allow injured players to be replaced during the course of play. A good rule. We beat Leeds 2-1.

The League was, again, always going to be something of a sideshow to our European adventures. Jenny and I decided to continue our first-round 'habit' of attending the away leg. So we took a late holiday in Greece, this time we would see the second leg tie against Olympiakos. We decided to fly out. A new experience for us and one that I handled badly.

The Hammers had won 4-0 at home, so this took the pressure off things a bit. But we saw a good match ending in a respectable draw, 2-2. Martin Peters scored both for the Irons. The Greeks were fanatical supporters. The Piraeus crowd wasn't the noisiest I've been in, but it was the most chaotic. Eye-bolting, screaming, arm-waving stuff. So the Poms are not the only football nuts in the world. We didn't do as much travelling this time, but Athens was fascinating.

As expected, West Ham did not make a great start to the League programme, but just before Christmas we found ourselves back in the League Cup semi-final, which ended up in a great 10-3 aggregate win over Cardiff City. This put us into the last two-legged Final of this competition (from 1967 it would be decided by a Wembley Final, just our luck!). We now had a rather crowded fixture list:

2 March, Cup-winners' Cup, 3rd round, 1st leg, FC Magdeburg (h)

5 March, 1st Division, Aston Villa (h)

9 March, League Cup Final, 1st leg, West Brom (h)

12 March, 1st Division, Blackburn (h)

16 March, Cup-winners' Cup, 3rd round, 2nd leg, FC Magdeburg (a)

19 March, 1st Division, Blackpool (a)

23 March, League Cup Final, 2nd leg, West Brom (a)

26 March, 1st Division, Fulham (h)

Eight games in 21 days

We beat Magdeburg of East Germany 1-0 at home (communist Germans — a difficult one for Dan, this). This was followed by 4-2, 2-1 and 4-1 victories over Villa, West Brom and Blackburn respectively. A 1-1 draw against Magdeburg gave us a 2-1 aggregate win. West Ham were through to their second European semi-final, but the potential opponents were awesome: Liverpool, Celtic or Borussia Dortmund of West Germany.

Great! And it didn't help the fixture pile up:

2 April, First Division, Burnley (h)

5 April, Cup-winners' Cup semi-final, 1st leg, Borussia Dortmund (h)

8 April, First Division, Tottenham (a)

9 April, First Division, Chelsea (a)

13 April, Cup-winners' Cup semi-final, 2nd leg, Borussia Dortmund (a)

16 April, First Division, Arsenal (h)

Six games in 15 days

The pace was beginning to tell. We lost 2-1 to Blackpool. At the Hawthorns goals from Kaye, Brown, Clark and Williams, all in the first half, finished our hopes of the League Cup. A 4-1 defeat. Fulham did us 3-1. We managed a draw against Burnley.

We were tied against Dortmund in the Cup-winners' Cup. Most were pleased to miss Celtic and Liverpool, but I'd been watching the Germans and I thought they had more class than any team left in the competition. They were one of the best teams in Europe at the time.

Billy and I went to Upton Park to see the first leg against Borussia. It was just spring time, and I was full of the optimism that this time of year usually brings to me. Martin Peters put us in front just before half-time. Greenwood had brought in the 32 year-old Jimmy Bloomfield, an old mucker of his from Brentford days. This seemed like lunacy to me. Totally the wrong player at the wrong time. We ran out of steam in the final stages and Lothar Emmerich, West Germany's leading scorer, put away two in the last five minutes.

Things looked as if they were turning round when we beat Spurs. If we could win 4-1 at White Hart Lane, we could do the same in Germany. But a 6-2 hiding at Stamford Bridge did not bode well. At the Westfelanstadion, Dortmund scored with the first movement of the game. Sigi Held crossed the ball to Emmerich, he headed against the bar, but banged home the rebound. Byrne managed to get on the score sheet, but we ended up well beaten, 3-1. The Germans went on to take the Cup, beating Liverpool in the Final. We then proceeded to win our next three games, against Arsenal, Spurs and Manchester United. By now even I was saying, "Typical!"

A hectic season had left us in 12th place in the League and nothing else, but it had been a thrilling ride.

Me and Billy are at Wembley again. It's a bright, English summer's day, half an hour to the World Cup Final. Martin Peters, Geoff Hurst and Bobby Moore are all playing. Moore and Peters had played 63 games for West Ham before the tournament, Hurst played just one game less. But the West Germans have Borussia Dortmund's Lothar Emmerich, the bloke who destroyed us in the Cup-winners' Cup, and his team mate Sigi Held. If this goes to extra-time, I don't fancy England's chances.

# Dreams
# That Will
# Not Die

# Chapter Eight

Marching Cadence
*I wanna go to Vietnam,*
*I wanna kill a Vietcong,*
*With a knife or with a gun,*
*Either way will be good fun.*
*But if I die in the combat zone,*
*Box me up and send me home,*
*Fold my arms across my chest,*
*Tell my folks I done my best.*

WHEN I got back from the war, I was out of the Corps for the first time since I was a kid. I had more Nam tours behind me than most, and being an 'expert', I'd been there from the start and could speak the language. In fact I was more Vietnamese than American by the time I made it Stateside permanent. Mom wasn't there any more and I had a Vietnamese wife. I tried to settle down. I got a job and a place in the city, but Chengsei took a lot. Hardly a day went by when we didn't have to take the 'gook' stuff, or else we got sympathy, which meant some kind of apology for Nam or digging up memories that we really wanted to forget. We had to get away from New York, but I nearly went nuts up-State, and, if anything, the attitude to Chengsei was worse.

*I am ordered to take out an old man who has dashed by, I miss.*
*Another guy tries to get him with a grenade launcher. He catches the*
*old guy as he is going through the door. But the place is full of*
*kids, some kind of school. He was making his way back to tell the kids*
*that we were coming. Kids screaming.*

I had visited my Dad in England a few times. He had been in touch with Mom since I was born. So I decided to try things there. This was not really much of a wrench. My step-dad, John, had been a marine and so, although I had hardly known the man, it was natural that as soon as I could I joined up. I had been all over the world. The States was just a place to touch base every now and then. After Mom died, I began to think more and more of England and London as my spiritual home. I got on with my Dad, even though we had very different political stand-points, this never got in the way. We both worked quite hard to bring out what we had in common rather than think about what separated us. As such, I was proud of the part my old man played in the fight for democracy in Spain. When I went out to Nam he justified my involvement through his problems with Sino-Soviet Communism. But Indo-China changed things for me anyway. By the time I had made my mind up to come to London, I guess I was not too far away from old Danny in political terms.

*We came through the tightly enmeshed jungle, we knew by the stink*
*that we were approaching something nasty. The soldier was hanging*
*from a tree-trunk. He had been pinned there by a flying bed of*
*sharpened bamboo. Not too long ago, maybe a day or so, it had been*
*he who had been unlucky enough to trip the wire that was to put the*
*well-crafted trap into motion. Maybe the thing had been up there for*
*months, just waiting for someone to make the mistake.*

Dad sorted me out a job with a transport firm and a little two-up-two-down in Canning Town and we moved. He and the rest of the family were great. East London was a huge ethnic melting pot, and no one really stood at the centre. So it was as good a place as any for us to be. At least there seemed to be a chance that we might get on with life and that the past could get out of the present. But some things just will not fade away.

*Although some traps were designed for instant death, being covered in poison, or with massively elaborate armour, the most effective, tactically placed traps would not kill a man instantly. Where spikes were placed, how many of them, the length and so on were important considerations. Charlie learnt just what it took to maim, yet not hush the victim with shock. What would entice comrades to disempale a man, and so cause them to slow down, having to carry a casualty.*

I had become interested in West Ham through my Dad's letters, although Mum had sung *Bubbles* to me when I was small. She always chuckled when she told me that it was a song she had picked up in Spain. I guess this affinity was symbolic of belonging to something. Dad sent me programmes and even a scarf. Soccer was not a big sport at high school. It was seen as a bit cissy, vaguely 'un-American', but I found a team, mostly made up of South American kids, and I played every Sunday. My Dad came to New York around a year after my step-father, John, had been brought back from Europe and buried in Arlington. I was about seven or eight at the time. My Mom seemed pleased to see him. She and I visited the following year and during our stay I made my first visit to Upton Park. The Hammers won 2-1 against Leeds United. Terry Woodgate and Eric Parsons scored for me. I was hooked. At the age of 11, I came on my own, by air. This time I was treated to a six-goal thriller. Bill Robinson got two for us, Harry Hooper and Gerry 'Pirate of Penzance' Gazzard scored the others.

*Traps that targeted lower limbs were sometimes favoured. Charlie would remember where every one of these kind of things were. GI screams would act like warning sirens. They would move out as soon as the 'alarm' was sounded. This meant that the whole patrol was now in danger. It's likely that all this man's buddys were now either dead or captured You can't help but hate Charlie, but you got to respect him too. No, he is not 'Charlie'. Neither is he a 'gook' or 'dink'. He is 'Nathaniel Victor'.*

I grew to love London. It was a great place in the 1960s. I'd taken my leave there just before going to Nam for the first time.

*A number of guys saw the NVA soldiers. About a dozen or so rifles fired at the same time, all the NVA hit the ground. When my squad got to the trees, we found that they were all dead. To demonstrate their willingness to die, some of the Vietnamese had tied themselves by a leg to a tree. They had patches on the front of their shirts which read: "KILL AMERICANS."*

Chengsei was an ethnic Chinese. Her great-grandparents on both sides of her family had come from Peking. She was an interpreter working for the South Vietnamese government. In '63 (I had been one of the first wave of 'advisors') I had put my name down for language training and was sent down to Saigon to take the starter course. Chengsei was my tutor. Her family were well-heeled business people. She had been to university in France, so apart from Vietnamese, Cantonese, Mandarin and English, she was also fluent in French. She taught me well, but I was a keen student.

Following my second tour I took Chengsei with Willow to meet the family for the first time. We arrived in the Fall of 1966. The family made a great fuss of us all, especially little Willy.

A great deal of hope had been invested in Ron Greenwood, a kind of new dawn was promised. Although Greenwood achieved some success early on, it is amazing, given the kind of players he had at his disposal, including the core of England's World Cup winning side, Moore, Hurst and Peters, fresh from beating West Germany, that success was so hard to come by. He also had other quality players, some with international credentials or potential like Standen, Bovington, Brabrook, Boyce and Byrne. They had beaten Tottenham Hotspur and Arsenal in the League Cup. What could be achieved was further demonstrated when the Hammers, having battered Fulham 6-1 in the League two days earlier, at the start of November 1966, met with Leeds in the fourth round of the League Cup and achieved their biggest-ever win in the competition. This was the foundation of the great Leeds side that included David Harvey, Paul Reaney, Billy Bremner, Jack Charlton, Norman Hunter, Paul Madeley, Greenhoff, Johnny Giles, Bates and O'Grady.

I was at the game with Dad and in the very first minute Harvey was forced to make saves from Byrne and Brown. Soon after 'Budgie' put the ball wide to Sissons on the left, and Johnny sent it curling back to open the scoring. Leeds hadn't come to Upton Park with the idea of being one down after two minutes. They had to come forward almost from the start which exposed their defence badly. The five minutes before and after the half-hour produced two more West Ham goals. First Byrne sent Brabrook away, he went through Willie Bell and sent the ball sideways for Sissons to score. The third goal was almost a carbon copy of the second. Peters put Brabrook through, he then picked up Sissons, who put a low drive into the net. Less than five minutes before the interval Sissons made a lengthy cross, it was cleared as far as Peter Brabrook and he sent the ball to Peters who headed to Byrne. 'Budgie' drove the ball hard, it hit Reaney and Charlton before going in. Hurst was awarded this goal although he didn't touch it.

Not 15 minutes after the half-time break, Byrne opened the way for Hurst who by-passed the defender to shoot low and hard to make it 5-0. We had to wait until the 79th minute for the next goal. Martin Peters left a couple of defenders floundering before driving a hard right-footer passed poor old Harvey. No more than two minutes later Standen booted the ball powerfully down the park for Brabrook to nod on to Byrne, who in turn provided Hurst with the perfect pass to send goal number seven crashing home.

Less than a week later we were at White Hart Lane facing another great team. Pat Jennings, Phil Beal, Cyril Knowles, Allan Mullery, Mike England, Dave Mackay, Robertson, Jones, Jimmy Greaves, Alan Gilzean, Terry Venables. Some called it the match of the year, others said it was one of the greatest exhibitions of attacking football ever.

They were all over us at first and it was a surprise when Peters and Boyce worked the ball to Brabrook. His cross was met by Byrne who sent a subtle chip past Jennings. Greaves was hacked down by Bovington only to get up and level the scores with the resulting penalty. Less than five minutes later Gilzean hit the post and while the Spurs players were still looking up at the skies in consternation, a rare shot from Bobby Moore had forced Jennings to punch the ball back out into play. Brabrook sent it straight back past the Northern Ireland goalkeeper. We made it 3-1 three minutes later when Sissons finished off a long run from deep inside West Ham territory with a blistering shot a few yards outside the penalty area. Venables replied almost immediately, launching a scorching 25-yarder that seared to its target with all the venom and blind exactness of a homing missile. Spurs should have gone level two minutes after the Venables screecher when Moore used his hands in the area, but Jimmy Greaves skied the penalty. Tottenham continued to pile forward. One minute past the hour their tenacity paid off. Gilzean did his back-header number from a Jim Robertson cross. All square going into the last quarter-of-an-hour. Bobby Moore sent the ball to Peters from deep inside the West Ham half. Peters released Brabrook down the right flank on a winger's mission, the inevitable cross found the head of John Sissons who deflected it to the lethal head of Geoff Hurst for the decisive fourth goal.

*We approached the hut, an old man came out of the bomb shelter. I told him to get away from the hut. We had to move swiftly on the sweep. I threw the grenade into the shelter. As I pulled the pin, the old guy went beserk and ran towards the hut and me.*

This was followed by a 3-0 win against Newcastle, a 2-1 defeat by Leeds, and a 3-0 win at home to West Brom. Then a 3-1 win against Blackpool at Bloomfield Road, took us to the League Cup semi-final. A 4-2 loss at Turf Moor was the prelude to a date at Stamford Bridge on 17 December. We shared ten goals with the Blues, letting them get on even terms twice in the process. Great stuff, but it didn't smack of good organisation.

The Irons took the lead in the 24th minute, after having a John Byrne effort called offside. The former Chelsea man, Brabrook, converted a corner from Sissons. This was followed by good work on the part of Byrne and Hurst to create a second goal via Martin Peters. We looked like going in 2-0 up, but Tom Baldwin pulled one back for Chelsea out of a goalmouth melee in the last moments of the first half.

With 50 minutes gone, Tony Hateley banged in a goal from a good 25 yards out. Chelsea went in front less than five minutes later by way of the immaculate Charlie Cooke, who picked up on good work by Baldwin and Hateley. Before the hour was up, Sissons beat Bonetti with a cruel, curving shot. Moving into the last half-hour Sissons struck again, this time from a massive 40 yards. A minute had gone by when 'Chopper' Harris handled in the area. Bonetti made a marvellous save from Byrne's penalty, but 'Budgie' picked up the rebound, swerved passed Eddie McCreadie and former West Ham man Joe Kirkup to restore the two-goal lead.

With ten minutes of the game left Moore was judged to have fouled Hateley. Bobby Tambling converted the penalty. Chelsea fought tooth and nail from then on and equalised in the last minute of injury time through Tambling with the last kick of the game.

This was all very dramatic stuff but it was obvious that something had gone missing. I was inclined to think that it was what Ronnie called the 'Allison effect'.

Like the League Cup Final of the previous year, we were well beaten by West Bromwich Albion in the 66-67 semi-final. I travelled up to the Midlands with Ron to see the first leg. Jeff Astle blew Ken Brown away. They won 4-0. We got a 2-2 result at Upton Park, but the first Wembley League Cup Final would not be graced by West Ham and a fourth successive Cup Final appearance for Moore and Hurst would not take place.

*My buddy shot him. Then I heard a baby crying from inside the shelter. Nothing could be done. After the grenade went off we found two children, the mother and an almost new-born baby.*

I went back home to the States just after this game, and soon after I was back in Indo-China, but I kept in touch with my family in London and what the Hammers were up to. That season, Greenwood's fifth year of stewardship, West Ham finished barely outside the relegation zone in 16th place. Flashes of natural genius from the players meant that the guys could get the kind of results I saw during my stay, but West Ham moved between relative brilliance to mediocrity.

*We burned the hut. The old man was wounded. He lay sobbing in front of the burning hut. The guy who had brought him down finished him off.*

This points to bad management. In the jungle you could get a long way with experience, but a marine survived because of his training and the skill of the platoon leaders. A self belief and a level of concentration had to be fostered. This is what West Ham didn't have and Greenwood did not have the personality, the steel, to engender it. Charlie could kill you without even seeing you by breaking you in the head, driving you crazy with fear. At the same time, that's how he motivated himself.

*There was no bark on the trees. They had written on many of them.*
*For example: DEFEAT THE AMERICANS, HERE WE TAKE OUR*
*STAND, and THE WHOLE NATION IS WATCHING. DO NOT DIS-*
*GRACE YOURSELF — STAY AND FIGHT. DO NOT RUN.*

I once took a tour of Liverpool's Anfield ground. Above the tunnel that leads out to the pitch, the visiting players read a notice that Bill Shankly had ordered to be put up. It reads:

*This is Anfield*

Above the players' tunnel at the Boleyn Ground another notice twitters, "Welcome to Upton Park." This does much to sum up the difference between the managerial attitudes that reign at the respective clubs.

The next Hammers 'success' was a long time coming. In 1972 we reached the semi-finals of the League Cup yet again. I could only read about this, but I got a good picture from the Hong Kong press, Dad's letters and what little coverage that was given in the news we got from the States. We had beaten Cardiff City, Leeds United, after extra-time at Elland Road, Liverpool and Sheffield United. Then the long struggle against Stoke City started. The first leg at the Victoria Ground went to West Ham, 2-1, Hurst and the big Bermudan, Clyde Best, got our goals. Apparently we looked good up there, but at Upton Park Stoke scored first through John Ritchie, which put the teams on a par. With just three minutes of time remaining, the great Stoke goalkeeper, Gordon Banks, fouled Harry Redknapp. I could not believe that Hurst had gone up to take the penalty. What did Banks, so long an England team-mate of Hurst, not know about Hurst's style? With whom, when on England tour or training, did Hurst, the England penalty taker, practise his penalties? This was Greenwood's shortcoming. Banks saved and it went to a replay. Of course we lost the toss and the next game was played in the north, at Hillsborough.

*We called in the choppers to clear the hill. Three of the birds came*
*over the rise. They were up high. Before they disappeared they had*
*killed 12 of us and wounded more than 20. Some of the crews have*

*so much junk in 'em that they'd gun down a picnic in Central Park
We'd screamed at them to stop, but Charlie screams at them too.
Killing's killing. It don't mean nothin' . . . It don't mean nothin'...not a
thing, not a single thing . . .*

West Ham won their two League games before the trip to Sheffield,
beating Tottenham Hotspur at White Hart Lane and Manchester United at
Upton Park (3-0) on New Year's Day. The game against Stoke ended in a
goalless draw, after extra-time. Again we lost the toss and the second replay
was set for Old Trafford. We lost 3-2. Ferguson got knocked out early on and
Moore went in goal. He saved a penalty from Mike Bernard, but could not
hold the shot and Bernard scored on the rebound. Billy Bonds equalised with
only ten West Ham men on the park. Ferguson came back on, still dizzy.
Brooking put West Ham ahead, but the dazed Ferguson was nowhere when
Peter Dobing and Terry Conroy challenged and they both scored to send
Stoke to Wembley where they beat Chelsea to take the trophy.

The most ironic thing was that after the World Cup Greenwood had the
opportunity to sign Banks, but instead he went for Ferguson ...from Kilmarnock. Not wanting to let down his old Brentford buddy, Malcolm McDonald,
the Kilmarnock manager, to whom he had promised a world record fee to
take the erratic Ferguson out of his hands. Think about that! Ferguson would
not have been playing for us, Banks wouldn't have been the Stoke City
goalkeeper, etc., etc.

We were in the last eight of the FA Cup when we moved into Canning
Town. A win at Southampton, brought Swindon to Upton Park. Clyde Best was
brought in for Bobby Gould. It was a poor display by the Hammers. They held
us 1-1. Their winger, David Moss was impressive. Like so many players from
lesser teams, he raised his game at Upton Park to heights few would have
thought possible. The replay at the County Ground saw Swindon take the lead
through Trevor Anderson. Brooking pulled us level with a dramatic diving
header. Pat Holland, in because of injury to Gould and the suspension of
Keith Robson, put us through to meet Queen's Park Rangers with just six
minutes to spare.

The game against QPR was a bit of a mud-bath, but Brooking was pure
poetry. Dave Clement had scored first for Rangers, making the most of a

mistake by Robson. Pat Holland got us on level terms and Robson made up for his earlier gaff with a headed winner.

The quarter-final took us to Highbury. Not a happy hunting ground for the Hammers. It had been a decade since we had won there. But the 21 year-old Alan Taylor, who looked like a stick man drawn by one of the slow kids at kindergarten, complete with yellow crayoned hair, was going to silence those who would have us steam-rollered. We had signed him in November from lowly Rochdale. He scored a quarter of an hour into the match. But a crucial moment in the game came about a minute before half-time when Frank Lampard made a weak back-pass that stuck in the mud. John Radford put it passed our charging goalkeeper, Mervyn Day. It didn't go in, but over Radford went. No penalty! The Gunners' heads were down after the interval. It was then that 'Sparrow' outpaced Bob McNab, Terry Mancini and Peter Simpson to move on to Brooking's pass. The net was at his mercy. Franz Kafka, the writer, observed that when a goal is scored most people feel sorry for the ball. However, he felt sympathy for the mouth-gaping net. I knew something of what he meant when Taylor scored. The happy Irons were through to the semi-final for the first time in over a decade.

Ipswich, the new favourites to win the FA Cup, made the semi-finals having beaten Leeds over a four-match tie. This was in our favour. However, they had six internationals in their side and had hardly been out of the top three in Division One all season. A terrible goalless draw at Villa Park, where although they totally outplayed us, neither team wanted to push people forward, was followed by a trip to Stamford Bridge just four days later. Ipswich had played six matches in 13 days and were carrying a huge list of injuries. Their manager, Bobby Robson, whined about the venue before and after the match, saying it favoured West Ham, being in London. I suppose he would have liked it played at Carrow Road! You would think a former England international would have more integrity. John Lyall, who had by now been appointed team manager, kept the same side that had beaten Arsenal.

David Johnson had two goals disallowed on an awful night. Sleet and snow soaked and froze us as we stamped on the terraces. But it was Taylor who put West Ham in front following our first real attack, half-way through the first period. A mistake by Billy Jennings lead to the scores being levelled just before the break. Ten minutes from time John Wark cleared, Taylor picked it up and shot. The ball skidded passed Laurie Sivell and slid in off his post. West Ham were at Wembley for the fifth time in their history. As we trudged out we heard that the Fulham v Birmingham semi-final in Manchester had gone to extra-time.

> *In an eagle flight the helicopter is loaded with a few picked troops and you circle around waiting for someone to take a shot at you. At that point you swoop down, the troops are disembarked in an attempt to police the village. This had been a good day. A number of strikes had been made. Around a dozen Vietcong had been taken prisoner, we had killed about the same. Fighting in a chopper is something like watching a football match from the top of the stand. One time we flushed out a VC, he was running frantically through a dry paddy. He was falling and stumbling. The chopper went after him, this big metal thing against flesh and blood. I did feel some sympathy, but at an outpost a few days before,I had carried out the dead bodies.*

It was an all London Final. We faced wily old Alec Stock's Fulham. At the start of the competition you could have got 500-1 on them to win the Cup. But this didn't look such a bad bet given our results in the League following the victory over Ipswich. We lost 3-0 at Leicester City, were beaten 1-0 at Derby's Baseball Ground, and experienced a 2-1 home defeat at the hands of Coventry. This was the first team debut of 21 year-old Alan Curbishley, a Forest Gate kid. Alan was something of a schoolboy prodigy, playing for England at that level. He was a leading member of our Youth Cup Final side and had gained six caps as a Youth international. Curbishley was a stylish midfield player, and looked almost arrogant on the ball. A real prospect if treated right. In our next game Ipswich got some revenge via a 4-1 trouncing at Portman Road. However, we won against Arsenal at Upton Park in our final fixture, 1-0. Pat Holland got the winner. On 30 April, Saigon was lost to the North Vietnamese.

The Final was Fulham's first appearance at Wembley. Stock had taken Bobby Moore to Second Division Craven Cottage. It was strange to see him lining up against us. Another former England skipper was also in the side, the one-time Spurs captain Alan Mullery. It had been a long haul for the Cottagers. Replays included, they had played 11 games and 18 hours to get to the Final. This was a record.

Patsy Holland played out of his skin that day. It was he who, on the hour, took the ball from John Cutbush and made a short pass inside to Jennings whose shot could only be parried by Fulham goalie, Peter Mellor, to Alan Taylor. 'Sparrow' made no mistake with the rebound, driving it back through Mellor's legs. Soon after it was Holland again who set up Paddon's shot from the left. Mellor failed to hold it, and for the second time it was the nippy Yorkshireman who picked up the left overs. It was his third double in the Cup that season. For the second time we had taken the Cup with an all-English team.

> *If someone took evasive action, they were fired on. Evasive action was never defined. It usually was taken to be anyone running away, from, say, a helicopter, even if they were being shot at. One unit had fixed MP sirens to the chopper, for 'psychological effect', this meant that it intimidated the people. Once, they flew over a big paddy field, it passed over the people working there a couple of times, very low. The peasants, maybe 20 of them, in the field looked nervous, but just went on working. The chopper then hovered amongst them, no more than a few feet off the ground. The police sirens were turned on and some of the Vietnamese started to jog away. The chopper opened fire.*
> *They were all shot.*

The Hammers started the 1975-76 season well, although our sixth Wembley appearance ended in defeat. Dave Mackay's League champions, Derby County, beat us in the Charity Shield. 2-0. However, we were top of the table in November, experiencing only two defeats in the first 15 matches. But once we got involved with the European Cup-winners' Cup, nothing else seemed to matter.

In the first round we were drawn against Lahden Reipas of Finland. We just about got a 2-2 draw in the frozen north. But a 3-0 win at home, with goals from Robson, Holland and Jennings sent us comfortably into the second round. I was planning to make the away trip with cousin Billy and

Ronnie, but we were assigned to play Ararat Erevan, in the Soviet Union, and this didn't seem such a good idea for an ex-marine. Dad and Charlie made the journey to the Soviet Republic of Armenia, near the Turkish-Iranian border and the Caucasus Mountains. For Dad it was a return. He had gone there during the final part of his stay over 50 years before. They stayed in freezing Moscow for a few days, then took the 1,500-mile flight south and found themselves sweating in temperatures of around 75 degrees.

We had to start without Brooking, who had gone down with gut problems. Pat Holland took the number 11 shirt and played a fine game, as did John McDowell in defence. Alan Taylor scored after 56 minutes, but the Soviets pulled the game level with a goal that Dad and Charlie went through again and again in the telling. Day went for a high ball and was fouled, the ball ran loose, a defender played it back to him. As Day stood holding the ball, he was harassed by Nazar Petrosian. Day went to throw the ball, but Petrosian lunged to head the ball from between his hands. After a scramble, the Armenian smacked the ball into the net. The German ref gave a goal, which, according to Dad and Charlie, had everyone in the stadium laughing. Justice was done at the Boleyn Ground with a 3-1 victory for the Irons.

Whilst in the area Dad and Charlie visited the nearby Mount Ararat, where Noah's Ark was said to have come to ground following the flood. I thought this was odd for Dad, a man who saw religion as an illusion. It was Chengsei who later asked him about this, quoting Marx's idea that religion is 'the opium of the people'. Dad, after a pause said, surprisingly quietly and gentle for him, that he remembered when opium was seen as a curative substance, a bit like aspirin. It relieved pain, like toothache, that was common when he was a boy, but difficult and expensive to treat. As a lad, he had often been sent out on errands to buy two penny-worth of laudanum, a tincture of opium, when someone in the family was in pain. He said that my Grandmother had used it to combat cramps during menstruation. He thought that Marx saw religion in the same way as opium was seen at the time that old Karl was writing his Manifesto; a benign thing, that had the power to alleviate pain and help poor people through their lives. But something more was needed.

In the quarter-finals we were up against Den Haag. A really quality team. Brooking was still suffering. At half-time, the Dutch were leading 4-0. Two of their goals were highly disputable penalties and the fourth was completely nutty. Mr Glockner, the East German referee (who had officiated in the 1970 World Cup Final), stopped the game after 40 minutes when a bottle was thrown in the general direction of Mervyn Day. Lex Schoenmaker, a Den Haag player, went behind the goal to remonstrate with the fans. Glockner restarted the game with a dropped ball on the centre circle, Graham Paddon stepped up for us, but the referee waved him back so Schoenmaker just took the ball, made for goal and scored. Perhaps even more bizarre than this was when Glockner stopped the game and demanded that Kevin Lock pull his socks up.

John Lyall had been taken ill earlier in the day, so it was Ron Greenwood who took off Mick McGiven at half-time and sent Keith Coleman out for the second period. This helped us score two second half away goals through Jennings, which proved to be decisive. 30,000 fans were shouting down the throats of the Dutch when they came to Upton Park and they visibly wilted. We won 3-1, going through on the away goals rule to face Eintracht Frankfurt in the semi-finals.

The West Germans were the best side we had played in Europe. Like many German sides, their players could work equally well in defence or attack. They had a very good team, that included Bernd Holzenbien, Nickel and for my money one of the best German players ever, Jurgan Grabowski. Graham Paddon gave us the vital away goal in the first leg with a beautiful 30-yard piledriver of a shot. They came to Upton Park leading 2-1. Paddon and Bonds on the left and Brooking on the right worked well for us. The ball moved quickly on the wet ground, which suited the West Ham game. 40,000 fans saw Trevor Brooking waltz in one and head home another, but it took a Keith Robson goal to make the tie safe (4-3 aggregate) and ensure that in the spring of 1976 West Ham would grace a sixth major Cup Final.

*They instructed us to level the hamlet if we received one round from*
*it. Three marines were wounded. So we went into the place, going*
*over the hedges, ditches through the bushes, then the destruction.*

Ronnie, Bill and me took a boys' holiday to the Final. We spent an entertaining, but clean (honest) night in Amsterdam, before making the trip to Brussels the following day. Ron knew the city well and we had a great lunch before the game.

At the Heysel Stadium in Brussels, we faced Royal Anderlecht of Belgium, a club with an impressive and proud history of European campaigns, and although we were about 10,000 strong, and giving it all we'd got, the rest of the 58,000 crowd were mostly Flemish. The stadium was a sea of the white and violet of Anderlecht.

We hadn't won a game since beating Frankfurt three weeks previously. In the League we had got a draw at home to Villa, and lost to Everton, Ipswich, and Sheffield United. Outside of Europe we hadn't won a game for the best part of four months: 16 games. We had won only 13 games during the League season, and just two in both the domestic cups. This form was of course reflected in our League position. We finished 18th. Everything had been focused on the Cup-winners' Cup. We'd won four, drawn two and lost two (both away) in Europe. This was a decent enough record, and an exciting campaign — we had scored 18 goals and conceded 11.

But Anderlecht were a powerful team. Not only did they have the star of a classy Belgium side up front, François Van der Elst, but two of the Dutch 'Total Football' World Cup side, Haan and the quicksilver Robbie Rensenbrink

Pat Holland put us in front just before the half-hour mark. It was a good time to score, and a second major European trophy seemed almost secure. But just before half-time, and an even better time to score, a rare mistake by Frank Lampard, misjudging a back pass to 'keeper Mervyn Day, gave Anderlecht the opportunity to take the advantage. Ressel swiped the ball and laid on Rensenbrink to smash the equaliser into the net. Not only did Lampard all but set up the goal, he injured himself in the process. Lyall replaced him with Alan Taylor, a forward, who had not been having the best of seasons, and this meant an entire reorganisation of the side. McDowell moved to full-back and Holland into midfield, thus drawing Paddon further behind the attack. So, almost inevitably, soon after, a couple of minutes before the break, Rensenbrink, who was now really turning it on, put Van der Elst through to score. We did draw level through a Keith Robson header, via the post, from a typically artistic 'Brookingesque' concave cross, sent in from the byline. But 14 minutes from time the French ref gave an unbelievable penalty after Holland had deprived Rensenbrink of the ball. At first I thought that Mr Wurtz was confirming the corner, but no, he was pointing to the penalty spot. Rensenbrink completed the formalities.

Now West Ham had to throw caution to the wind and go hunting for a goal. With Lampard gone, this left great gaping holes at the back. This situation was exploited by the free running Anderlecht attack, and with just a couple of minutes of the game left, Rensenbrink found Van der Elst with a long through-pass. The little winger darted round McDowell and Day before finishing us off.

It was a terrible ending. That draining feeling came back. I was so empty.

*In a day, 150 homes were burned. Three women were wounded and a baby was killed. One marine was wounded. We took four prisoners. Old men who could not answer questions. They had no notion of what an ID card was. Today's activity is Vietnam. Our fire-power is awesome, but for the rural Vietnamese, their home equates to generations of toil.*

*How are we on their side?*

For all this, it's been a good season. I can never escape from Nam, but there is respite. The Hammers shield my dreams just a little from 'Nathaniel Victor', my constant companion. But it don't mean nothin', not a thing, not a single thing . . . Roars of hope dilute screams of war.

*If you are able,*
*Save for them a place*
*inside of you*
*and save one backward glance*
*when you are leaving*
*for the places they can*
*no longer go.*
*Be not ashamed to say*
*you loved them*
*though you may*
*or may not have always.*
*Take what they have left*
*and what they have taught you*
*with their dying*

*and keep it with your own.*
*And in that time*
*when men decide and feel safe*
*to call the war insane*
*take one moment to embrace*
*those gentle heroes*
*you left behind*

Major Michael Davis O'Donnell
1 January 1970. *Dak To, Vietnam*

# Nothing to do but blow bubbles

# Chapter Nine

*"It's hard to explain what the club is, but I do know that it's **my** club. I've been brought up with it all my life. One thing is for sure; it's something that has always been there. You can't explain it ... People that don't understand think that you're bloody stupid, that you're crackers getting so involved. It's hard to understand yourself, especially when your ulcer starts acting up ... but you can't tell yourself not to get involved."*

*Long-standing West Ham supporter*
*From West Ham United by Charles Korr.*

29 April 1978

Happy 14th birthday Willy girl. West Ham needed one point yesterday to stay up. Easy. A draw against European Cup Finalists Liverpool, who needed a point to finish runners-up to Forest. I went to Upton Park with more than 37,000 other twits to watch them blow it ... 2-0. I got involved in the hundred-a-side football on the pitch as soon as the players went off.

We started singing *Bubbles* about ten seconds after Liverpool scored their second goal and went on for a good half-hour after the match. I sat in the emptying stand with two guys of about 30. We all had a good cry. The big feller held me, and kept saying, "It'll be all right." The other one, sort of Asian looking, but with a broad, almost South London accent, constantly patted us both on the back, repeating variations of, "We'll be back. Next season. Wait and see," and "We'll show 'em, bounce straight back we will. Second Division champions!" We parted as we had met. Anonymous. Aunt Jenny calls it *Agape* ...

What a completely crap season! Do you know who I feel really sorry for? Alan Curbishley. He is not getting any help. He's a maturing player and could be the best type of replacement for Brooking or Devonshire one day. What a waste!

This was only the second time West Ham had been relegated. The first time was the 1933-32 season (we got one more point this time, 32!). The only person who can remember this is Grandpa and he reckons that the 1932 team was the better side. We nearly went last year. In the last game we faced Manchester United. They were on their way to Wembley (they were to beat Liverpool in the FA Cup Final), we were fighting for survival. We started in the first minute by letting Gordon Hill score, then we missed a penalty. That looked like it, but Lampard, Pike and 'Pop' Robson turned it around for us. Stuart Pearson did pull one back, but with about 15 minutes left Robson scored his second and we stayed up. We wouldn't go home that day either, calling the team out for an encore.

But no such triumph this time round. The bearded wonder Derek Hales, yet again proved West Ham to be the dumping ground for the surplus camels of Derby and the like. Ten goals all season from the ex-Charlton super star. We had to wait until nearly Christmas before we got a win at home, by which time we were well stuck in the basement of the First Division. David Cross was dragged in from West Brom at about this time. He did all right, but we were doomed. We went out of the FA Cup on a 6-1 fourth-round replay bashing from QPR. The first game had ended up 1-1, Ernie Howe got a late equaliser to Bonds' opener. Half-time at Loftus Road we were playing well, but Martyn Busby had a great second half and scored two. Stan Bowles was out of this world. Why couldn't we have got Stan Bowles instead of Hales?

Last season had seen us get away with it by a 'Pop' Robson whisker. It was not going to happen again, not even with hairy Derek's face.

Anderlecht are in the Cup-winners' Cup Final again. They got beat last year 2-0, by SV Hamburg, but this will be their third Final on the trot. It is not right to pray about football matches and it is less right to pray for vengeance, but then, none of us are perfect.

*U.N.I.T.E.D.,*
*United are the team for me ...*

26 March 1979

Last game Alan Curbishley plays for West Ham (sub against Leicester at Upton Park, 1-1). He's gone to Birmingham of all places. Only 24 years old and we get rid of him after only 74 games. Shortsighted or what? What did Brooking look like after 74 outings? Alan was the perfect local hero. He could have been great for this club and England. If he had played on the continent he would have been a phenomenon. I mean, he looks like a Dutch player doesn't he? Sometimes nothing at all makes sense. Apparently there was some argument about his role in the team. I'd say he was right. If you can't use skill like his, something is wrong. It's not as if we are floating on talent. The likes of Curbishley are the heart and future of any team, they need a patient base, in an area that can identify with them. We have to have a Curbishley, someone who has come through the ranks; one of 'us'. You nurture his like; you build around him. He scored seven goals for us. He made many more. It is the goals that he will now never score or make that we will miss. Jake says I fancy him, but I don't! It's not that. Be lucky Alan. One day, come back. We are always yours. You are always ours.

*Alan, Alan Cur-bish-ley,*
*Al-aan Curbish-ley.*

8 January 1980

Uncle Charlie died. On Boxing Day it was. Aunt Daisy had his ashes spread on the pitch. The first game played 'on Charlie' we've beaten First Division West Brom, 2-1 in the third-round replay of the FA Cup. Phil Parkes was truly magnificent in the first game, but he didn't have much to do in this match. A misty night. Shame Billy B was out injured. I suppose you could say that Charlie had a part in both Piko's and the Brook's goals. That wasn't meant to come out like that. Hope you enjoyed it, Chas. I miss you!

Me and Jake went over the Brisbane Road for the next round. He goes with me, even though he supports the Arsenal. We got to the ground about an hour before the game. This is usual. We played 'Alphabet Disco'. We give each other a letter and we have to come up with ten titles of Top 40 records beginning with that letter. We also have to name the recording artist for each title. So he gives me 'B'.

1.   *Baby, Baby My Love Is All For You* ...Deniece Williams
2.   *Babylon's Burning* ...The Ruts
3.   *Bad Moon Rising* ...Creedence Clearwater Revival
4.   *Baker Street* ...Gerry Rafferty
5.   *Bare Footin'* ...Robert Parker
6.   *Boys Are Back In Town* ...Thin Lizzy
7.   *Baby Come Back* ...The Equals
8.   *Bridge Over Troubled Water* ...Simon and Garfunkel
9.   *Brother Louie* ...Hot Chocolate
10.  *Breaking Up Is Hard To Do* ...The Partridge Family

Something for everyone there I think. Jake always goes along the same track. Sixties, soul, Tamla. Me, I like to be more catholic. But I put a stop to him with 'Z'. He got:

| | |
|---|---|
| *Zing Went the Strings of My Heart* | — Trammps (Arsenal supporters?) |
| *Zoo* | — Commodores |
| *Zorba's Dance* | — Marcello Minerbi |
| | (weren't Dundee drawn against this lot in the first round of the Fairs Cup in 1968?) |
| *Zabadak* | — Dave Dee, Dozy, Beaky, Mick and Titch |
| | (the Orient midfield) |

Pretty good, but not good enough. So I won! 'Z' along with 'X' is now outlawed

We're a funny pair me and Jake. Me the Hammers, him the Gunners. I'm a product of Vietnam, China, Black America and England. Jake is half Trinidadian and half Irish, but born in Holloway. Turn's you off of having kids don't it?

Jake isn't really a boyfriend. I've never had a boyfriend. He's like a mate, a buddy, a pal. I met him on a bus last year. I was coming back from Grandad's and he'd been on the buses all day for something to do. He'd bought a day pass. I had my scarf on. "Hammer?" he asked. "Yeah." "Gunner," he said, pulling his scarf out of his tatty old jacket. "Right," I said. "Right," he said. Start of a beautiful relationship. No. Not really.

No Brook tonight. Ray Stewart moves into midfield, Paul Brush and Lampard at the back. Billy Bonds comes out with a bandage round his napper. Looks like 'the mummy'. 'Traitor' Tommy Taylor scored for Orient first. Penalty. But we won 3-2. Ray Stewart got two and Nigel Gray of the O's decided to score for us. The talented Nigerian winger John Chiedozie, 'the new Laurie Cunningham' (no, there'll never be a second Laurie, now he is more than special) scored Orient's second. Whoops, fifth round! Swansea at Upton Park. League form less than tasty. Fourteen famous victories, eight unlucky defeats, three droopy draws.

I haven't gone to school much over the last few months. In fact I don't think I've seen the place for about a year. I don't see the point anyway. Maggie's army awaits. I think Jake must be a general by now. He's never had a real job. He does an Avon round, though, and he delivers newspapers. He says he's 'a street-wise opportunist'. He lives with his aunt in Hackney. Don't get any better than that does it? Dad gives me a few quid a week and I've got a morning job with a greengrocer. That's how I get to buy records and go to matches. I've never got much money after Saturday.

Not going to school doesn't mean I'm stupid. We are a family of readers. Grandad got me into some heavy stuff early on. Sometimes, when he was visiting us, he used to read me Shakespeare at bedtime (great for sending kids to sleep that; now, of course, I'm an addict). It wasn't long before I was tucking into his library, stimulated by the 'debates' between him, Uncle Charlie, Aunt Daisy, my older cousin Jenny and her hubby Ron. Cousin Billy bought me the classics, Swift, Melville, Robert Louis Stevenson and so on. He thought you needed your own copies. *If you're gonna get anything from books girl, you gotta abuse 'em.*

They all ruined school for me. It was such a boring and dictatorial form of education in comparison. I remember telling a bemused teacher that the metaphor of Swift was the natural forebear of Defoe's *Robinson Crusoe* and Carol's *Alice in Wonderland*. She blinked for a bit and then gave me lines for interrupting her. I was 12.

Jake didn't have any money to come to the Swansea game, and I couldn't take him and me, so I went on my own. I could have gone with Dad and Grandad, but it's not the same with them, I feel ...restricted ...no, inhibited. As well as this, I've got to say it, I get embarrassed with them. It was all right when I was little, that's how I started going to matches, with Dad, Grandad, Uncle Charlie, sometimes Aunt Daisy and Jenny. Mum hardly ever comes. She don't like the noise. But, for the last four of five years I've found that I prefer to turn up on my own. I stand on the North Bank. But I quite like going with Jake. He wants us to go to Highbury together, but unless they play West Ham I wouldn't have any interest. That sounds unfair, but I don't know, it would be like ...being unfaithful. Two-timing. He don't feel like that, but I do, so that's it.

You get some funny stuff at times. Once when I went with Billy, Charlie and Dad, some guy called me 'a Chink'. Dad got mad. I thought he'd kill the jerk. A couple of this twerp's buddies looked like they were going to get involved, but Bill had a bit of a reputation and when they saw he was with us they changed their minds. It was Billy that told the bloke to apologise. He said sorry. But I couldn't deal with that stuff now. I'd rather ignore it. That's another reason why I go on my own. Jake takes a bit of that too. Someone made a remark when we were at the Chelsea game (we got beat 1-0). I surprised myself. The mouth was about twenty-ish, with a bunch of others. Said something about monkeys. I just got really angry. I said, "Hey! What you saying." They looked at me. Jake wilted. He turned ventriloquist and growled, "Shut up!" I had to carry on before they answered. "What they teach you in West London? To talk like poxy fascists? We don't like that kind of stuff here." A bloke behind me said, "Too right!" Then about 30 others started singing and pointing at the mouthy guy, to the tune of the *Dad's Army* TV show;

"*Who do you think you are kidding Mr Hitler,*
*If you think we're on the run,*
*We are the boys who will stop your little game,*
*We are the boys who'll keep Chelsea down again*"

I was scared witless, but the Chelsea crew all blushed and moved off. Odd, but I felt a little sorry for these boneheads, or perhaps it was contempt. They were locked into their identity, they were prisoners of their colour (white not blue). I thought of the Montague and Capulate feud in *Romeo and Juliet*, and the stupid war depicted in Jonathan Swift's fictional world of *Lilliput,* premised on which end an egg should be broken. *What's in a name?* What's in a colour? Racists strap themselves to something. It doesn't allow them to build an identity of their own, organise their uniqueness. Jake felt much the same way about ideas of black separatism. He saw it as taking on the categories of the racists. For Jake it was saying they were right. He said it was a *"backdoor way of giving in; accepting the status given to 'house' blacks by the plantation owners".*

I had given up trying to decide if I was American, Vietnamese, British, or Chinese. Yellow, black, white or 'a person of colour'. I'm me. I build what I am with that which is around me. I will not be defined by yobs, college professors, the past, silly ideas about race or colour. I make my own affinities with who I want. Sod what other people think. I am unique and I will not have the 'we' or 'us' I identify with sorted out for me by other people who have their own agenda, based on their **personal** interests, be they black, white or yellow. The Chelsea boys might like to think they are Anglo-Saxons or something, but their genes are full of Semites, Mongols and Negroes. That's why they have ever so slightly different skin tones, different shades and curl of hair, why they have varying eye shape and colour.

Race! The whole idea is a nonsense, born in the warped mind of some rabid Victorian eugenicist. You could say I'm something of a hypocrite, given my affinity to West Ham, but this is a symbol *I* chose. Grandad told me that a French philosopher, Emile Durkheim, reckoned that we take up things that distinguish us from others. We want to be seen as different, *apart,* but also *part of.* At the same time we want to be in control of ourselves. Although according to Emile, when together we can get out of control. Grandad showed me a passage. I wrote it down. *"When they are come together a sort of electricity is formed by their collecting which quickly transports them to an extraordinary degree of exaltation."* I think this is more so when you have decided to be in the collection. Nothing makes me go to Upton Park, unless there is a little, Cockney claret and blue gene knocking around the double helix ... Nah! Being ascribed or conscripted to a type, or category is not choice, and it is a way of *controlling.* I'm not going to be conscripted to anything. I chose West Ham and West Ham accept me. I am Iron: of the Hammers. North Bank faithful. One of many. Last of the few. Perennial. Lasting.

Given this attitude, you would think that I'd be a bit isolated. But I never feel alone. I think football grounds are full of people who would be lonely without football. Not sad cases, but everyday people. That's why I think you get so many younger people going. On the North Bank you can scream, shout and rant, and most people around you will agree, more or less, with what you're saying. Where else could thousands of people sing silly songs together, no matter what type of voice you've got? Swaying, jumping up and down. What Grandad calls '*solidarity*'.

A football crowd is a kind of protest against all the petty conventions of society. Men, strangers, can kiss and cuddle when a goal is scored. A few weeks before Christmas I nearly got my ribs crushed by a guy when Cross scored his second and the winning goal against Bristol Rovers. He just picked me up and held me and I held on to him, someone else had their arms around us both and we were all leaping around inside a great big ball of humanity which was so pleased to be West Ham. He put me down, we smiled and nodded at each other, clenching fists high above our heads, and that was it: **U-NITE-ED, U-NITE-ED!** You're holding on to another human being, but it isn't, like, *personal*. What you're holding on to is West Ham, in flesh and blood.

Hard work against the Swans. Brooking was back. It was late on, though, when Paul Allen got our first. A minute later David Cross got the second. No reply from the Welsh. Second time this season that we've beat Toshack's lads. I should think so, the times him and that overrated little squirt Keegan have done us up in the past.

The night before the Villa game I went round to Jake's place. His aunt had gone to church or bingo or something. Anyway, she was out. We'd snogged a bit, but we'd never really been on our own before, not like in a house or anything. We weren't planning to get up to anything, but neither of us had much to do and all the dough we had would be taken up with the next game. We watched the tele for a while, then he suggested that we played 'Pick a Team'. This involves picking a manager, 11 players, and a sub, for the 'Eternal Life Cup'. You both also pick a ref each (one for each half) and two linesmen. Each player is given a group, job or whatever to draw players from. For example, women jazz singers, dictators or National Hunt Jockeys. This evening I got characters from James Bond movies, I stick him with stars from Carry On films. This is what it looked like:

## Carry On XI

*Manager:* Phil Silvers — Authoritarian, wheeler dealer.
*Coach:* Arthur Mullard — Concentrated.

Playing 4-4-2
Terry Scott — of course, in goal.
Sid James — hard man at the back.
Barbara Windsor — link defence and midfield, can push up-front (oooo Mrs).
Peter Butterworth — last line.
Bernard Bresslaw — stopper centre-half.
Joan Sims — someone to put their foot on the ball.
Kenneth ("Stop messin' about") Williams (captain). — silky midfield genius
Kenneth Connor — nippy, just behind the attack.
Harry H.Corbett — pugnacious midfield destroyer.
Una Stubbs — Flair, balance.
Jim Dale — Athletic and good in the air.
*Sub:* Charles Hawtrey — quick-minded midfielder, can play forward.

*Ref:* Frankie Howerd — Puts up with no tittering.
*Line:* Fred Ipititimus — Unpredictable.

## Licence to Kill 007

*Manager:* 'M' — Likes to see fair play. Tactician, but relies a lot on the captain.
*Coach:* Vesper Lynd — Hot blooded, passionate, likes it on the ground.

Playing 4-3-3
Ernst Starvo Blofelt (captain 'The Cat') — Intimidating. All high knees and elbows. Leads from the back. Always got a plan.
Emillio Largo — Ruthless. Tackle from behind a speciality.
Red Grant — Physical. Throws caution out of the window (you've got to have seen the film).
Rosa Klebb — Sharp with both feet (ditto).
Oddjob — Hatful of tricks (ditto …again).

Holly Goodhead — Fantastic service up front, especially good with a big man as a target.

Pussy Galore — Stirs things up in the middle, but likes to be involved with penetrating attacks.

Plenty O'Toole — Likes to play deep. Moves in and out of the game, but a superb ball player. Flashes of genius in tight situations.

Drax — Completely uncompromising, looks to dominate the park (and the rest of the world).

Dr No — Cold, single-minded. Ruthless. Sort of Thatcher with a good left foot.

Gold Finger — Greedy player. Bit of a predator (you've got to etc., etc ...), but laser sharp.

*Sub:* Le Chiffre — Anything possible.

Ref: 'Q' (See 'M' above) — Inventive. Sees trouble before it has started.

Line — Miss Moneypenny — Sharp-eyed (now if you get this you really are a fan, and very sad).

## Match Report:

Williams wins the toss (as usual). Carry On, being at home, start the game with the Double-entendre end behind them. Immediately, Largo cuts into Stubbs. Mr Howerd blows up. He books Largo (for a panto season in Bridlington) and gives the free-kick. James sends in a powerful cross for Dale to head passed the flailing Blofelt. Vesper Lynd is on her feet (for a change) complaining to Miss Moneypenny, claiming offside. Moneypenny is impassive, but Mr Ippititimus on the other side of the park waves his flag hopefully.

Play becomes bogged down in a dour battle for midfield supremacy. Goodhead goes down following contact with James, but Mr Howerd blows in response to Oddjob mouthing it off. The big man throws his hat at the ref and is sent off the field. James chuckles, but Mr Howerd warns him too, saying, "Titter ye not."

Play restarts with a bounce up between Galore and Windsor. The ball flies out of play and into orbit after a titanic struggle. Mr Ippititimus gives the throw to 007, but as Drax puts the ball back into play, the linesman flags for a foul throw, to the cheers of the home crowd. Dale tries but is also penalised for the same offence. Goldfinger and Butterworth fare no better. Mr Howerd has a word with his official, then signals to Galore to take the throw. As she bends down to pick up the ball, Mr Ippititimus gives the thumbs up to the ref.

Half time: Carry On XI 1  Licence to Kill 007  0

Licence come out like a hurricane. Red Grant makes a buccaneering run down the right wing (in memory of the old Robert Shaw TV series) and sends in a powerful cross that Dr No heads against the bar. Scott can only stare at it cannon back into play where it is volleyed into the net by Gold Finger, who drops his shorts and moons the entendre faithful. 'Q' ignores the gesture to the annoyance of Arthur Mullard, who lumbers on to the pitch and nuts Gold Finger. A huge fracas ensues. By the end of the battle Williams is also prostrate next to Gold Finger. Mullard is ordered to remove himself from the touchline. As he leaves the field Drax leaps on his back, biting his left ear. Mullard hurls his assailant into an advertising hoarding. Butterworth takes advantage of the opportunity and places a boot squarely between Drax's splayed legs. The L to K forward screams as Mr Ippititimus tries to get between them. Butterworth, now in feeding frenzy, turns on the linesman. Yet another incident involving both sides takes place. It tops up with both subs being brought on as the injured are stretchered off. Butterworth is consigned to an early bath.

Play now becomes much more open and the game swings wildly from end to end. Le Chiffre pulls out a wonder save from Scott after jinking past James and Windsor, while at the other end Stubbs comes close with a lob only just headed out of the goal by Klebb.

In injury time 007 win a disputed corner from Miss Moneypenny's flag. Drax connects well with Galore's inswinger, but the shot is parried by Scott out to James, who starts on a sprint towards the Licence goal. The whole of the Carry On team push forward with the full-back, who, moving infield, makes a terrific pass to Hawtrey. The waif-like wonder boy holds the ball up, allowing the forwards to get into position. The referee looks hard at his watch, bringing whistle to lips. Charlie looks to lay the ball out to the wing just before O'Toole is on him, gaining possession. But before she can make the most of things, Corbett slides into her. Her gasps and moans can be heard all around the ground. Dale collects the ricochet right on the corner of the 007 penalty area. He looks up to see Bresslaw charging in on goal like an enraged wildebeest. Dale smacks in a chest-high pass, directly into the path of the galloping centre-half, who dives to connect his bald pate to leather. Blofelt touches the ball, but such is the power and pace, he hardly slows its course. 'Q' blows-up as does James, Scott and Connor. Phil Silvers tears over to Vesper Lynd and grasps her by the throat, screaming, "The mines. Again!" Mullard and Butterworth appear from nowhere. Arthur pole-axes 'M' who was endeavouring to dart down the tunnel, but before Butterworth, who is stark naked and dripping, can get involved he is eaten by a shark. Lynd downs Silvers with a concealed Luger. Everything is eventually brought under control by a platoon of spear-gun wielding divers parachuted in by the UN.

Final Score:  Carry On XI 2  Licence to Kill 007 1

After the game both Silvers and 'M' concede the match was hard-fought, but played within the spirit of the game. Silvers criticises the referees for over-use of the card, and 'M' agrees saying, "This is a man and woman's game. If the oven is too hot put the chips on the stove." Although Silvers has injury problems for the Cup match against the Heavy Metal Rock Stars on Tuesday, he feels his team can recover in time. He has lightning winger, Hattie Jacques, and Bob 'on me head' Monkhouse on the way back. Apart from this, Silvers can call on club scout William Hartnell to sort out any number of out-of-work comedians, literally at any time. 'M' states that he will have to speak to the managing director, Cubby Broccoli, about making another film before he can talk about replacements.

Back to reality (or is it?).
Biggest gate for a season and a half against Villa. Over 37,000. First Division club, see. Franky Lampard took over as skipper from the injured Bonzo. It was a very close game, nip and tuck, backward and forward. Again it went to the dying seconds. Brooking took a corner and as the ball curved into the area a hand, not 'keeper Jimmy Rimmer's, came up and pushed it away. Ray Stewart walked up to take the penalty. Ray Stewart, a firm, accurate spot sharp shooter. Focused.

No distractions. Everyone's eyes were out on stalks. Ray hardly ever misses; has he ever missed? Yes. No! He's scored six this season so far, but I can't remember if he's ever ... He can't miss this. Jimmy Rimmer sets himself, he just can't miss this, don't miss it Ray, do it for Scotland, do it for London, do it for West Ham, do it for me, but just do it! Yhhhhhhheeeeeerrrrrrrraaaaaa! He did it.

I didn't see another game between beating Villa and going up to Villa Park to meet Everton in the semi-final. I saved up every penny. Jake was taken up with Arsenal's exploits in the other semi-final. They had to deal with Liverpool, so he wasn't going to make it up to Birmingham. But we queued together. Most of the night at Highbury, all night at Upton Park. Surely we were not going to meet in the Final. I didn't want the Scousers to beat his team, but since we had met we had never been rivals. Oh well! If it had to be, then that was it.

I had a great journey up with loads of other Hammers fans. I met a crowd from Belfast, Protestant and Catholic, who knew everything anyone never wanted to know about West Ham. Apparently there's been an Ulster supporters' group for years. By now the chances of promotion were pretty remote, but you live in hope. We were not doing badly, eighth place, and one of the Irish lads had it all worked out how we could still go up, and had sorted out all the scorelines, but it involved Leicester losing 8-0 along the way, so I was not encouraged. 47,000 stuffed into Villa Park. Everton scored first, after 42 minutes, through a penalty by Kidd. Mr Steel had penalised Alan Devonshire for a straightforward tackle. There really was nothing wrong with it. For all that, Stuart Pearson pulled us level on 68 minutes. Kidd got himself sent off (good!), so we had the advantage. Yet again, in the final moments, Paul Allen scored ...no he didn't ...offside. Come on ref. Who was offside? Replay.

Now I had three days to find the money to get myself to Leeds. As with the Villa Park game, I had the chance to go with Dad and Grandad, but I couldn't take that. I didn't want to go with them, I wanted to go on my own. I worked my butt off for the next few days, begging work in the shops down Green Street and Queen's Road Market. But I just could not get it together. I'd got the ticket, but I didn't have the fare. I was doomed to hitch it. I dare not tell Mum and Dad. I had to set out the night before the match to be dead sure of getting there on time. What to do? Where to start from? I decided just to go. I'd phone home on route. They'd go crazy, but it was that or go with Dad, Grandad and Billy in the morning and I wasn't going to do that. So I figured that if I just walked down to the A13 I'd get something.

I'd had my thumb out for about an hour without any luck. I was quite anxious about the whole idea, and half of me didn't want anyone to stop. But this was something I just had to do. I had to get where I was going under my own steam, I couldn't say exactly why I didn't want to rely on my family to 'take' me. I get on with them all really well, but this was my business and my journey. It was now 11pm. Mum and Dad would be expecting me to be home. Just then a little white van stopped about ten yards from where I was standing. I went up to the passenger window and peered in. The driver was about 20. Big thick glasses and spotty, gawking out from under a big sticky, oil-slick of hair, that stuck thinly across his pin head and pinched, pallid face. "Wh, Wh, Where you off to d,d,d,darling?" he stuttered through insanely buck teeth. He was stooped over the wheel. He must have been six foot six, but he was painfully thin. "Leeds." I startled him. I must have shouted for some reason. "Ha,H,Hop in. I c,c,can ta, ta take you as far as W,W,Watford." Without another thought I clambered in. The van smelt of strong cheese. Thank goodness it's not summer, I thought.

As it was getting late, we moved quite fast. My driver kept looking at me out of the corner of his eyes, not moving his head. "Reg," he blurted. "What?" I didn't see what he was trying to tell me. "R,R,R, I,I,I mmmy nnnnames Reg." "Oh, right." "Y,Y,Yoooooooo?" He's yodelling, I thought. Then I sussed it. I saw a sign 'Bromley-by-Bow', "Eh, Bromley. My name is Bromley." This seemed to trouble him, but he soldiered on. "So its L,L,L,Leeds you s,s,say?" he strained, "Yes, Leeds." He jumped again. The van was rattling like no one's business. "Why L,L,L …" "The match. West Ham." He nodded exaggeratedly. "S,S,Sup, Sup,Sup...Fan?" he inquired. No, I thought, "Peanut seller." "Yeah." He nodded enthusiastically again, mouthing, "Oh, oh, oh." We spent an uneasy half-hour in a kind of silence with him humming short snatches of unrecognisable tunes from time to time, straining his magnified eyes to their leftward extremes, checking me out, nodding to himself, and me pressing hard against the passenger door, with my head out of the window, trying to get some relief from the pongy cheese smell that seemed to get stronger by the minute. Was this such a good idea? "R,R,R, Rugger mmmmmmman myself," he spluttered after an age. "Oh," I said out the window, "great." "MMMMM,More f,f,f,iszzzzzical." He nauseated me, so I couldn't help my reply. "Game for frustrated middle-class dorks with silly balls if you ask me."

His head ticked back and forth between me and the road. "You

Cho,Cho,Cho?" "Train?" I asked, "N,N,No. CHINESE!" "No. This is a rare complaint. It's called Foo-Man-Chu syndrome. You slowly turn mongoloid. They think it's a Communist Chinese plot to take over Plaistow. My Dad won't eat anything but chow mein and pulls a rickshaw up and down the Barking Road all day. That's what I've got to look forward to." He nodded slowly. Was he considering this? He returned to the excruciatingly annoying humming, but now added tuneless whistles through his great yellow gnashers. I sang *Chinese Laundry Blues* out of the window, just to keep him thinking.

After what seemed an eternity, he dropped me off at a service station on the M1. "Th,Th,This is wh, wh..," "Cheers" I shouted. He jumped and hit his head on the roof of the van as I dived out and slammed the door. The van didn't move for about 20 seconds. I thought he might have knocked himself out. Then he pulled slowly away. I seemed to stink of cheese.

I found a telephone, with every intention of calling Mum and Dad, but as I picked up the receiver I lost my bottle and put it down. Without thinking I called Billy's number. It rang for ages, then a tired sounding Bill answered. "Where are you?" he asked. "Can't say. Will you tell Mum and Dad that I'm on my way to the match Bill?" "Why don't you tell 'em yourself?" "They'll kill me," I winged. There was a pause. "All right girl. I'll sort it. But take care. If you get in trouble I'll personally throttle you." "Cheers Bill. You're a pal." "Yeah. Do you wanna meet after the match. I can take you home." I didn't even think about it. "No. I'll be all right." "Okay. See yer when I see yer then. Think we'll win?" "We'll stuff 'em," I asserted and put the phone down. I was starving, but didn't have anything to spare to spend on food, so I picked a pitch at the start of the slip road north and got the thumb in gear. I waited for only about ten minutes when a woman in a beat-up Volkswagen beetle pulled over. I jogged up to where she had stopped and looked in the passenger window that she was leaning towards and winding down. "Hi ya blue, where yer headed?" she said in an accent not unlike Ron's. "Leeds," I replied. "Well, I'm going that way," she smiled and I got in.

Dotty was making her way around Europe. She had bought the little beetle in Naples after flying in from Sydney six weeks previously. She was a dentist, but had taken a couple years out 'ta see the world before it ends'. She was making her way up to Scotland before moving on to Ireland. She laughed about my cheesy exploits. Dotty was a tall, dark haired, good looking woman, a fact whch couldn't be disguised by her wire-rimmed glasses, old tee-shirt and tatty jeans. She had fantastic teeth and a mouth the size of the Great Barrier Reef. She was really interested in my addiction to West Ham and how I needed to make my own way to the match. "Good for you girl," she told me, "The world's full of people doing it the right way, that's why the whole place is crook."

We had done about 40 miles when Dot told me she was making for a camp site for the night and that she could drop me off or I could bed down in her car for the night. It was about 1am, so I agreed to take up the kip option. When we got to the site we found that we were the only inhabitants. I helped her set up. My stomach was rumbling. "Christ, thunder!" exclaimed Dot. "You need some tucker girlie." At two-thirty in the morning we were tucking into bacon sandwiches, fried bread, sausages and great pint tankards of tea, with the little car radio blaring out a Dutch pop station. Dot danced as she ate, making final preparations for the night.

When we finally bedded down I was exhausted and slept soundly. We got up quite late. So by the time we grabbed a coffee and some toast in the site cafe and ambled our way up north, we got into Leeds just a few hours before the game. We spent some time strolling around the centre together and before dropping me right outside Elland Road, Dot bought us a late fish and chip lunch. We parted as I went into the ground. Dot kissed me on the cheek and said, "Look me up some time digger, but not this year, I won't be home." With that she pressed a card in to my hand, "That's me practice, just ask for Dot." And off she went. What a nice person.

I had put aside enough for a programme. I read it twice from cover to cover to take me up to the kick-off. Our centre-half, Alvin Martin, was out with throat trouble, this meant that John Lyall was obliged to ask Stewart and Bonds to play in the middle of defence, move Lampard to right-back and bring in Paul Brush to cover the left side of defence. Alvin was our answer to Everton's big Bob Latchford, the England international centre-forward, in for suspended Brian Kidd. This posed a problem. Neither Bonds or Stewart were masters of the skies.

There was no score after 90 minutes so it went into extra-time. I was getting my money's worth. Four minutes of extra-time gone and we were 1-0 up. Alan Devonshire scored after looking our most effective attacker for most of the match, raiding down the left. It looked as if we were going to hang on, but half-way through the second half of extra-time Latchford got free of Stewart and Bonds a put away a superb effort. Predictable! Not another replay. I had no idea where I would get the dosh from. But it was not to be. Trevor took a throw, he got the ball back and crossed to Cross, who headed it back towards the centre of the box. Up popped Frank Lampard to head it home, save me pain and send West Ham to the Final. I just love Frank. He had made my pilgrimage worthwhile. Somehow he knew about all the trouble I'd gone to in order to come and see him and he'd scored the winning goal for me. And as he danced round the corner flag, I shouted, "Thank you Franky." He looked up at the West Ham supporters and spotted me. We caught each other's eyes and he raised a hand and waved. Walking back into defence, the wave transformed into a raised thumb. That's Frank for you! That'll please Grandad. Revenge for 1933 at Molineux.

Getting back was easy. I cadged a lift from a guy who had gone up with his buddy and their two boys. Home for them was in Dagenham and they, in good spirits, were happy to drop me off on their way. I even got treated to supper at a service station. All the way we talked about the match and the Final to come. But first I had to face Mum and Dad.

My travelling companions dropped me off at the Green Gate and I slowly meandered towards home, not looking forward to the coming encounter. Dad was waiting. I went to say something but he put his finger to his lips. "All right Willy. Just go to bed. I'll tell your Mum you're home." He hugged me. "We'll talk about it sometime," he said. I didn't expect that. What did Billy boy say?

I now had just over six weeks to sort myself out for the Final. I got a loan from Dave, my greengrocer employer, for the ticket. This came to four weeks' pay, including ten per cent interest, so I had a fortnight's earnings for fares and spending money. But no more League matches. The *Mirror*, *Newham Recorder* and Dad's old programmes had to do. Jake was in the same boat. That being the case we had a few nights in ahead of us. So what's new?

Less than a week after beating Everton we played Birmingham at the Boleyn. Still having a slim chance of promotion the lads, and particularly Psycho, went for it. A win would have put us in second place. Just after the break, with the score at 1-1, Bonzo got involved in the light middleweight championship of the Second Division, with Colin Todd, the England international defender. Both got sent off. This meant a suspension that would rule Billy, our skipper, out of the Cup Final. Oh good! And we lost the match 2-1.

Lyall and Bonds went up to Lancaster Gate. Bert Millichip, the chairman of WBA, the team we had knocked out in round three, was in charge of the appeal. Chances? Pork pie in synagogue thought I. But it seemed that perhaps Bert may have liked our man's right hook. Bill's one match out of it was seen as punishment enough and we had Captain Nutter back. With Alvin returning too, and old big head Brian Clough's remark that Trevor Brooking "stung like a butterfly", everybody was up for it.

Arsenal made the Final. They had taken seven hours to beat Liverpool and had been taken to three replays by Coventry. Oh dear! How were me and Jake going to square this?

Being with Jake, I'd got to know Arsenal pretty well. The Gunners had taken four games to beat Liverpool and then managed to beat Coventry 1-0 in the third replay. This had to be in our favour. They were a well balanced side, but their shape in defence was quite inflexible. I thought we could wrong foot them. You had to play David Cross as the main striker. He would tie up O'Leary and Young. But a positive midfield, with Pearson just behind Cross, would give us a lot in reserve and draw the Arsenal defence out of their offside tactic. Unless they put a midfielder on Pearson, they would just leave him alone (which would be my bet). This, I thought, would break up their organisation. Jake stared at me when I put all this to him. He was definitely an Arsenal man.

Another 'Cockney Cup Final.' I hate that stuff. The rest of the world thinks we're all a cross between Arthur Daley, Alf Garnett and Dick Van Dyke in *Mary Poppins*. North and East London are different places. North and south of the river are even more different. Accents change. Things like the width of streets, height of buildings and transport all have an effect. West Ham used to be part of Essex, and it shows. The docks have given the place a feeling of transience, but this is placed alongside families like mine, that have been around, but, essentially, are fixtures. The Arsenal supporters come from a very different background. From all over the world people have come to North London to serve the city, taking up the old middle-class, housing that has been divided into flats. These people have mingled with the poor who were moved out of the Kings Cross area before and after the First World War.

There's a big Irish population, reflected in their side. Jennings, Rice, Nelson, O'Leary, Brady and Stapleton are just the latest in a long Gaelic tradition. In the same way, West Ham have their share of Essex boys and East Enders. Manager John Lyall, Paul Brush, Lampard, Paul Allen, Pike and Brooking for instance.

I must admit, I didn't feel terribly confident as the teams came out at Wembley. Arsenal were the European Cup-winners' Cup Finalists. They were holders of the FA Cup and this was their third straight Final. Both teams were at the end of a long season, Arsenal with the better part of 70 matches under their belt. This would be West Ham's 59th game. Arsenal had played the better opposition but had a bigger squad.

The midfield competition would be telling. They looked powerful, with Liam Brady at the hub. We looked competent, especially if Dev had a good day alongside Paul Allen, the youngest-ever player to start an FA Cup Final; just 17 years and 256 days old, but he would have to face Brady on the left. If Brooking needed to take on responsibilities in attack, as I thought he might, the Gunners, on paper, had the edge in the engine room. I think our defence was better though. Phil Parkes was worthy company for Jennings while Stewart, Lampard, Bonds and Martin were, if anything, slightly more daunting than Rice, Devine, O'Leary and Young, although their defensive record was better.

Things started off really slowly. Both teams seemed to be pacing themselves, but it couldn't last with these two teams. It was about ten minutes into the match when Devonshire started a long sprint out on the left. He out-paced Talbot and Pat Rice before reaching the by-line and making the cross. Pat Jennnings got a hand to it, but the ball ended up with Cross on the right of the box. Dave sent in a shot that ricocheted off of the Gunners' centre-half, Willie Young. Pearson got through. For an instant his effort looked wasted. The angle was very tight and the instinctive shot was not well directed, but Trevor, one of only three survivors from the 1975 Cup winning team (with Bonds and Lampard), down to waist height, darted in and headed (yes, he headed the ball!) past Jennings from close range, falling backwards in the process. Brilliant! Brooking had been 16-1 against to score the first goal. The underdogs from Division Two shock the favourites.

Arsenal began to grind forward. Brady created openings for Rix and

Stapleton but both headers were off target. It became more and more obvious that Allen was on Brady's case. He harried him where ever he went, taking away the time Liam wanted. It was getting to the Irish genius, who had crippled Manchester United in '79. This was a brave move on the part of our manager, showing a great deal of faith in his young player. We went in at half-time one up and full of optimism.

We defended Parkes' area for most of the second half, but Psycho and Alvin were not going to let much past. Both Devonshire and Brooking were getting forward only on the counter, drawing the Arsenal defence in the process (how did Lyall find out about my game plan?). Now, apart from the shirts, we looked like Arsenal. The Gunners were clueless, it must have been like playing their own reflection. Young was reduced to deliberately bringing Allen down from behind. There was just two minutes to go and the goal was at Paul's mercy, with only Jennings to beat. Willie should have been sent off, but Mr Courtney, who up to then was having a good game, only booked him. Not great behaviour for a Scottish international.

But Allen proved himself the better man, getting up off the ground to shake Young's hand. In the end, as I had thought, Arsenal could just not figure it out and were pulled all over the place. We had won the Cup for the second time in six years.

Their long run-in to the Final had taken its toll on the Arsenal players. Frank Stapleton and Alan Sunderland looked tired throughout the second half. They went on to be defeated by Valencia in the Cup-winners' Cup. It was 0-0 at full-time, but in extra-time they lost 5-4 on penalties. But this said, the FA Cup Final was a masterful tactical victory for John Lyall. It showed his intelligence and sophistication. However, it had all relied on the ability of David Cross to take on the combined defensive force of Rice, Divine, O'Leary and Young on his own for much of the time. Cross was a tower of strength and handled his role like the consummate professional he is …I listen to too many football commentators.

Well, just two days after our triumph we lost 2-0 at Roker Park. Still, if we had won it would have meant promotion for Chelsea. At least we kept them in the Second Division (as predicted). We ended six points short of a promotion slot in seventh place. Leicester won the League, Sunderland got just one point less than them and Birmingham finished in third place with 53 points, one point short of Sunderland. We'd beaten Leicester home and away in the League, honours were even with Sunderland. We'd managed a draw with Birmingham at their place and I've already been through the home leg involving 'Sugar Ray Bonzo'. Make sense of that?

What had I got to look forward to now? Oh yeah. Leaving school. I couldn't wait. No qualifications, no ambitions (beyond West Ham), a relationship with a losing Finalist. Perfect!

My first day at the Job Centre. "How about a lift attendant?"

"Sounds great, I've always seen myself going to the top. When do I start?"

"You have to go for the interview first. That's if you get short-listed. Now let's have a look at your exam results. Oh. I see."

Short listed? Exam results? Interviewed? For a lift attendant? The ups and downs and ins and outs of the real world! I suppose I could go to college and get a degree in lift attending, that would sod up the opposition. I never got short-listed. "Due to the quality of applications …" It's hard to get into lifts apparently. Basement bargains please.

# Heroes and Villains

# Chapter Ten

*"STERN ALL!" Exclaimed the mate, as upon turning his head he saw the distended jaws of a large sperm whale close to the head of the boat, threatening it with instant destruction.*

Wharton the Whale Killer

*Suddenly a mighty mass emerged from the water and shot up perpendicularly into the air. It is the whale.*

Miriarm Coffin or the Whale Fisherman

I F YOU CAN'T get a job you have got to do something. The dole does some, but not me, I can't do it. I can't have some scummy little clerk down at the job-shop talk to me like I'm so much muck and stick me on some lousy training scheme, or get me working in a warehouse in Wapping for a pittance, including all but sleeping hours overtime. So, I do what I can.

I started locally when I was still at school. I did it for a laugh. Anything really. We'd bash down front doors and nick silly things, boots, kettles, I even took a sofa once. But you can't live on that. I walked round East Ham and Upton Park with half a hundredweight of cheese after doing a school kitchen. I ended up flogging it for a quid to a Greek cafe on the Barking Road. Not viable. I had a few near misses with the cops. A couple of my mates got nabbed. It wasn't worth it. But I had learnt my trade and those who had avoided the Old Bill were the best. Sort of survival of the fittest. You are, of course, attracted to your peers and you share expertise and knowledge. You begin to trawl in the most beneficial places. Like, not the East End. By the time I'd reached my 21st birthday, I was part of an elite team of thieves. We did everything. Houses, lorries, big firms. I don't do any physical stuff now. I am purely a dealer. I find customers for goods: paintings, antiques, coin collections. You name it. I do what I can to find what people want – the details of documents, rare books, whatever.

When there is no work, there is no economy, but trade will happen. That's human. Trade is basic. You will seek out commodities and place them on the market, where there is a demand. It's what the Tories and Maggie are about. That's all I am, a trader. I am what I am because I merely respond to a demand. You may say that I am dishonest, but I am made so by those who would get what they want through dishonesty. I'm just doing their dirty work, and you'd be surprised at the identity of some of my customers. By no means all villains. Villains mostly do their own villainy. Bishops, MPs, actors, sports people, anybody. I do a lot for Yanks and Arabs. Of course, for the most part, you're not meant to know who the customer is. Most of them find themselves an 'agent'. They don't have to soil their hands with the likes of me. In the same way, the bent art dealer, the less-than-honest antique shop owner, the mendacious stamp dealer or whoever, avoids contact with the obviously miscreant. I am the man in the middle for the middle man. But, for something specialised, you get to know the market; the most likely candidates. To cut down on the risk of detection you are often used to not only get things, but also deal with the delivery too. Not directly to the door you understand, but certainly to the country of the new owner, sometimes the state or the district. No questions asked or answers given. Add this to the hints which the go-between drops, purposefully, in boast, or otherwise, and you have a very good idea of where 'the merchandise' will end up.

I am like a managing director of a company. I have a small number of employees who work for me full-time and they contract out work to casuals, specialists from time to time, part-timers and temporary people. As Ronnie Reagan, the new American President might put it, it's trickle-down wealth, but it could also be called redistribution of resources. I mean, who loses? The rich. Who gains? The not so rich. The rich steal from the rich and the labourers, mechanics, technicians and the likes of me, the managers, get paid for the transit activity; the taking and dealing with the risks. The cops and the prison screws also get a job out of it of course. It's a whole industry. Don't think that Thatcher, the Home Secretary and the Commissioner don't understand this. Crime, I mean theft of one type or another, is one of this country's biggest employers and brings a load of foreign exchange into the economy. Penalties are high. A tea-leaf of the highest order will be most profoundly punished. Much more than a violent offender. But this acts to raise talent and skill. It is more an incentive than disincentive. After all, most industry works like that now; perform or you get punished with lower wages, demotion or the sack. In the world of crime, prison has much the same effect.

I should get the Queen's Award for Industry the amount of exporting I do. Monetarism is founded on the principles of crime or 'free market' forces. Shareholders get payments that are generated by the labour of others. That is, workers sell their labour on the 'free market', the price they get must be lower than the cost of what they produce so that shareholders can get their dividend, the bit that is taken from the workers. This is just what old Karl Marx was on about. The shareholders steal part of the product of the workers' labour. If the workers got everything they earned, then the shareholders wouldn't get a brass razzoo. How is what I do any different? You will say 'but the worker consents to this, whereas the victim of crime does not'. But what choice does the worker have? Most of them know nothing of shareholder dividends or the concept of 'surplus labour'.

Tort is a world industry. It is structural, it's cultural. The economy in places like Colombia are dependent on the drug trade for example. Without the employment that is based on servicing the traffic and wealth it generates, you would soon get an increase in poverty and civil war that would likely produce a left wing government or the doorstep of the United States. This is understood. Crime is intimately related to capitalism. After the Second World War the Americans freed Mafia boss 'Lucky Luciano' from jail and sent him back to Italy. The fascist 'National Socialist' regime had stamped out the Mob, but a crime syndicate was needed to start the economy rolling again following the Allied victory and destruction of Mussolini's state. One of the first things Thatcher did when she got into power was to make huge cuts in the Customs service, the most efficient block to criminal trade. In Northern Ireland, the illegal activities that surround and facilitate the violence, everything from protection to cornering the drug market (a fine source of income) are central to the economy of the province. Many legitimate jobs rely on this hidden economy. You will not get peace in Belfast until you come up with an alternative structure and/or culture that generates a comparable level of wealth. But who wants peace other than poor people? The state? Ulster is the perfect exercise ground for warfare against an army immersed within the population. If ever there is a revolution, the technology developed and lessons learnt in Northern Ireland will stand the army in good stead. And don't think the Americans haven't been watching. If ever Black Americans do what the Panthers got near to doing, the experience of Belfast will be called upon.

I am but a small cog within a huge international crime system which operates alongside and within the overt world economy. My operations are legitimate in a world that produces illegitimacy.

I know, like any boxer knows, and any business person worth their salt, that what I do has a life. If I fail to diversify, the market will be exposed, through competition. As more people are driven into the market, more chances have to be taken for less return. You take on more business, in response to lower profit margins, the result of competition, but this just means more risk. The inner circle of the organisation, which must remain tight, has, by necessity, to be widened. As it grows, *spiritual* make-up erodes. The emotional bonds become extended as organisations overlap. The 'grass' has a bigger, and so more vulnerable target group, as they occupy a more or less fixed space. The cops have more information and can establish patterns of operation more easily and swiftly. The Thatcherite climate, that energises crime, at the same time makes it prey to forms of monopoly capitalism. Those who cannot diversify, and by this I mean out of the crime sector altogether, will be overtaken by larger, more efficient organisations, and become the criminal equivalent of bankrupt ... nicked.

That's why I keep going back to Moby and Ahab. It is a kind of tale of everyone's life. If you choose to chase your obsession, the big one, whatever it is, it will destroy you as who you are, because, even if you find it, you'd kill it. Then you wouldn't have it any more, so you might as well be dead as well. I know a bloke who was a mountain climber. His whole life was about climbing. When he was at his peak (so to speak), as strong as he was going to be, he made it to the top of Everest. That was it for him. No point any more. Took to collecting china. I got a piece from a big house in Shropshire for him. He couldn't show it to anyone, it was pinched. He couldn't sell it. But he just had to have it. He got the whole range of whatever it was he was after. You know what he did? Smashed the lot. It was the collection or him you see.

This is it. This, or like young Willy and Jake. Sort of urban rebels who attack the system with their own apathy. But that takes them nowhere. You just end up old, poor and, as you would expect, apathetic. It's a kind of suicide or kamikaze activity. Futile, but I understand their satisfaction. The same is true of the joy-rider, the drug addict or hooligan. They're all reactions. Rejections. Have you ever looked at a smashed-up bus-stop or burned-out car? No. Really looked? These sights are kinds of art. You'd pay good money at the Haywood to see some of it. Such things are expressions of dissatisfaction, hate or even the sheer fun of reshaping, or reflecting the nature of the world. What else is art? What good does it do? What does it change? Ask the same of a Hockney, a Turner, a Constable or perhaps more obviously a Pollock. I've looked at all this stuff. I see nothing different from what I see walking down the streets where I grew up. The violence and passionate rejection or portrayal of the way the world is through the eyes of the 'artist'.

Apathy is different to boredom. Apathy is assertive; it involves doing something. If only annoying other people. The alternative is escape. That's what most people do. They get ripped off day after day and gain solace from religion, booze or the tele. This is why I think I still follow the Hammers. Perhaps this is why everyone puts up with the trash at Upton Park. You have no real control you see. They are never going to do what you want them to do. They will always mess up or at most, do so much and no more. But you keep wanting them to, hoping that they will come good. Take this season. We make a record signing, Paul Goddard from Queen's Park Rangers. David Cross finished the season with 22 goals, including four against Grimsby. We knocked in 79 altogether, Cross and Goddard scored 56 of them. Cross, way different from the West Ham ideal. A hard man, not prone to compromise. Goddard, an intelligent player, former Boys Brigade sergeant, schooled by Tommy Docherty at Loftus Road in a similar style to that traditionally employed at West Ham. Phil Parkes, one of the best 'keepers in the country,

Ray Stewart, Scottish international. Alvin Martin, Billy Bonds, Frank Lampard and Trevor Brooking. Full of promise?

The season got off to a start that would be sort of symbolic for the whole campaign. Back at Wembley for the Charity Shield, we lost to Liverpool. Terry McDermott scored the only goal of the game after 18 minutes. The FA Cup is shown off before the first League game, which we lost 2-1 to Luton. But come the end of October we had not tasted League defeat for a dozen games. We beat Barnsley 2-1 to make the fifth round of the League Cup. On 1 November we topped the table after beating Bristol Rovers.

In December we entertained Ossie Ardiles, Ricardo Villa, Glenn Hoddle, Steve Archibald and uncle Keith Burkinshaw and all — Spurs in the League Cup. It had been four seasons since last they had visited our humble East End abode. Oh how we had missed them! And now they turn up with the scalps of Orient, Palace and Arsenal under their belts. Veritable butchers of London were they. I had some business over in North London, so I was unable to make the game, but I caught it on closed circuit at the pictures. It was a 'right cracker' as we say amidst the rookeries of ye olde Cockney land. I've never heard a cinema so noisy. It wasn't sorted out until nine minutes from time when Cross sent in a lofty, long-range shot. Barry Daines, the Spurs 'keeper, was out of position and in she went, sweet as the proverbial cashew.

Coming up to Christmas, we opened up a five-point gap over Chelsea in second. We'd clocked up a club record of 11 straight wins at home with a 3-1 victory over Derby. Boxing Day we got beat at QPR, 3-0. Silkman, the fantastic Tony Currie and Stainrod did the damage. We were dreadful. The worst game of the season.

Early in the new year we got bounced out of the FA Cup by Wrexham. At Upton Park, Ray Stewart had put us ahead with a penalty on the hour, but just before the whistle Gareth Davies (a Welshman) had pulled the Robins level, which meant a replay at the Racecourse Ground. There were no goals after extra-time. Lyall lost the toss with Arfon Griffiths (another Welshman) for the venue. After two postponements because of the terrible weather, Wrexham took the second replay with an extra-time goal by the ancient Dixie McNeil (the Arch Druid of Liverpool). What a way for the holders to go out. At an Eisteddfod.

However, February was better. We won our five League games, including a lovely 4-0 tonking of Chelsea. Blue is the colour ...very blue. We went into March as League leaders, eight points clear of Notts County. The Youth side also got into the semi-finals of the FA Youth Cup. We really dominated the League for the rest of the season. Overall, we lost only four games in the League, establishing a club record for points gained, 66, (it had previously been 57) and ended up champions ...by 13 points ...from Notts County. Yes, the Second Division.

We reached the League Cup Final ...twice. We lost the replay by the odd goal of three. Both the semi-final and Finals were typical West Ham performances. In the last four we were paired with Coventry. West Ham were 2-0 up at Highfield Road, via Bonds and an own-goal by Garry Thompson. But they must have had something in their half-time tea. Thompson decided to go the right way and scored two, and Gerry Daly made it 3-2 to the Sky Blues.

The second leg was Psycho's 600th game for the Irons. On the hour Goddard made the aggregate score level. It looked like yet another dose of extra-time when in the final minute Jimmy Neighbour, brought in from Norwich to cover Pat Holland, who was injured, sent us to Wembley for the third time in less than a year.

It was Liverpool in the Final. Clemence, Dalglish, Souness, Hansen, Ray Kennedy, McDermott etc., etc. It was like Snow White and the Seven Jocks. Without doubt the best team in Britain. They did away with Manchester City in their semi. We decided to copy them, as we had done against Arsenal in the FA Cup Final (it worked once, why not again?). We held on to the ball, playing a passing game, and talked in Glaswegian accents. Alan Kennedy scored first, moving in on a poor clearance, with three minutes of extra-time left. I was amazed that this was given. When he hit the ball, Sammy Lee was offside, crouching down in front of Parkes. The linesman was waving like a windmill, but your pal and mine, referee Clive Thomas (a Welshman), unbelievably pointed to the centre. With just seconds left the Scousers were having a knees up. Then Alvin Martin rose high for a header which was gliding towards the top corner of the net. Clemence was beaten. McDermott stretched out a hand to push the ball on to the crossbar. The penalty was the last kick of the game. Stewart (our very own sweaty) scored with his trusty right peg. He sent the England 'keeper the wrong way with a side-foot effort. Unusual for him. He generally smashed them in with tartan steam coming out of his ears.

Honorary Scouser Clive, always the star, made the headlines the next day, claiming that John Lyall had called him a cheat. Unlikely. Lyall wouldn't call Rasputin a cheat. For me, Clive was not a cheat, more of a complete and utter dilk. Johnny boy was cautioned for the first time in his life and faced a charge of bringing the game into disrepute. A fate worse than death for Saint John. Thomas acknowledged that Lee was in an offside position, although, in his opinion, not interfering with play. But as Bill Shankly put it, *If he's not interfering, what's he doing on the field?* Thomas also confessed that he was mistaken in not consulting the linesman. So why wasn't he charged with bringing the game into disrepute? See what I mean? There is no justice folks, just us. Anyway, sense prevailed and Lyall was cleared by the FA. But why did Thomas keep the replay? Had he not admitted his inadequacy? Had not Lyall's vindication indicted Thomas? At least he should have been forced to have his first name changed to John.

The reply took place at Villa Park, for some reason three weeks later (it could only happen to the Irons). Liverpool had been beaten by the Gunners the Saturday before the game and were on their way to a European Cup semi-final against Bayern Munich. They didn't seem to care much at first, and it looked plain sailing when Goddard put us ahead before ten minutes of the game had gone. A neat near-post header from Jimmy Neighbour's hawk-eyed cross. But then Lee began to play like a man possessed in midfield. It was his free-kick that resulted in the newcomer, Ian Rush (a Welshman) rattling the angle of Parkes' goal. This was followed by Kennedy heading on to the bar. Dalglish put the Pool level, picking up McDermott's clever pass. He tore past the disappearing Bonds and put a sizzling hooked volley past Parkes. Three minutes later Hansen headed Case's corner in at the far post off Billy Bonds. In the second half Brooking and Devonshire pushed forward, but, like Mike Yarwood, we didn't really make an impression.

But there was still the Cup-winners' Cup. We'd won that before, of course, so, as I have said before, why not again? Never push your luck. If you learn one lesson in life, learn that. We beat a Spanish Second Division club, Castillia, who are like Real Madrid Reserves. The second leg was played in an empty Boleyn ground following some high-jinx on the part of some West Ham supporters in the Bernabeu Stadium. This was UEFA's punishment. The Bernabeu is light years away from the Boleyn Ground. It holds 100,000 and I didn't even notice our lads making a fuss that night. There were around 40,000 people in the ground and they looked a bit lost in all the space. Perhaps all the room went the heads of one or two of the Upton Park faithful. They probably thought they were on the Costa Brava. I did see some trouble outside, though. I heard that one West Ham bloke had been knocked down and killed in a road accident.

So, at 7.30pm on Wednesday, 1 October 1980, everyone listened to the second leg on the radio and then went out and smashed up bus stops. Pike pulled one back before the 20-minute mark with a blinding 25-yard scorcher. We drew level over the two legs when Cross got his noggin to a free-kick taken by Trev. Close to half-time Cross obliged to provide Paul Goddard with his first goal of the tournament. The Spanish lads came out for the second half steaming and Miguel Bernal, their skipper, scored from 30 yards in the 56th minute. Extra-time. Cross got two more for his hat-trick. On the night 5-1 and 6-4 overall. A tale of two cities. So much for the supporters' crucial role. We should play to more deserted grounds.

When we next get punished UEFA will order us to play in front of a full stadium. Uncle Dan ignored the whole tie. I didn't figure out why ...sort of homage to 'Catatonica'.

Following the victory of the phantoms we knocked out the Romanians, Politechnica Timisoara. Sounds like a dessert in a cheap Italian restaurant, but this was their second European campaign and they had put Celtic out in the first round. The second leg of that tie, in Romania, had been a humdinger. Three players were sent off and five were booked. It was Culloden all over again, but without the English ...and with Romanians. What would our fans do (apart from the conga)?

Timisoara had players in the international side that had beaten England 2-1 in the World Cup in Bucharest, shortly before our first leg tie. On top of this they had contributed to the Under-21 team that beat their English counterparts 4-0 the day before the senior side bit the dust. Billy Bonds converted a Stewart free-kick in the 24th minute and before the half-hour Goddard and a penalty from Stewart had made it 3-0. David Cross completed the rout with a goal seven minutes from time. Shows you how really crappy the England set up was. Who was in charge of the England team? The Right Reverend Ronnie G!

I travelled to Romania with the team on the charter plane as no other means had been made available. It was a different world. A strange, agricultural atmosphere. Peasants working in the fields, but the fans singing *Yellow Submarine* with rejigged lyrics in praise of their team *Poli*, that sounded like:

*Poli-shoooor, Poli pooooore,*
*Poli, Poli,*
*Poli ploore,*
*Poli-paaaa, Poli pen,*
*Poli, Poli,*
*Poli ren*

This provoked a section of our supporters to recall yet another variation of the ditty in reminiscence of our beloved brothers at arms, the Arsenal:

*We all piss in a red and white pot,*
*A red and white pot,*
*A red and white pot,*
*And Charlie George, has got no balls,*
*This doesn't worry, Bertie Mee at all,*
*And the band begins to play …*
*I'm forever blowing bubbles etc., etc.,*

This must have crushed Poli. They won the match 1-0 but went Poli-well out of the Cup.

Top of the League and through to the quarter-finals of the European Cup-winners' Cup. Then we lose. Who to? Yes, of course. The mighty Luton.

Dynamo Tbilisi next. No slouches this crew. Last season they beat Liverpool 4-2 in the European Cup as champions of all the Russias. But what an impressive team. At Upton Park it was clear from the first quarter of an hour that they were masterful technicians. Very cool on the ball, they kept it simple off the ball. We found it almost impossible to keep up with their movement across the pitch. Magic names too, like mythological warlocks: Aleksander Chivadze, Ramaz Shengalia, David Kipiani. Just over half an hour gone and they were two up, Chivadze and Vladimir Gutsaev. Cross, whose name is more like a hot-bun than a warlock, got his sixth goal of the competition about five minutes off the hour, but Shengalia banged in two to make it 4-1 on the night. 35,000 East Enders applauded the Soviets off the pitch. They were great! They were the best team that I'd ever seen at Upton Park. It was an honour to watch them.

I went to Georgia for the second leg. Timisoara and back had taken 35 hours. A jaunt compared to Tbilisi, not far from the Iranian border, via snow-bound, minus 16 degrees Moscow, where we arrived for what turned out to be a ten-hour stay at 2.30 am British time. A total distance of 4,000 miles. But it was worth it to be in the fantastic 80,000, all-seater, Lenin Stadium. A completely different experience to the Bernabeu. West Ham played intelligently, holding on to the ball, looking for breaks as the Soviets came forward, but it was no match for what I had seen at the Boleyn. Pearson, who was brought on in the 65th minute, scored the only goal of the game in front of about 2,000 West Ham supporters and 78,000 others. It was a very tasty volley from a right-wing centre by Cross

As the archetypal West Ham fan, I decided to become a temporary supporter of Tbilisi and went to Dusseldorf with about a dozen other 'resting' Irons fans, to see them win the Cup against Carl Zeiss Jena, an East German fridge. We were well at home. With only 9,000 in the stadium it was like playing Castillia all over again, this time with *There's only one Sydney Puddefoot* (to the tune of the Sandpipers' old number *Guantanamera*) ...*There's only one Sydney Puddefoot, One Syd-ney Puuud-defoot, There's only one Sydney Puddefoot* at half-time and *Bubbles* at the end. We managed to teach about 40 ex-pat Tbilisi supporters something like the words: "*Eyes fur-heffas blo-isk bubills, pity bubills isk de aar,*" and offered free coaching in the *Hokey-Kokey.* "*U doo da Oky Cockney han uoo ter aron, han daz vot eats halls abot.*" They took it very seriously. I'm sure they saw it as some mad Cockney ritual to summon up the spirits of the ancestors or something. A potential gold medal team we thought. Cultural exchange and all that.

West Ham played 60 matches in 1980-81. In May the Youth team beat Spurs 2-1 on aggregate in the FA Youth Cup Final and Alvin Martin played his first game for England, at Wembley against Brazil. They had never seen anything quite like him. He scared them to death. They were all crossing themselves like mad, crying, "El Diablo." Liverpool won the European Cup against Castillia's big brother, Real Madrid. It took Liverpool only 90 minutes to do to them what it took them 210 minutes to do to us. So, it took the European Cup winners, the European Cup-winners' Cup winners and Wrexham (a Welsh team) to stop us in our tracks.

But, now playing in the First Division, we have gone nine games without a loss. This run has included the tonic of beating the Spurs. David Cross got all four goals. I bought an old FA Cup runners-up medal today. They're very rare. 1923 this one. Worth a few bob. Comes from a collection that used to be housed in a vault in the West Country. I suspect no one had seen it for years. I've found out that a son of the original owner is still alive and living in New Zealand. I sent it to him today in a plain brown packet. Got it delivered with a batch of innocuous legitimate stuff in Norwich. Funny old team West Ham. There's always hope.

# Relegation, Death and Football

# Chapter Eleven

*West Ham United's existence matters to thousands of men, women and children, many of whom have never seen a professional football match ...the seven-year-old girl who witnessed the electric tram in 1923 never forgot that it was something to be proud of and that it was connected with West Ham United ...West Ham was rooted in the various communities and subcultures that made up the East End ...The club has touched the lives of tens of thousands of people in ways that have nothing to do with what happens on the field. The Hammers have been part of something much larger than the club, the League, or even the game of football ...it has been a way of life*

From *West Ham United* by Charles Korr.

IFE FOOLS YOU. You go for years just ambling along, almost convinced that nothing will change and then the whole lot seems to cave in. At such points you look to stable things, aspects of your surroundings that have always been there. Pieces of furniture, shops, pubs, photo-albums ...football teams. Odd moments mark more profound incidents. What you were doing when Kennedy was shot — something mundane, ordinary, then, from out of nowhere, a history-changing event promotes the insignificant activity into a seminal moment in your personal catalogue of events.

Ronnie, Billy and I went to Highbury for our 1-0 win over the Gunners, an FA Cup third-round replay. 'Rosie' Rosenior scored. We were 7-1 against to beat them. Ronnie had £10 on that. He gave us a history lesson. The last time the Gunners were beaten in an FA Cup replay at Highbury was in 1957. West Brom that time. 'West' must be an unlucky direction for Arsenal; anyway, they went west in that game too. Rosenior's next goal put Swindon out and sent us into the fifth round. By this time Ron was dead, Billy had been arrested and placed on remand.

I was stunned by the loss of Ron. We had lost Mum just a little while before. I was a widow and an orphan. This had been hard, but everyone had time to prepare, as best you can, for the death of a mother. Heart attacks are well named. Sudden assaults on the heart, giving no time for entrenchment or reconciliation. They kill the loved one, and emotionally rape the survivor. One minute he is there, laughing and pontificating on the trivial history of his team, the next he is no more. All he was, all we had, seemed lost.

I took a term off work. I got lost. I went to see Bill but, selfishly I suppose, I couldn't connect with what was happening to him. I must have resented him. 'What a time to get yourself put away, when I needed you most.' I never said this, but I guess I must have felt it. Resentment is powerful at these times. I resented Ron as well. Stupid Aussie drongo! Why did he die? Why did he leave me? Senseless questions asked in dreams. As if he had died on purpose with some malice towards me. We are mad at such times.

I didn't mope, everything just slowed down. I couldn't read, not even a newspaper. I'd stare into the television, but I wouldn't take in a word. The only thing that could hold my attention was football. In accord with both Mum's and Ron's wishes we had their ashes spread on the pitch at Upton Park. We had done the same with Dad's remains, so I suppose I felt a bit closer to them all over there. I found myself, mostly in the North Bank, watching games with an intensity that I had never experienced before. Being in the crowd, surrounded with sound was comforting. Everyone concentrating on 'the event' of the match. It was also where I had stood with Dad so often as a girl. This was helpful. I recalled how he put his arm around me when they lost and how he would lift me up when they scored. At half-time, I lined up and got myself a Bovril, just like we used to. I folded my hands round the plastic cup and was a little girl again, with my Dad to protect me.

The Division One campaign was not going at all well. Right from the start of the season things had looked bad. We took a 4-0 strapping at the Dell. The first home game was against Charlton. Paul Williams got a goal in both halves. Kevin Keen pulled one back for us from the spot, but Stewart Robson made it 3-1 with an own-goal. Perhaps he was still playing for Arsenal. By the middle of October we were bottom of the table. We had lost 12 of our 20 League games, winning just three. We could do no wrong in the League Cup, though, winning five games over four ties, including a 5-0 drubbing of Derby at Upton Park and a memorable match against Liverpool, the reigning League champions, sixth in the table at the time. It was one of the few occasions that we had Brady and Devonshire fit to play together. Under the lights at Upton Park. The smell of the pitch, the ground filling up on a cold November night. Freedom. In my mind the green of the field is quite vivid, much deeper and brighter than I can recall noticing before. Mum didn't have long left now. It was to be her last game. We all went. The idea was to book seats in the West Stand, but no, she wanted to stand on the North Bank, where, since a girl, she had stood with my Dad. So we chose our spot and surrounded her, propped up on their favourite barrier. Danny lent on the support in front of her, with young David. Billy, Ron and Danny formed a triangle behind her. Willow and Dot stood to her left, Chengsei and I to her right. I held her right arm.

West Ham lost the toss and so had to play towards the North Bank in the first half. Our midfield passing was quick and accurate from the kick-off. We were all over them. With 20 minutes gone, Liam curled in a cross, Paul Ince caught it beautifully on the volley. 1-0.

West Ham still came forward in waves, as if they were playing for my Mum. The ball glided round like a comet dancing between the gravitational pulls of a claret and blue universe. Ince charged forward from the void and connected perfectly with Dev's corner, entering another paragraph to the poetics of headed goals. The Scousers got one back through an Aldridge penalty about ten minutes before half-time. Alvin was supposed to have held him, but the referee must have been blessed with superior vision because his eyes saw what 60,000 others had missed.

The Hammers came out in the second half like the Horsemen of the Apocalypse (plus seven). Just over ten minutes gone and Kelly delivered a searching cross. Staunton headed straight into his own net. 3-1 to the Irons.

We had them most definitely on the retreat. A quarter of an hour before time, the doyen of central defenders, Tony Gale, bent a succulent free-kick around the Liverpool wall making it 4-1. We had inflicted upon Liverpool the biggest defeat they had experienced at the hands of an English club for half a century. It was their worst Cup result since February 1939. The old lady was happy. At the end the team turned to the North Bank and applauded, hands clapping above their heads. Seventy years of loyalty, a life-time of fidelity, acknowledged.

So, by the time the League Cup fifth-round game against Aston Villa came around, I had lost a mother and, a few days prior to the match, a husband. I imagine that not many newly-widowed '50 somethings' find solace in football and this was not purposeful on my part. It was the first game I had attended alone. I just wandered over on automatic pilot so to speak. Although I still had Billy and did a lot with his boy David, him not having a mum, I felt closest to the ones I had lost by attending games. We had shared so much emotion at Upton Park. Joy, sorrow, anguish. Intense feelings shared without inhabitation. It was an escape but also an archaeology of feelings.

The League position was getting quite serious. With only four wins from 21 starts, we looked prime candidates for the Second Division. But, to me, it didn't matter. I understood. Massive injuries, disastrous luck. Just as well we were at home because we had to start the game without Ray Stewart and Alvin Martin. Goals from Ince and Dickens sent us through 2-1. To my surprise I was looking forward to something. A fourth-round FA Cup tie and a League Cup semi-final against the holders, (oh no!) Luton.

Well, you can always rely on Luton. 3-0 at Upton Park. Mick Harford, Roy Wegerle and Danny Wilson did the damage. On the way home I met Willow. She was coming out of a chip shop. She had been to the match and was on her way to work. I asked if I could walk her to the station and she said that she would appreciate the company. I hadn't noticed what a distinct Australian accent she had developed. She had been to the match and we chatted enthusiastically about the possibilities of the second leg. I ended up accompanying her on the Underground all the way to Leicester Square. She signed in to her project and introduced me to her co-ordinator, Carl. "Welcome sister," he said, in his deep Jamaican brogue. "You wanna watch this woman, she trouble." He pointed at Willow and laughed. "You late again Willy," he raised his voice in mock anger. " You been watching that football again? Cha! You got no betta way to waste your bread girl?" He laughed again and we got infected. "Get yourself out of here. Get yourself to work!" he chortled, pointing at the door. Willow asked me if I'd like to walk around with her for a bit. I spent the evening as a detached youth worker. I was taken with Willow's skill with the kids she worked with. She made good use of me too, drawing regular clients round her aunt. "You got an aunt Willy? I fort day jus turn'd the likes of you aat ready made dan at Dagnam." I got on well with them. I saw a lot that night. Kids who had never known a family's love, who had found nothing but brutality and abuse in parental and sexual relationships. These were the kids I missed as a teacher. Some of my inexplicable resentment of Ron turned to appreciation. The loss of Mum started to be interpreted as 50 years of love that I possessed.

As we made our way home at dawn, we were still talking. I was weary, but not really tired. Willow asked me if I would like to attend the away leg with her. I jumped at the chance. We decided that we would make our way to Kenilworth Road by train, as this would allow us to be part of everything. According to Willow, you get cut off from 'the pilgrimage' in the car.

Fish and chips before the game, discussions about our prospects with fellow travellers. Willow was right. It was a much broader experience. I understood now why she often avoided family parties to games. It's the nearest you can get to democracy. Inglis in his book *The Name of the Game,* saw football as a common culture of equality that cuts across all cultures. He saw it as offering a moment when 'the democratic dream condenses as fact'. I recalled what Yi Fu Tuan says about shared space, how support makes us more and as such one does not have to be diluted in the crowd: "When people work together for a common cause, one man does not deprive the other of space; rather he increases it for his colleague by giving him support." Being in a crowd, with a shared enthusiasm, is a kind of liberty; a place to be human. In college I read the work of the great humanist and educator John Dewey. I remember once coming across his question: "How do the fruits of liberty compare with the enjoyments that spring from a feeling of union, of solidarity of others." I thought about this in the context of being a West Ham supporter at that time. I considered that the fruits of liberty come from the feeling of union and solidarity.

Poor Allie Mc-Fright-Night, as Willow christened him, played, she assessed, 'like a washing machine'. 2-0. We came home despondent but hopeful for the FA Cup home draw against Norwich. West Ham fans learn to look forward. As the fans thinned out as we approached London, she began to talk about Billy, Mum, Dad, Ron, Jake and Dot. I never knew how great the loss of Jake was for her. It was a deep, hard blow. The last time Willow had seen Jake was before he went to the Falklands. He'd been killed on the way to Port Stanley. He had joined the marines mainly because he could not get a job in civilian life. He had no will to fight. Jake was a gentle young man, artistic and sentimental. He had hoped that the marines would give him some kind of late start to his life and provide him with the opportunity to see a bit of the world. As it was he got the South Atlantic and an early end. As she was not related to him she found out about his death weeks after he was killed. She picked out his name in the newspapers. Willow said that she had loved him more than she had understood at the time. She, like me, had felt lost and had sought out Dot in Australia. Having spent some time in Sydney working in Dot's practice, the couple came back to the East End, Dot joining the exodus of Down Under dentistry that seemed, like salmon, to have a genetic need to return to the city of their initial training.

We were knocked out of the FA Cup by Norwich in a sixth-round replay. Now all that remained was the struggle against relegation. Five days later the Canaries beat us again 2-0 at Upton Park. This was followed by a 3-0 defeat at White Hart Lane.

With only ten games to go West Ham were stuck fast to the bottom of Division One. Seven points off Newcastle. The very minimal bright point was that we had three games in hand. Frank McAvennie was brought back from Celtic. Where there's life …

The 'run-in' started with a home draw against Derby. Then, at the Boleyn, with ten minutes to go against fellow strugglers Middlesbrough, we're one up, a terrific goal by Keen. Bernie Slaven scored twice in half a dozen minutes against our makeshift defence of Hilton and Potts. Martin, Gale and Strodder were all unable to make the game through injury. 2-1.

For all this, I was surprised that I was enjoying the season. The football was good and the crowd were always behind the Hammers. The situation was worsened by a 2-1 home defeat against Southampton who were also threatened with the drop. This was the beginning of the end for us. But things got put into perspective a few hours later. 15 April. It had been a hot, sunny, beautiful spring day. In Sheffield it was the FA Cup semi-final. Liverpool were playing Nottingham Forest. Ninety-four people, including several kiddies, had been killed at Hillsborough. About 150 people were seriously injured. It transpired that a senior police officer had ordered a gate to be opened, allowing fans to surge into the Wednesday ground. Thousands of people were crushed on the overcrowded terrace. Liverpool fans, frustrated by the time it was taking to get into the ground at the Leppings Lane entrance, pushed towards the turnstiles a few minutes before the kick-off. To alleviate the problem the police opened the metal gate and the fans poured in through the narrow, dark 100-foot-long tunnel in the centre of the stand. The fans immediately in front were crushed, although there was room to the sides of the tunnel. People, unaware of those dying at the front of the terraces, pushed forward for a better view of the game. This caused more problems for those at the bottom of the terraces, pushed up against the fences which prevented people from getting out, although a few climbed over or got through a small gate on to the pitch. The dead and injured, who were at the Liverpool end of the ground, were buried under falling people. A number of children died after being pinned against the security fence. They were there for the view. The crowd tore down advertising hoardings and perimeter boards to use as stretchers.

Looking at the TV pictures it seemed that the police didn't fully grasp what was going on for a while. The game was playing for six minutes while people were being killed. It took ten minutes for the first ambulances to arrive.

At our next home game, against Millwall, the 16,000 crowd donated nearly £6,000 to the Disaster Appeal. Fans had been taking flowers up to Hillsborough all week. A memorial service was scheduled for 29 April. On Sunday, 23 April I took Dad's old scarf and Ron's one that he had bought for the start of the new season, and went up to Sheffield in the car. I bought some flowers near the ground and wrapped them in a claret and blue nest after asking the flower seller to soak the scarves. I laid the tribute between a red and white Arsenal teddy bear and a sheaf of irises marked 'Tears from Chelsea'. I wandered around for a while. Football, just a game? Go to Hillsborough, see how much more than a game it is. They were all there. A giant reef, half green and white, half royal blue, read, 'Celtic and Rangers. A City Unites in Sympathy.' The great Lion of Millwall alongside the subdued red and solemn scimitar of Charlton. Real Madrid, Barcelona, Juventus and Benfica, the Eagles of Lisbon hung their heads, the Stadium of Light was darkened. Rotherham, Barnsley and Orient. River Plate, Estudiantes De La Plata, Racing Club Buenos Aries, Moscow Dynamo, Brentford and Luton. Hillsborough was a holy shrine of care, sympathy and respect.

This had happened partly because of stupidity and greed. Packing supporters into out-of-date, filthy stadiums. But this kind of thing has happened before. The Ibrox disaster of 2 April 1902 was the first big carnage. Six minutes after the start of the Scotland-England game a wooden stand fell apart. Hundreds of people fell through a 25-metre hole. Twenty-five were killed and 300 injured. The match was restarted. It ended in a draw. At Burnden Park on 9 March 1946, at the start of the Bolton-Stoke FA Cup sixth-round, second leg match (that season ties were being played home and away), a very similar tragedy to the events at Hillsborough had occurred. The Wanderers were 2-0 up from the first leg and a massive crowd had turned up to see Stan Matthews and others. Two crash barriers collapsed. Spectators piled on top of each other. The match kicked-off as bodies were being carried off. The referee called the players off the pitch as soon as he understood what was happening, but the police wanted the game to resume to avoid panic. So play was continued without an interval or a score. 33 people died. More than 500 were injured. Bolton went on to be defeated in the semi-final by Charlton (2-0). The controllers of football and the newspapers of the day quickly forgot this 'incident'. Nothing was done about stadiums, as it was left to the boards of individual clubs to make 'arrangements'.

Sixty-six people died during the 1971 New Year Glasgow derby game between Rangers and Celtic. On 11 May 1985, the final day of the League season, Bradford had won the Third Division championship. They were playing Lincoln. It was half-time. A ball of fire spread quickly across the 76-year-old wooden main stand. Fifty-six people perished. Two hundred suffered burns. Unburned rubbish found afterwards included a copy of the *Bradford Evening Telegraph and Argus*. It was dated 4 November 1968. The wrapper for a packet of peanuts was also found. Its cost had been six old pennies. Fires had destroyed or damaged stands not long before the Bradford inferno, notably at Nottingham Forest, Bristol Rovers, Brighton, Brentford and Norwich, and although there had been no loss of life, the warning signs were there. Thirty-nine died and four-hundred were injured at the European Cup Final game in Brussels between Liverpool and Juventus. It was 29 May 1985. The Liverpool fans were made the scapegoats for a while, a group of people that had no domestic or European record of violence. Later poor segregation, inadequate searches, a lack of concern for the way tickets were sold, weak walls and barriers and insufficient communication and co-operation between clubs, stadium officials and police were all identified as factors leading to the panic that caused the majority of the deaths. As so often seems to be the case, the owners of football were determined not to lose out financially. The game was started 85 minutes late. Juventus won 1-0.

At least the level of consciousness shown at Hillsborough demonstrated that this time things would not easily be swept under the carpet. Fans could no longer be the cannon fodder for those who seek to drain the life blood out of football; crush its bones and kill its heart. Again, the action of the support-ers will be what makes the impact. We cannot rely on the government and certainly not the boards and football authorities. Ibrox, Burnden, Valley Parade, Heysel and now Hillsborough. All are testament to the exploitation of supporters. Now it has to end.

A lot of people were quite dispirited by our performance over the season, but of the 20 matches we lost, eight had been by the odd goal. This, added to the fact that we had been involved in eight draws, shows that we were unlucky. If just half of the draws had have been wins and half of the odd-goal losses had been draws, things would have been different. This sounds silly, but if injuries had not been so crippling, it might have been possible. 'If', 'if', 'might'. The patois of West Ham.

In the final home game of the season we beat Luton. Dickens got the only goal of the game. I went with Willow. We didn't finish bottom, we finished second from bottom, humbling Newcastle. Middlesbrough also plummeted, so it was a bad season for the North-East.

I'm sad and not a little frightened now that the last whistle has blown. I'm going to have to face life in the summer without the support of football. But I'm stronger now. I have a lot to be thankful for. I've started voluntary work with Willow's project. It's hard, I do Wednesday evenings and all night Saturday, but I love it. I've done a bit of training. 'Informal education'. Now that's tough for a teacher.

There's a lot of lonely, unhappy kids in the world, but at least most of them know it. We have to stop treating them as if they are sick or, in some way, lacking. This is what Willow calls 'the deficit model', it is the contemporary version of the old colonial mentality; the 'native' needs 'empowering' by us. This assumes that those we work with have no power, or what power they have is 'less' than our power. At the same time it implies, like the work of the well meaning European missionary in the days of Empire, that those we work with can only get power (civilisation, religion) from us. I have learnt that these young people have tremendous potential; they survive. Every day they are faced with things that I could never cope with. Willow, Carl, me and others seek to create an 'empowering environment', wherein individuals and groups might 'empower themselves'. You see, the nature of power dictates that it cannot be given, it can only be taken. The proposition 'to give power' is an oxymoron, it is a contradiction in terms. Young people, by their own devices, can take power. This is how they undertake powerful acts. By power I mean 'responsibility'. If they take responsibility it is likely that they will begin to learn about dealing with the consequences of their actions. This is a person of power. A person who has their responsibilities dealt with by others, who is protected or diverted from managing the consequences of their actions is disempowered. Unfortunately this is what many teachers, youth workers and social workers end up doing to those they work with.

Young people can do something about their situation and they do. In the main people are strong and good. They find a path. Sometimes it means having to work through a desert of drugs or a sea of booze, but most of them get there. Don't assume weakness just because someone has had a rough patch or made a mistake. We all need something to lean on at times. Even if it's just an old barrier on the North Bank.

I'm an art teacher. Teaching art for all the years that I have, you tend to think about things in artistic terms. As Inglis has it, "Sport is the art of the people ... To call a shot powerful or a pass delicate or a save marvellous is both to describe and to judge it." This is appreciation and critique; the making of art. Art is made by its audience. The artist may produce a painting or a sculpture, but it is those who view it, who give it meaning, that make it art. Solid support of a club like West Ham means solidarity, fidelity, care and love. It is to *be with* others who have the same passion, based in a feeling of integrity and respect of who you, and others, are. It is not founded on hate, but the feelings of having things in common with others. All this includes supporters of the opposition; they, after all, are indispensable in the creation of identity. At the same time subtle differences are noted, the differences that make each of us unique. Football support does not promote uniformity. If you go to matches, listen to fans and look at players, you might notice that they celebrate their support by promoting both their collective obligation and personal expression. This is how the 'event' of the football match is acclaimed, as a kind of symbolism, in as much as it is the representation of something almost sacred and certainly not totally material, by means of the very concrete match and the players that contest it.

In art, symbolism takes ideas about things and tries to present these to the world. Objects, 'things', *symbolise* feelings, hopes, and fears. This can happen in a conscious or unconscious way. Dreams, for the symbolist, are one source of these ideas. Thus dreams and real life find a space to coalesce. Imagination becomes the most important source of creativity. In much the same way, the ideas/dreams the supporter has about the game and the team, are symbols attached to the 'things' happening on the pitch. In this manner the club becomes one of the symbols of the fan's inner world represented in reality.

The aim of the symbolist was to clothe the *idea* in sensual, seeable form. The symbolist poet Gustave Kahn explains:

> We are tired of the everyday, near-at-hand and the contemporaneous; ... The essential aim of our art is to objectify the subjective...

The 'objective' is reality. The 'subjective' is the idea. What Gustave was looking to do was to make life more meaningful by elaborating it with imagination and the hopes, and wishes, found in our inner worlds; our ideas, our fantasies, our dreams. He sought to externalise ideas; get them out into the world. Feelings, ideas and dreams became the place where symbolist art starts. Ideas dominate rather than the mundane 'real' world.

West Ham is a veritable mine of symbolism. The Hammer is a real object in the world. It is hard; it does things. It has a strong presence; it can be held, displayed and used. A bubble is ephemeral; it envelops no more than an empty space, yet in cartoons it often contains an idea. We send it away on its short life at the mercy of the elements. Its time in the world is short. Dreams are even less tangible and sometimes more transitory than bubbles, but they contain elements of our background and experience. They can direct our lives and are the basis of all action.

However, even the hammer, for all its solidity, is itself a symbol with a history. It started out as a plain representation of West Ham's origins, the Thames Ironworks, but that solid connection has been lost. It is now associated with dreams; a player in claret and blue rising high above the crowd to head home a cross, a golden-haired youth raising a silver cup to teeming thousands and bubbles, pretty bubbles in the air. The real making of dreams, dreams made real.

Most people at school think I'm mad. Going to matches alone, wandering round the streets of the city with 'prostitutes and drug addicts'. We *find* ourselves in such places. Life gains its meaning through the extraordinary in the everyday. The crowd singing, clapping, chanting. The whistle blows and the ball is kicked, 'Tump!' We roar, we roll. We, as one, are thunder. And swing, and hold, and ooh and arrr. We are here. We 'are'.

At some point, the floodlights will catch a glistening ball that falls out of the deep, deep East London sky. Our centre-half, who has arrived on his long journey, just for this moment, crouches, waiting the time when he will take off. In mid-air, at the arc of his climb, Alvin, Marc or Tommy, connect, and possibilities merge with hope, in a silent snatch of time. And everything we are, all that we know, is captured in expectation. The near, the ever-so near, fills the mind.

Our memories and dreams, wrought in the process of living are what make us human. They are what make the mundane special, the commonplace unique. Reduce life to its mere concrete process and it is no longer living. You have hard existence set before you. Call football '22 men running round chasing a ball', and you call poetry 'just words'. From this dull, material perspective painting is no more than 'marks on canvas', theatre is 'play-acting'. Fact, actualities, may define life, but it is the ephemeral world of our dreams, and our imaginings, woven together with our experience, that make life worth living. The fear of the future is turned into hope. Out of this emerges concepts like justice, freedom, loyalty and love. I miss Ron. Every moment of my life I miss him, but I'm glad I miss him. I hang on to that feeling, it shows he and I were, are alive. What we have has not died with him. My missing him, my love for him, keeps that alive. I miss the man he was, but he comes to me in my dreams. Not in sleep, but between the events of my day. That fantasy, or illusion, as some would call it, is oh so sweet. If I lose it my life will be poorer. Perhaps, like Willow, I will meet someone else, but I will not forget Ron. What we had will be no less. With every new experience all other experience matures, become more part of us, until everything becomes a single entity.

> Then he asked, "After you have finished your true stories sometime, why don't you make up a story and the people to go with it?
>
> Only then will you understand what happened and why.
>
> It is those we live with and love and should know who elude us"
>
> Now nearly all those I loved and did not understand when I was young are dead, but I still reach out to them.
>
> Of course, now I am too old to be much of a fisherman, and now of course I usually fish the big waters alone, although some friends think I shouldn't. Like many fly fishermen in western Montana where the summer days are almost Arctic in length, I often do not start fishing until the cool of the evening. Then in the Arctic half-light of the canyon, all existence fades to a being with my soul and memories and the sounds of the Big Blackfoot River and the four count rhythm and the hope that a fish will rise.
>
> Eventually, all things merge into one, and a river runs through it. The river was cut by the world's great flood and runs over rocks from the basement of time. On some of the rocks are words and some of the words are theirs.
>
> I am haunted by waters.
>
> From *A River Runs Through It* by Norman Maclean

# Iron Bars

# Chapter Twelve

*...every prison that men build*
*Is built of bricks of shame,*
*And bound with bars lest Christ should see*
*How men their brothers maim.*
Oscar Wilde *The Ballad of Reading Gaol*

*"The first 25 days of April 1990 saw the worst series of prison riots in*
*the history of the British penal system."* The Rt Hon Lord Justice Woolf
The Prison Disturbances April 1990 — Report of an Inquiry.

OPPRESSION, brutality, squalor, substandard conditions, i.e. food, minimum time out of cells, pathetic prison wages, lack of opportunities to use telephones, draconian visits, being sent to prisons far away from home where family and friends cannot visit. Only one half-hour visit every 28 days. You end up totally alienated from your family. My people were always kept waiting at least an hour to see me for 15 minutes. One or two officers would make offensive remarks about my Jenny and David. The first time that happened she had to watch me dragged off, screaming. End of visit and punishment to boot. If you try to complain you get, "Mess with us and we will mess with you."

This routine is typical of a day in the life of a male prisoner in one of Britain's local prisons:

7.30 Cell unlocked. Prisoners get hot water and slop out (empty plastic chamber-pot). Razors are handed out and applications to see the governor, probation officer, doctor etc., are made.

7.50 Prisoners collect breakfast from the hotplate and are locked in their cells to eat it.

8.30 Unlocked. Breakfast trays collected and slop out. Back to cells and details of work shouted out. Prisoners taken to exercise, where they walk around a small garden or yard for an hour.

9.45 Prisoners who are working go to their workshops or other place of work. Unemployed prisoners return to the wing and are locked in their cells.

11.45 Working prisoners return to their wings. Dinner served at the hotplate and eaten in cells. This is the main meal of the day. Cell doors remain locked for prison officers' lunch break.

2.00 Slop out and return to work. Unemployed prisoners remain in the cells.

4.00 Working prisoners return to the wings and collect their tea which is eaten in their cells. They are also given a small cake which they can save for supper. They then slop out — the last opportunity until the next morning — and are locked in their cells.

6.30 Some prisoners may be allowed out of their cells for a recreation period. Facilities are very restricted and this tends to be a privilege allowed only to those who have been there some time.

8.00 Recreation period ends. Supper (a cup of tea) is sent to everyone in their cells.

9.00 Lights out.

*From a leaflet produced by the Prison Reform Trust, 'Prison Facts and Figures'.*

The most terrible thing about prison is the boredom. You can be in a cell, with one or two other blokes for anything up to 23 hours a day if things are going badly in the nick. This makes time grind away. Cells are often dark, the one window is not much bigger than a generous letter-box and this can be shut off from the sun by a block opposite or the prison wall. This being the case, much of the day can be spent in the sick yellow light of one dying bulb. The stink of the bodies and slop bucket pressing hard against the solid steel door.

The prison was built for around 750 prisoners. It had a population of 1,600 in April. Three men to a cell of only eight by 12 feet. A remand prisoner has no work, so he has to stay in the stuffy cell with two other men, who he probably hates the sight of, for 24 hours a day. Many cells have only one chair, maybe no table, so you are forced to eat off the bed. Try sitting on a lower bunk and eating a meal, it makes you frustrated and angry. Meal time over, the prisoner has to lay on the bed. Just for a change he could maybe sit on the bed. If he walks up and down the floor he is told to sit down or be put down. He has a head full of worry and problems about the forthcoming court case. One of the other inmates has a radio on full-blast, driving him mad. He needs to use the toilet but the staff won't let him out and he dare not use the bucket because he'll get beaten by the others. Would you be depressed?

There are no toilets in the cells. If an inmate rang his cell bell over the dinner period, seven days a week, he would receive no response from staff for that period of time, 1 hour 45 minutes. At night, often nine o'clock, the same rule is in force. A prisoner only receives attention in these periods by smashing cell furniture against the cell door — a common practice — especially if the prisoner is suffering from diarrhoea. We were only allowed one shower a week, even after working all day. The exchange of clothing (once a week) only happens if clean items are available. Sometimes there is clean underwear, sometimes there is not. A prisoner's bedding is never changed if it is blankets. But we are allowed to change one sheet a week. The quality of the wash would shock anyone outside prison. Five minutes to slop out? It's not enough.

The toilets and washrooms are degrading, filthy and out of date. Time allocated to using them is very short. The water, hot and cold that you get in buckets and jugs, is used to wash your body, items of clothing and cleaning your cell. These same jugs and buckets then have to contain water for drinking and washing knives, forks and spoons.

*Like so many other institutions of its type, the prison is a Victorian hulk, divided into three main wings A, B, and D. These wings are the original buildings knocked up around 1830. A and B are galleried and linked at right angles to a centre from which they can be separated by gates on each landing. D wing is cut off. A and B wings are for adult prisoners. D wing is for young offenders on remand.*

I had got three years. Much better than I expected, but still the prospect is not a happy one. I know about bird, but this is not an open prison, this is the real thing. Hard bricks and mortar. Unforgiving and full of the most nasty types. If I let myself think about it too much, I swear I'd top myself. Most of my 20 months in prison I have always worked. There are less fortunate prisoners who are not working and are locked up 23 hours a day.

Being shouted at like a dog, constantly verbally degraded and belittled is part of the game. Nobody can understand just exactly what sinister goings on actually take place in prison. Officers bullying, telling lies at adjudications, disregarding rules. They seem to thrive on enforcing to the limit the often petty rules which constitute the prison rule book.

I dream that I'll never get out of here and that's when I wake up screaming. This is pretty common, so Ted, my current cell mate, doesn't often complain. He's a lot younger than me, but unlike me has done a fair amount of bird and knows how to do time. His nights are spent amidst earthquaking snores and deep, profound farts that belie his five-foot six, eight-stone frame. The meals that we have to eat are mainly stew seven days a week. It's like living with a minute but particularly noxious volcano. Still, just two of us and we get on.

*Recreation, Education and work time had been restricted in the prison for some time due to a lack of discipline, staff, the result of high levels absenteeism and sickness.*

If it wasn't for the books that Jenny brings in I would not survive. I've always been a reader, but now I spend most waking hours with my head down. This, and the Hammers of course. Ted is an Arsenal man. Rabid. He knows everything about them, right down to players' wives and girl-friends. Typical of a peter merchant; obsessive. I obtain any Arsenal type pictures, George Graham etc., and place them in the bottom of our slop bucket before use. The irony is hardly ever wasted on him. Although his waste is often piled on the irony.

*The most common complaints of prisoners were the quality of food, time banged up, inadequate wages, poor attitude of the staff and inadequate visiting arrangements.*

Being in here so soon after Mum and Ron dying, and being away from young David for so long, got to me. West Ham getting themselves relegated didn't help either. I resented every minute of the spring and summer slammed up in the cell. Prison ends up making you hard and mean. I'd seen a bit too much of this place. The routine deadens you. At first you do your time, try to make the best of it. But eventually, sooner or later, what you want is revenge. It can be focused on a screw, or an individual or a group of cons, but mostly it's aimed towards the people who put you here, that is 'them out there'. No one in particular, everyone in general. For the first time in my life, I lost all interest in football. I never even made any special effort to listen to the scores on Saturday and I steered clear of newspapers altogether. I got lost in literature. It was as if I had rejected the outside totally and moved inwards.

> *The prison is grossly overcrowded. At the time of the riot there were 458 inmates in a wing certified to have no more than 337. On 8 April there were 203 prisoners on A Wing. The cells did not have integral sanitation. The sanitary facilities that were provided were limited (e.g. there is one toilet for 13 cells in the segregation unit).*

By the end of March the last light went out for me. The early spring sunshine brought me down further. That's when I had my difference with Officer Taker. If you treat us like animals, we'll behave like animals. Officers treat inmates like outcast degenerates. The governors and officers are on a par with the Gestapo.

There comes a point when have got to get back at the screws who bully, cheat and generally abuse you.

He had taken a dislike to Ted, you see. Nothing serious, just wind ups from time to time. He was a Geordie, a keen follower of Newcastle United, sort of black and white shite. When the Hammers had got gated I was chuffed that our double over the Magpies had dragged them down with us. He was truly irked by Arsenal's success. He had a very concentrated contempt for 'Southerns' and Cockneys were the worst of all the pansies below the Tyne. This was fuelled by Ted often quoting Steven Berkoff in *McVicar*, alluding to the alleged devotion of native North-Easterners (a.k.a. Maggots) to the nether lumber regions.

*It started on 8 April 1990. A week after the riots at Strangeways and
the day after Glen Parva. Dartmoor was into its second day. Bristol
had been going for five hours. Cardiff started at the same time.*

It was morning and we were bringing back our breakfasts from the
hotplate. The standard of food is poor here as well as the quantity. Some
mornings we would be able to eat our portions of cornflakes out of an egg-
cup. Taker laid into Ted heavily, shouting that he had been attacked by him.
Then three other screws began to give the skinny little Gunner a good hiding.
At first I hesitated. I'd lose all my remission and perhaps get another portion
of time. I would only come off worse physically anyway. I was still thinking
this when I sank a boot deep into Taker's groin. He fell like a bag of manure.
The two others left Ted alone in a bleeding heap and leapt at me. I caught the
first one in with a straight, hard right. His nose busted open, splattering his
mate with blood, snot and bone. He slumped against the door-slam of the
cell, causing the second screw to tumble over him. I hurdled over the two just
in time to catch the full weight of Taker's truncheon on my right shoulder.

*The first fight started at 08.40 coming back from breakfast on
landing A2. The idea spread and things started to get thrown about
on A3 and A4. Keys were taken from one of the officers. The officers
retreated and A Wing was taken. There was an attempt made to re-
enter the wing, but the prisoners drove the officers back. Everything
in the wing that could be destroyed was destroyed. The control and
restraint teams came in at around midday.*

I yelled out in pain, but in reflex launched myself at him like a torpedo.
The flying head-butt caught him straight in the temple. The fat lump spun
round like a bloated Nijinsky and fell heavily to the deck. I heard a scream
behind me. The screw who had fallen over his mate was on his knees holding
his head which was foaming with blood. Ted stood leaning against the rail
behind him. He'd grabbed the fallen screw's truncheon and smacked his
partner on the bonce with it. Oh the irony. We looked at each other and he
smiled with broken teeth through a red veil of vomit, sputum and blood
…"Goona's!" he muttered before crumbling down the wall. Five screws were

flying up the stairs. I felt the pain in my shoulder and the blood drain from my head. The screws faced me. Very trepidacious. I passed out.

*The riot took place in A Wing. At the lower ground level of that wing, the landing is separated into two halves by lockable gates at the foot of each of two flights of steps. At the end nearest the centre is a segregation unit.*

When I woke up the whole wing was in turmoil. Everything that could be ripped up and smashed was flung over the landings. I felt sick and my shoulder hurt bad. I guessed that I must have been out for half an hour.

*The possibility of prisoners gaining access to the roofs had been a long-standing problem. At the time of the riot, extensive scaffolding had been erected. During the riot, access to the scaffold was gained from above.*

The screws had been driven out and must have dragged the fallen screws out with them. I couldn't see Ted anywhere. I looked down from the landing and saw that barricades were built around that gates. I pulled myself to a standing position. I couldn't move my shoulder. The screws were trying to get back in, but the old turtle formation wasn't moving much due to the debris. The cons were raining everything they could find down on them from the landings so it wasn't long before they were obliged to retreat.

I needed to lie down. I staggered back into the cell. It went relatively quiet outside. What was I doing here? I would be marked out as a 'ringleader' now. I thought about outside. It was the first time in months that I had allowed my mind to wander beyond my internal world and the everyday crap of stern. I reached for the scrapbook that David had brought in for me. To my shame, I hadn't opened it. It still had the green plastic string around it.

I spent ages, one-handed, unpicking the childish knots. Dave had filled the book with West Ham press cuttings. The first page detailed the Lou Macari saga. Wonderful stuff. The board really made a ricket there. Always so straightlaced, they had hired a bit of a 'ducker and diver', the Syd King of the 1980s, except Macari would not obligingly do himself in. Was Lou a villain? I had a surprising thought. How much Upton Park and most other football grounds had in common with the nick. Largely Victorian structures that locked people in, often in overcrowded, dangerous and unsanitary conditions. The stewards, like the screws, were underpaid power-freaks. The food was unfit to eat. It was run by people who were out of touch with reality, words like 'segregation', 'control' and 'violence' underpinned the language of football. Behaviour was mostly rowdy, but occasionally spilled over into aggression. The crowds were, in the main, male, working class and, disproportionately, in terms of the population, young. Home from home! Much later I followed this up and came across Michael Foucault's ideas in *Discipline and Punish* about how control can be exerted by the building in which those who need to be controlled are placed:

> *...but to permit an internal, articulated and detailed control to render visible those who are inside it; in more general terms, an architecture that would operate to transform individuals: to act on those it shelters, to provide a hold on their conduct ...*

Up the Hammers!

Billy Bonds had taken over in February. A popular appointment but, wonderful swashbuckling, raider that Psycho was, he seemed a strange choice for manager. I never got the impression that Bonzo was a great tactician. As captain he had led by example, and on the field this has its place, but strategically he was John Lyall's faithful sergeant major.

David had practically ignored the League. He had included the last two home games at the end of the book, both wins against Leicester (3-1) and Wolves (4-0) and the final Division Two placings, showing Leeds as champions, Sheffield United (on the same 85) points and Newcastle promoted. West Ham finished in seventh place eight points adrift of promotion with 72 points. Bournemouth, Bradford and Stoke were relegated.

Dave had concentrated on the League Cup. The first tie took the Hammers to Birmingham and we won the away leg 2-1 and got a draw at the Boleyn, Julian Dicks scoring against his old club. The two legs against Villa produced a single goal from Dicks. We then beat Wimbledon and then there was an epic struggle against Derby: 1-1 at Upton Park (Jules again), 0-0 at the Baseball

Ground in the replay. We won the second replay 2-1 at home. This set up an all-Second Division semi-final against Oldham.

Amazingly we lost the first leg at Boundary Park. I stared at the scoreline for a while, then read on. Dave had underlined two words in red ink: 'Plastic Pitch'. Apparently they had put together an unbeaten 32-match run on this stuff. It seems both Arsenal and Southampton had been equally overrun. Andy Richie did well, though, keeping up a record of scoring in every round with two goals. The report of the Upton Park leg confirmed suspicions. Alvin Martin, Dicks and Kelly scored with no reply from Oldham. Dave included a match report of the Final. Forest won by the only goal.

I turned the pages back and forward for a long time. I forgot my shoulder and the riot. This was fascinating. I had missed all this, ignored it even. Not just West Ham, but my son's passions and his attachment to the stream of my own life. For the first time in my life I hadn't been there. The riot and Dave's scrapbook had, in some way, small perhaps, but not insignificant, set me free. I must not lose touch again. I will not let this place do that to me again.

Ted came to the door. He looked a mess. Dirty, filthy even. His head was covered in dried blood. "We've been on the roof. Asking for help. They're coming in again. I think this is it."

*The commanders and their units were fully briefed on the inter-vention plan and took up their positions by the Governor's passage. Two sections approached A Wing. Two more sections went to the Chapel entrance. Another section used a borrowed police vehicle in an attempt to reach the entrance at the other end of the wing. There was some confusion as to what went wrong with this aspect of the attack, but there is no doubt that it came under an onslaught of missiles thrown from the inmates. As a result, it was difficult for the occupants to emerge safely and two officers were injured attempting to do so.*

*The units moved in after the tactical use of hoses at 11.16. Most of the prisoners surrendered by 11.50. The wing was cleared by 13.45*

*The damage caused included the destruction of the recesses and their fittings, 27 cell doors ripped off their hinges, and five cell fires.*

*The cost of repairs was approximately £30,000.*

*As a result of the riot, the staff lost confidence in their ability to maintain control. They were therefore reluctant to restore the relaxed regime which had previously existed.*

The riots were caused through overcrowding, diabolical food and disgusting sanitary conditions. I agreed with the riot. Something had to be done. Because of the inhuman treatment of every inmate. We are treated like animals.

The problem with the prison system is a simple one; it's the prison system and the conditions you ask us to live in. No one listens to us. No one answers our questions.

**The details of prison conditions and the prison riots of 1990 used above are based on the work of Woolf & Tumin, in *Prison Disturbances April 1990 —* HMSO 1991**

100 Years

# Chapter Thirteen

*The first meeting of the West Ham supporters club was at Cave Road School in the late 1940s. Twenty-six of us attended following the placing of an advertisement in the Stratford Express. We paid 2s 6d each. No interest was shown from the club. Charlie Paynter was a tyrant. He didn't want to know. These 26 had the courage to start something. In that first meeting we decided on our motto: 'Help not Hinder'. We set up our headquarters in The Duke of Fife in Katherine Road.*

Mr Fred Noakes, 1997 — Founder member of the West Ham United Supporters Club.


7 September 1995.

AND WEST HAM are one hundred years old. The day I was born the Hammers got a 1-1 result in a friendly at Hermit Road against The Royal Ordnance. On 11 September 1995 the game nearest to our birthday was played against Chelsea at Upton Park in the Premier League. The first four games of the season hadn't produced a win. This was to be the fifth in that run. We lost 3-1.

We played 47 games in that first season. We won 30 and lost 12.

West Ham United officially came into being in June 1895, but the team and supporters — the real club — didn't come together until the first match. Of course, I don't remember that season. I went to my first match with my father in 1899. It was a decent 4-0 early season home win against Chatham. Ken McKay and Albert Carnelly got two each. It was Albert's home debut, having joined us from Bristol City. He scored 14 goals for us that season. Harry Bradshaw, the club captain, died on Christmas Day and this affected everyone quite badly. We finished bottom of the Southern League, having won the championship the year before. It took a test match at White Hart Lane to maintain our place. We beat Fulham 5-1. Bill Joyce, the former Tottenham player, got a hat-trick. For the rest of our Southern League years we were never much more than an ordinary team, but we had some memorable moments.

It was the first day of September 1900. The day before the British Army had occupied Johannesburg as conflict with the Boers continued. We were playing as West Ham for the first time on the first day of the season. It was a wet and cold day at the Memorial. We were entertaining Gravesend United. Before five minutes were up, Bill Grassam, our inside-right, had put one away. Fergus Hunt and Fred Fenton on the wings were devastating that day, as was Lou Raisbeck and skipper Roddy McEachrane. Fred was like a whippet. Early on he got a bit carried away. He outpaced the boys from Kent but the rest of our team could not keep up either. Without looking up he sent in a cross. Only Albert Kaye was within a street of the ball and he missed it by yards. It travelled all the way to the opposite wing before Hunt picked it up and banged it in from a sharp angle.

Fenton was having a fine time, but poor old Kaye was being run ragged. He couldn't get to the next centre either and just managing to connect with a third, shot the ball into the side netting. The Gravesend 'keeper, a second choice by the name of Wilcox, was having a bad game. He had managed to stop a shot from Jim Reid, but Jim beat him a bit later.

So, at the break we were 3-0 up. Right from the whistle to start the second half Hunt laid on Grassam for the fourth goal. Fenton and 'Fergie' continued to torture the opposition and it wasn't long before Reid got his second after a scramble in the Gravesend box. Gravesend rallied a little and managed to get Henderson up and force a good save from Monteith, but it was shortlived. Bill

Grassam put away another couple before the end and in the process became the first Hammer to score a hat-trick. 7-0. It was to be our best victory that season. It equalled our 7-0 FA Cup win against Dartford in October 1899 and was our best Southern League win since the 10-0 defeat of Maidenhead in April of the same year.

West Ham was born out of one man's paternalism. The Thames Iron Works FC was one of a number of works societies looking to cater for the leisure of its firm's employees. It was part of an overall strategy for securing peaceful industrial relations which the owner of the biggest Thames shipyard of the time, Arnold Hills, had set up following the dock strike of 1889 and other disputes. It was a device to placate the workers and the background organisation has never quite lost this founding culture. No supporter of any standing has any illusions about this. It fits in with a more generalised use of sport since Rome, as Rousseau was probably aware when he said that games should be used to create 'a deep love for the nation'.

There's very little that the person in the stands has in common with members of the board. Football for the latter is essentially one way to pursue a profit and status. Old Arnold was never too sure about the team turning professional. That's not what it was about. Great gatherings of working folk in one place would always make certain groups of people feel uneasy. But it had the pay-off of deflecting concentration into a mere game. However, human beings are not that easily manipulated. Feelings still get expressed, although they may be diverted into particular channels. Every football match becomes a demonstration. Police are called out in force, work places, whole cities come to a halt for a match. That's why football becomes the focus of control and establishment concern from time to time. Thatcher seeking to bring in identification cards via the back-door of football is just one example.

For me, the real history of a football club can only be found with its supporters. They interpret this through the games and those who played in them. The ambitions of directors or governments for their team rarely impinge. Memories mix with mythologies to produce history and dreams of the future. The White Horse Cup Final, the 'Academy' devoted to entertaining play, the 'family club' made up of local players, and most of all the games and the personalities who played in them.

For example, George Kitchen came to Upton Park in 1905. He was a flamboyant goalie and a mainstay of our 1911 Cup run. Kitchen, and the matches he was part of, marked us out as more than just another Southern League side. West Ham made the fourth round, taking the scalps of Forest, Preston and Manchester United, who won the Division One championship that year, on the way. The game against United was the biggest thing that had happened to the Irons. Thousands of people surrounded the ground. People were trying for every vantage point, up telegraph poles even. The whole crowd invaded the pitch after the game. Everyone wanted to congratulate the team. It was just after this that George Webb got his call up for England. Our Cup run was only thwarted by the eventual 1911-12 Division One champions, Blackburn. It was close as well, with Rovers going through by the odd goal of five. George Butcher got both our goals. Less than three weeks later British shop workers won the fight for the 60-hour week.

Kitchen and Webb brought some sophistication to West Ham, but in the years before I went to Russia, the player I liked to watch was Danny Shea. He was a brilliant inside-forward, a fine ball player, always hard to get off the ball. Out of Wapping, he was our first really big local player. Between the end of 1907 and the start of 1913, Shea scored 121 goals in 201 games. Danny was our top scorer for five seasons from 1908 and despite moving to Blackburn half-way through the season, for a transfer record £2,000, he was again the best marksman of 1913. He got representative honours for the Southern League, being the League's top scorer from 1909 to 1911. With Shea alongside Herbie Ashton, West Ham had a devastating pair of wingers. At Rovers he won three England caps and represented the Football League. He scored 27 goals in Blackburn's 1913-14 First Division championship side. Dan hadn't finished with the Hammers, playing quite a few guest matches for us while I was in Russia, and in 1920 he came back for one last season with West Ham. He only managed to score once in 16 games. That was in one of only four games in which he, Syd Puddefoot and Vic Watson played together for the Irons.

Syd Puddefoot, however, was *the* West Ham player of the club's early years. Alongside players like Hufton and Kay, he scored goals at a tremendous rate.

An outstanding 'Puddy game' was our encounter with Crystal Palace in 1918. It was the final game of the London Combination for that season. I didn't see the game myself, of course. I was still in Russia, not thinking much about football, the revolution was fighting for survival in the face of foreign interference, but I had Charlie's reports. I've still got the clipping he sent me saying that Puddy had been in particularly good form and that the Hammers scoring was 'extraordinary'. According to Charlie:

"With little more than three minutes on the clock, Syd opened his account, giving notice to Rae, the Palace man between the sticks, that this was going to be an end-of-season fireworks display. With a quarter-of-an-hour gone, Jack Macksey's thunderbolt drive could only be parried by Rae and Cadet A.Cunningham slotted the ball home. Driver F.Burke did not make the most of a straightforward opportunity to put Hammers three up. Palace cleared their lines as far as Puddy, who took the ball the whole way down the pitch, before making it 3-0 to the Irons. It was now plain that a rout was on the cards, it was just a question how Palace were going to limit the avalanche. Puddefoot was awarded his third and West Ham's fourth, darting through to beat the offside trap. Palace's appeals were ignored by referee Neale as the linesman stood to attention.

"The second half had barely started when Burke scored. Soon after Syd picked up the leftovers from a Piggott drive that Rae had done well to deflect. Puddefoot got West Ham's 99th goal of the season, before Burke made the century. Goal number 101 for the season, nine for the game, and six for Puddefoot was next, before a fracas involving Macksey and most of the Palace defence stopped the game. When the smoke cleared, Jack was flat out. He eventually rose like Lazarus, but was amazingly sent off. He looked too dazed to protest.

"Hammers being down to ten men may have given Palace a glimmer of hope that the torrent of goals would abate, or maybe some pride could be retrieved by getting one back. But it was not to be. Herbie Ashton and Puddy took on the whole of the Palace side and Syd put the Irons into double figures for the day. It was still not over. Ashton closed in quick following Rae's effort to stop a tricky drive from Cunningham. West Ham 11 Crystal Palace 0.

"This is the biggest win in the London Combination's history, Dan. Syd equalled Robert Thomson's record seven for Chelsea against Luton two years ago."

When Syd went to Falkirk for £5,000 the supporters were devastated. I think the board would have been lynched had a player of the calibre of Vic Watson not been ready to come into the team. Reaching the 1923 Cup Final also did much to pacify the fans, but we never really forgave the board for getting rid of Puddefoot.

The Wembley team was a mixture of old hands like Hufton, Tresadern and skipper George Kay and new boys like Watson and Jimmy Ruffell. Jimmy eventually got half-a-dozen England caps over four years. Jim Barrett signed in 1925 and up to the start of the war played over 400 games for the club.

Barrett, Watson and Ruffell were still all at the peak of their form when we played host to the Arsenal in the early spring of 1927. Games against the Gunners were always a big attraction. There had been 40,000 at their place earlier in the season, when we came away with a creditable point, the match finishing at 2-2, Watson and the smart, former amateur, Vivian Gibbins, got one each in one of the few occasions they turned out together. Gibbins got a fair bit of stick over that name. 28,000 turned out for the meeting at the Boleyn Ground. Charlie Buchan, Hulme and Baker were all out of the Arsenal side, which had got through to the semi-final of the FA Cup the week before.

From the start, you could see that West Ham were going for the kill. Only two minutes into the game Ruffell and Johnson sent Watson on a run that ended with a goal, chipped in with the outside of Vic's right boot.

We hadn't got to the 20-minute mark when Watson tried a shot that spun viciously. It struck the Arsenal right-back Tom Parker and went twirling passed the Gunners' goalkeeper. Danny Lewis in goal did not have a bad game and indicative of this was his block of a terrific shot by Ruffell. I don't think anyone could have done better, but the rebound went to Watson who calmly put it away. Shortly before half-time, the other Arsenal back fell victim to a Watson shot. Bob John did the right thing by trying the block, but the power of the drive meant that John just helped the ball past Lewis.

The second half got under way with Joe Johnson, our inside-left, waltzing passed a couple of defenders to glide the ball into the net. Watson made it six for the Hammers, getting his hat-trick in the process despite what was, by now, a very heavy pitch. He laid back and slammed in a pin-point pass from Ruffell. Jimmy got the final goal right at the death to make it 7-0 to the Irons.

It turned out to be our biggest win for over six years. We wouldn't have another like it for three more years. We finished top team in London in 1927, sixth in Division One. Arsenal went on to the FA Cup Final only to let it go out of England for the first and only time. Cardiff won 1-0. Billy Hardy, the only

Englishman in the Cardiff side, marked Charlie Buchan out of the game. Lewis, a Welsh international goalkeeper, fumbled the ball into his own net following a Ferguson shot. I don't know. Arsenal!

It was important to put up a good show against the Arsenal. Because they were a big London club, but not like Spurs. At this time, Arsenal, more than any other club, represented the football 'establishment'. For West Ham to beat Arsenal it was like the servants beating the masters. It's true that the rank and file support of the Arsenal was not much different to our own, but the football match is more than just a game between two teams of working class people or rivalry between their supporters. The event signifies the continuing tension between the managers and the managed, and this can be signified in a number of, sometimes contradictory, ways. Games dominated by working people at the organisational end do not rouse the passions found in football. Bowls, darts, Rugby League for example. Football, in part, is a sublimated political encounter carried on primarily at a psychological level. So you can resent your own board, and at the same time you can resent the Arsenal, as **'the'** big-money club, more. Perhaps it takes a hundred years to build up this type of perspective. It's easy to reduce everything to jealousy or rivalry, but if it was just this, why would anyone bother? More emotional energy needs to be generated if interest is to endure — motives have to be a continuing, underlying, dynamic. Football carries a lot of baggage.

Part of this is how it divides people with similar interests and backgrounds. It can reiterate religious divisions. In Glasgow, Rangers and Celtic are echoes of more profound problems. The 1919-20 semi-final of the Irish Cup between Belfast Celtic and Glentoran saw both sides disqualified. The trophy went to the other semi-final winners, Shelbourne. The problem involved 'crowd disruption' following shooting in the stands. Belfast Celtic eventually disappeared following a huge sectarian riot in 1949 at Windsor Park. It was during a match with Linfield. Football hooliganism a modern invention? Don't underestimate this in terms of the divide and rule philosophy of Empire. It worked for the Romans, along with beer and circuses, and football has its place within this schema.

Much has been made of the local attitude of 'us and them' that has always existed around the West Ham area anyway. The legendary 'North/South' confrontations for instance. What Northerner does not like to put one over on their Cockney cousins? The 1923 Cup Final was promoted as this type of conflict. In the second match of the 1930-31 season Liverpool came to London with ambitions to teach the Southerners a lesson. Both sets of supporters were in need of some distraction as the Depression was approaching its height. West Ham were in the mood for another North versus South confrontation, having disposed of Huddersfield in their first match of the term. We were two up in the opening ten minutes through good goals by Stan Earle and Watson.

Liverpool appeared to be confused. Bob Done had come in at right-back for the crocked Jimmy Jackson and their attack just couldn't get going. They looked a pace slower than our forwards, but their lack of penetration was in no small part due to Jim Barrett's fine form at centre-half. At half-time we were quite pleased with a two-goal buffer and the Hammers were expected to come out and consolidate a comfortable win. But boy, did they consolidate. Bert Cadwell sent a telling pass through to Watson and Vic made it count. Earle took his second following a magic, swerving run through the Liverpool defence. Wilf James then did the honours, taking advantage of good work by Earle and Yews, who had together obliged Liverpool's 'keeper, the South African Arthur Riley, to commit himself, leaving the net open to the Welsh international inside-left. Vic Watson got numbers seven and eight, chalking up a personal tally of four goals in the process. But the lads from 'up north' had the last laugh. They ended the season ten places ahead of us, beating West Ham 2-0 on the last day of the season at Anfield.

As much as the game can be used to divide people, it promotes solidarity. It would be pitiful, pathetic to spend your life involved in watching, not even playing, an empty 'game'. What engages people in such commitment are wider feelings, perhaps even cultural feelings. The working person who has no interest in football is often quite depoliticised. The recent gentrification of the game, ridding grounds of terracing, charging more than half the national pension rate for entrance, can be understood as an attempt to finally rid football of its subversive potential and it may have worked. But it will just go elsewhere. Kids take to the endless virtual acres of the cyber space or street hockey and asphalt basketball.

You will have to excuse the rantings of an old socialist. The Russian Revolution, the Spanish Civil War and standing on the North Bank have taken their toll. But there is something about the individual, within the wider team; the person in the crowd. We come together to find our potential and express ourselves. Football facilitates this. As such, it is not 'just a game', an end in itself. Everything happens around the match. Feelings and ideas are based on and lead to games. One such was the Leeds visit to Upton Park in the February of 1929. West Ham were soon on the march when Jim Collins set up Watson for his first goal and Ruffell carved the way for his second before Leeds could reply. But the Yorkshiremen roused themselves and pulled one back through England's inside-left Russell Wainscoat. Soon afterwards Tommy Jennings made it all square. The Tykes now had the momentum and with half an hour to go looked likely to take the points. Ernie Hart, the England centre-half, didn't look like he was going to give anything away, while it was obvious that Hufton had a problem with his wrist. But just on the hour Stan Earle made a super position for Gibbins and we were in front once more. From this point the ball did not seem to go out of the Leeds half. Watson caused the Leeds goalie to commit himself with a left-foot dummy and then shot home with his right. Shortly afterwards he forced Wilson to make a fine save, but he couldn't hold it and Vic smashed in number five. This was followed by a good goal premised by a jinking run by Tom Yews. Watson notched up two more before the end, setting a club record of individual goals in a single match. It stood for nearly 40 years until Geoff Hurst equalled the performance. Watson got a hat-trick at Elland Road at the start of the next season. Early in 1930 he put four past them in the Cup and by the spring he had knocked in another three against the Northerners.

Hurst matched the record during a game that gave every indication of being a bit of an average match. By that October of 1968, West Ham had only won five of their first 14 games. We were without a victory in the previous seven games. Although Sunderland were to go down the following season, this team was the seed bed from which the 1972-73 FA Cup winners grew and included the heroes of that side, Jim Montgomery and Ian Porterfield.

Hurst's first goal came in the 19th minute, on the end of a cross from Martin Peters. I was standing behind the goal and could plainly see that he handled it. He did confess to this later. It would be easy to criticise Geoff for this, but he was a professional. He understood that many goals are unjustly disallowed, and that this is balanced by those that are incorrectly given. The universe, in the main, moves towards a state of equilibrium. Such is the poetry of football, Hurst was a part of this.

Not five minutes later, Bobby Moore scored his first of the season. Hurley gave away the free-kick that Moore dealt with in splendid fashion. It was his 20th for the club in ten years, the second and last one for the season came a couple of weeks later against QPR. Bob went on to score another six before he left in 1974. In another team he would have scored more, but his defensive duties at West Ham preoccupied him in most matches.

A few minutes past the half-hour Hurst clocked up his second, a back-post header, and a little before half-time, he got his hat-trick by way of a Harry Redknapp corner.

A really nice movement between Sissons, Trevor Brooking and Peters opened the second half, ending in Geoff's fourth. Less than a quarter-of-an-hour later he had made it 6-0 to the Irons, following the ball into the net. Brooking cut through the Sunderland defence like butter, to make it seven. No more than 60 seconds later Brooking picked up on a poor pass from Herd, Trevor let Redknapp carry it off to cross for Hurst to equal the club record.

Two months later we would be beaten by Sunderland, 2-1 at Roker Park.

Hurst was awarded the match ball. Just as well really, I don't think anyone would have got it off him that day anyway. Hurst was a great player. He was a better goalscorer than Vic Watson, the holder of the club record for goals scored. Although Hurst did not get as many, he played at a much higher standard than Watson, mostly against top-flight opposition. This is not to say that Vic was not one of the best men to ever pull on a West Ham shirt, he was, but Geoff Hurst is the greatest forward we have ever had. He is certainly one of the most gifted English strikers, perhaps **the** most talented attacking athlete in the history of football. Internationally, Hurst is held in much higher esteem than he is in England. He was near to Pele at his best, maybe not quite as skilful, but stronger and, in certain situations, faster. He was just as feared and as difficult to control.

Strange as it may seem the Sunderland 'keeper, Montgomery, didn't have a bad game. Without him we would have been well into double figures. We did just that against Bury at Upton Park in '83. West Ham's biggest win in their history. The Boleyn Ground looked deserted, though. We didn't make 11,000 that night. The worst attendance ever for a Cup game at Upton Park. It was the second round of the League Cup, at this time in its 'Milk Cup' incarnation (I'm just waiting for the 'Egg Cup'). I went with Dan that night. He was pretty down, just a couple of days before 300 Americans, mostly marines, had been killed, along with 200 French soldiers in two simultaneous suicide attacks in Beirut. Dan had worked with and trained some of the men who were in the marine headquarters when the lorry containing 5,000 pounds of explosives crashed through the perimeter fence. He had no idea if any of those he knew personally were among the dead, but to a long-serving marine, every other marine is family.

We were 2-1 up from the first leg, so we couldn't afford to be too comfortable. It would not be unusual for West Ham to be taken to a replay and defeated by the likes of the lads from Gigg Lane. I thought I could relax a bit when only two minutes into the game Dave Swindlehurst headed the ball down, allowing a very young Tony Cottee to bang it home, but then Bury were given a penalty by Mr Letts. It was a relief to see Bramhall hit the post.

Big Alvin headed a fine second. Then, with 23 minutes gone, Billy Bonds opened things up for Brooking on the left. The 'Maestro' glided like a ghost past two defenders and threaded the ball just inside the far upright. The half-hour had barely ticked by when Bonzo caught a cross with his head and in came T.C. to clear up. Cottee got his hat-trick not five minutes later, scoring a fine headed goal from a Paul Allen cross. Brooking grabbed number five. The sixth goal was the result of a fine centre from Dev' that found Martin. Alvin, freed from the cares of defence, created the chance that 'Cotters' took.

Devonshire got a deserved reward with goal number seven following good work from Swindlehurst. This was followed by a Ray Stewart penalty, reaping revenge for a foul on Devonshire. With less than ten minutes left, Brooking shot from just outside the penalty area. The drive hit a Bury defender and went in. It was just not the Shakers' night. We were into the 85th minute before we got the magic ten. Brooking made a clever pass to Devonshire who produced a chip for his second of the game.

These are examples of great wins. The elation attached to them by those who watched them is beyond measurement. There are also painful moments. Knocked out of cups by lesser teams or the loss of valued players. I don't think players, managers and the board have ever really understood what the club means to local people. It is more than a business or a group of men kicking a piece of leather filled with air. When you see that what exists between supporters and what the club represents to them, you recognise it as a *relationship,* and you can't be 'unsentimental' about it. Your feelings and memories might not be based in fact or 'truth', but in that so many people believe that 'truth' is created by them.

West Ham directors and management have, for the most part, held the fans in contempt. The most recent manifestation of this was the bond scheme of the early 90s. Many supporters, approximately 10,000, went on strike; they just stopped going to home games. The board was asking us to fork out between £500 and £1,000 for a bond, or debenture, just for the right to buy a season ticket, something we already had. It's a bit like buying and selling shares in a nationalised industry. It amounts to people selling something that is not theirs, to people to whom what is being sold, already belongs.

I've still got the 1947 programme where they asked for suggestions about how the club might repair the wartime bomb damage, the Ministry or Works having blocked the purchase of materials. I decided to reply. About a week went by and then I got a letter, informing me that 'mass protest would not be advisable'. I was being flippant, but this was typical of the short shrift given to supporters. When the Supporters Club offered their help, they were informed that the board had 'decided against having anything to do with a supporters club'. This was confirmed no more than a month later when the Supporters Club approached the board about options for the name of the Supporters Club – 'West Ham United Supporters Club' or 'West Ham United Football Supporters Club'. The reply was what I would have expected, saying that they were not interested in what title the Supporters Club gave themselves. This attitude did change by the 1950s, particularly after the arrival of Ted Fenton, who during his time as manager of Colchester had seen the benefits a supporters club could bring. The Supporters Club became a useful source of fund-raising for projects designated, not by the fund-raisers, but by the board.

As older West Ham supporters go, I represent the rather radical section. Many are benign, long-suffering and sensitive people. When you talk about West Ham's relative lack of success, they will often defend the club, generally citing a lack of finance, something many of them can identify with. They talk about how players express their love of West Ham, and although this is often the case, many players have been more than keen to get away, Paul Ince is a notable example. Up to the 1960s, if you took a regular seat in the stands, it would be saved for you (no need for a season ticket). For the most part, I have been a North Bank regular, but on a couple of occasions, just after the war, I paid my 4s 6d to get into D Block and once splashed out five bob to sit in C Block. However, even on the terraces you saw the same people in the same places every game. For much of the club's history each part of the ground has had its own atmosphere, what today might be called 'culture'. The Chicken Run was always entertaining to watch. They would sing and sway together as one and, even today, the East Stand houses some of the most vocal and ardent fans.

It was the Supporters Club that started to hire coaches to take people to away games. The first match I went to with the club was at Luton. A group of us searched the area for a cafe after the game, but the place was a wasteland. We finally gave up, but found that the coach had left without us. This was the start of a lasting hatred of Luton. The Supporters Club also encouraged a good number of women members and for a long time this meant that West Ham had many more females attending games than most of its rivals.

For a time, after the first couple of years of Greenwood's reign, team members never acknowledged the supporters. There were some exceptions to this, most notably Geoff Hurst, who always showed a sympathy with the supporters, but in the main, players became remote, self-absorbed figures. This changed with the coming of John Lyall, but the likes of Bobby Moore and Martin Peters always gave the impression that they were doing the fans a favour by playing. Moore seemed to have never forgiven the club for not selling him to Tottenham early on in his career. Peters, of course, did find his way to White Hart Lane and ignored the Spurs fans with equal dexterity. There was a feeling of resentment from such 'star' players. Peter Eustace got the cold shoulder off to a fine art. He was every inch a Ron Greenwood player. Totally cold, remote and passionless. He said he missed the dressing rooms at Hillsborough. The complete opposite were the likes of Bobby Gould, Julian Dicks and Alvin Martin. Small gestures mean a lot in any relationship. Gould and Dicks, for instance, would always acknowledge the supporters at the end of a game and Martin would never end a season without some physical approach to the fans.

Of course we lost Bobby Moore in February of 1993. It was a tragic, untimely death. As a young man, Moore had been a bright boy, now and then showing a sense of humour and fun. But the unrequited cuddles he gave to Greenwood after the first Cup win and Ramsey following victory in the World Cup Final, for me became indicative of the rest of his career. Always studious in his attitude to the game, he became very concentrated and serious on the pitch. He loosened up late on in his career, but for the most part, he made the detached coldness of Greenwood and Ramsey his role model. However, I do not believe that this was Bobby Moore. Some of his off-the-field exploits betray something of a cavalier attitude, befitting the greatest player ever. Yes, he was better than Pele, he proved that by getting the better of him during the Mexico World Cup. Unlike Pele or Best, the usual candidates for 'the greatest' tag, Moore was not physically gifted. He was blessed by a mind that could adapt to the requirements of football better than any other; he had to make his body come up to pace. Bobby could not head a ball, he was slow in terms of speed across the ground, but he compensated by the use of his intellectual understanding of the physics of the game. To this extent Moore made himself a footballer. Any boy in the street, with the same application, could do what he did. That was his appeal. But such application is more than rare. It is likely that we will not see his type again for a hundred years. Beckenbauer was close, but Bobby was just that bit better, a tad more sophisticated all round.

Thousands of tributes were placed at the main gate to Upton Park after Bobby passed on. I wanted to do something, but not in claret and blue. I took a train to Wembley, his real home ground. I stood at the top of the Wembley Way and meditated on those twin towers for a while, I then read silently a poem by Robert Frost, first recited to me by my beloved Cala:

> The Road Not Taken
> Two roads diverged in a yellow wood
> And sorry
> I could not travel both
> And to be one Traveller, long I stood
> And looked down one as far as I could
> To where it bent in the undergrowth
> Then took the other, as just as fair,

And having perhaps the better claim,
Though as for that the passing there
Had worn them really about the same.
And both that morning equally lay
In leaves no step had trodden black.
Oh, I kept the first for another day!
Yet knowing how way leads on way
I doubted if I should ever come back.
I shall be telling this with a sigh
Somewhere ages and ages hence:
Two roads diverged in a wood, and I —
I took the one less trodden by,
And that has made all the difference.

When Bobby Moore died, part of West Ham died. He, alongside Peters and Hurst, should never have been obliged to stay at West Ham. Ron Greenwood has confirmed that he would not let them go even when they wanted to. This was poor management. After 1966 West Ham won nothing with the World Cup trio. One of the club's worst-ever results came shortly after the World Cup, in 1967. We were drawn at home to Swindon, then in the Third Division, in the third round of the FA Cup. Three goals from Hurst got us a draw. That took us back to the muddy County Ground for a 3-1 drubbing. Don Rogers, the Swindon winger, was devastating. The World Cup trio were not built around and were not allowed to develop by joining other clubs. Peters was released not too far off of his prime, but Hurst and Moore stayed throughout their best years. You can't hope for success from just two great players who feel a level of resentment about their situation. Although neither Hurst or Moore did less than well for West Ham – Bobby never had a bad game – their best performances were when they were wearing an England shirt. In a sense the national team became their club. This is where they, surrounded by quality players, could shine.

The best team to leave British shores was the 1970 World Cup squad. It might have been the greatest football team ever and Bobby Moore was their captain. But back at Upton Park mediocrity reigned. The Cup runs of the late 1960s and early 1970s are a fine examples.

In 1968 we had beaten Burnley and Stoke away from Upton Park to set up a visit from Sheffield United. We lost 2-1. Although they had Alan Birchenall, Mick Jones and the youthful Tony Currie, they were a young side and should have been beaten. In 1969 we had seen off Bristol City and Huddersfield, then we came up against Mansfield Town from Division Three. After a postponement due to snow, we lost the midweek match 3-0. In 1970 and 1971 we were eliminated from the FA Cup in the third round by Middlesbrough and Blackpool respectively. In 1972 we got as far as the fifth round before being knocked out by Huddersfield.

Billy Bonds and Harry Redknapp, both at the West Ham during the Moore-Hurst-Peters era, learnt from all this. In recent years no player who has not wanted to play for the club has been retained. It is better for the club and them if they go.

It has to be said, the West Ham establishment have always treated their supporters with more than a hint of patronage. In the first part of the club's history the board saw their work as something of a civic duty. Whilst managers Syd King and Charlie Paynter were pushed forward as 'men of the people', so protecting the board from any association with the riff-raff, and Ted Fenton cultivated something of the same thing through the media, the Ron Greenwood era represented an almost total cut off from contact with the fans and seemingly the rest of the world. Greenwood became a coach before he had finished his playing days, a rather 'soapy' thing even now. He gained employment at Oxford University, with all that institution's traditional connections with the FA. This led to work with the English Youth and Under-23 teams and the assistant manager's job at Arsenal. So Greenwood came to West Ham with a background as a sort of footballing ghillie (his father had been a maintenance man at Wembley, a 'good family record on the estate'). His attitude to 'the great unwashed' of the East End had everything of the Victorian butler about it. He saw it, "An area of swaggers ...they would love somebody like Allison ..." This shows how out of touch he was with the fans. Allison was never much liked by the crowds at Upton Park. Arrogance has never gone down well, hence the general low level disdain for Ron:

*They don't understand sincerity and intelligence. This community and this area doesn't appreciate anything the club stands for. Put this*

*club in another area and the appreciation would be tremendous
. . . People just don't have the same standards of respect . . . They just
want to be the biggest and the best and to boast . . .*

Greenwood strove for a kind of 'know your place' respectability, not
success. What the supporters wanted was irrelevant. An example of this is
made in his own book *(Yours Sincerely Ron Greenwood)* where he boasts
about not taking the opportunity to sign Gordon Banks at his peak.
Apparently he had made an agreement to bring Bobby Ferguson down from
Kilmarnock at a world record fee for a goalie. Needless to say Ferguson
turned out to be a less than ordinary player. But the point is that **him** keeping
**his** word meant more than providing the fans with the best possible options.
However, more than Ron's word was at stake. If only he could have seen
himself as changing his mind in the event of a changed situation for the
betterment of the team, much of West Ham's history could have been
different. But he was not that type of man. For example, he sent his whole
team to watch Munich 1860 prior to the 1965 Cup-winners' Cup Final. They
were put in an open stand in the pouring rain. Greenwood stayed at home. It
was important to **him** that **he** was confirmed in Loughton.

The ego of the quiet man often outweighs the seeming arrogance of the
likes of Allison, whose first priority, wherever he went, was the success of the
club.

For Greenwood, the supporters were simply supposed to turn up, be loyal
and put up with whatever the board thought was good for them:

*Success at a club like this is frightening. It would attract a lot of the
wrong people, the kind of people who will disappear as soon as
you're not at the top any longer.*

This, what Malcolm X might have called 'House Nigger' attitude, extended
to the rest of society. Greenwood the social philosopher:

*Football is a reflection of life . . . unfortunately, there's a lack of
respect in life in general and all that shows up in football.*

Greenwood's lifetime of forelock tugging servitude and doing down of those who paid his wages was not forgotten by his masters. Hence his reward as England's stop-gap manager. A reign of stolid mediocrity given the talent at his disposal (look at what English clubs were doing while Greenwood was in charge of the national side). His demeanour, a sort of 'Alf Ramsey light', was perfect for the job that would recruit a veritable parade of personality deficients in the future Bobby Robson, Graham Taylor and Glenn Hoddle (Venables was recruited through the tradesman's entrance in desperation when success was paramount. He was quickly shown the door when talent ceased to be the priority).

Still, Greenwood's feelings for the fans existed within a reciprocation of contempt. Not many managers could spend 16 years at a club, that spent most of its time in the top flight, and gain so little regard from the supporters. Never was his name chanted. He will never be associated with the team with which he spent the best years of his managerial time. Perhaps he despised the likes of Shankly, Busby, Stock, Stein, Stokoe and Clough, whose respect for the fans was repaid a thousand fold.

The players often had equal disregard for the man. After West Ham's famous win against Manchester United in the FA Cup semi-final of 1964, the team coach left without him. Bobby Moore would ignore his team talks.

West Ham have had their share of ups and downs, particularly in recent years. Relegated in 1932, 1978, 1989 and 1992. Promoted in 1923, 1958, 1981, 1991 and 1993. Since 1919, we've been in the top flight for 40 seasons. It's not great, but it's not bad, I'd guess much better than average if you look at all the teams that have been with the Hammers. In 76 years, never lower than the Second Division. But with our support and our location we should have done better. Moving north and east of the London Borough of Newham, the nearest big teams, if you don't count Norwich and Ipswich as big teams, are in the Midlands. To the south there is Charlton and Millwall, but that's about it until you get to Southampton (or Spain). To the north and west there are Arsenal, Spurs and Chelsea, and they, alongside Wimbledon, QPR, Fulham and Palace, should cover most options to the South and West. This gives West Ham a potentially massive constituency. But instead, because or our failure to break into the real big names of football, we find ourselves in competition for support with the likes of Orient, Southend, Charlton, Millwall and Luton. We end up pitting ourselves against clubs with far fewer resources in dog fights against relegation or for promotion.

This is not to say that this does not provide some moments. One of my proudest moments supporting the club came in the spring of 1991. We had reached the semi-final of the FA Cup. Billy had just got out of clink and he had got two tickets for the game up at Villa Park. We went up in a car he'd rented. It was a beautiful, sunny April day. Prison had taken its toll on Bill and he took in the whole journey with some relish, commenting all the time about the fresh air and the freedom of 'just being able to go'. But the game itself did not go well for the team. Keith Hackett sent off Tony Gale and we lost our shape. Forest scored four and we didn't get a look in. But as the goals piled in, the 20,000 West Ham fans chanted louder. They did not pause to acknowledge the growing scoreline, *Billy Bonds' Claret and Blue Army,* stamp, stamp, stamp, stamp *Billy Bonds' Claret and Blue Army* ... A constant, non-stop, mantra of loyalty. On, on and on. No one cared, it was just about West Ham. Forest and the score were irrelevant.

But the other side of things is also sweet. On the last day of the season, 1993. Cambridge came to Upton Park with us needing at least a win to get into the Premiership; goals scored were also going to be crucial. The U's needed three points to escape the drop.

Long before the start, the gates were shut and with over 27,000 in the ground, it was the largest crowd of the season. The game was preceded by the award of the Hammer of the Year. The little Yank Steve Potts got it ahead of Kevin Keen.

From the kick-off it was obvious that Cambridge were not going to give much away. They were time-wasting already. You don't know the tension of such affairs if you are spoilt by guaranteed Premiership football. Not only are you on tenterhooks watching the match in front of you, you are also waiting to hear about situations hundreds of miles away. In this case we were waiting on the result of the Portsmouth-Grimsby game. Every third person seemed to be intermittently listening to a transistor. A cheer relayed around the ground as the Mariners went one up.

There was no score at half-time so things were still tense. If the score stayed like this, West Ham would go up, but if Portsmouth scored they would be promoted and we would be stuck in Division One for another season.

Just a couple of minutes into the second period and the Irons went ahead. A good volley from David Speedie, on loan from Blackburn. The crowd hated the little Scot, not being able to get his Chelsea credentials out of their collective mind, but at that moment he was made an honorary saint. If everything stayed like this, though, we would be dead level with Portsmouth, same points, same goals scored. What then? Billy Bonds versus 'Bald Eagle', Jim Smith, over three rounds?

With less than half-an-hour to go, Leadbitter finished a Cambridge attack with a shot that beat Miklosko. David Elleray saw a signal from his linesman. A team man is Elleray and an intelligent ref. He doesn't so much officiate at games as manage them. Offside against Bartlett. Then word went round that Portsmouth were now 2-1 up. Things like this shouldn't happen to a 98-year-old man! With only a couple of minutes remaining, the 'Terminator' stormed through the Cambridge defence down the left flank. An accurate and cultured pass meant that Clive Allen, a sub that day, only had to touch the ball to score. This caused many of the fans to run on to the pitch, which would have been worrying if some other officials had been involved. But Dicks and Co soon got the supporters off, as far as the touchline in front of the main stand anyway. Finally it was over, the match, the season and our exile in Division One. We were back in the top flight by a single goal. *Bubbles* echoed around the ground.

What a silly little song. People think it is supposed to reflect the way the team play – flamboyant, light. But it was adopted when we had a local lad with a clump of curly blond hair playing for us. The song was a worldwide favourite at the time. His nickname was 'Bubbles'. For most of West Ham's history, we were regarded as a hard team. The 'academy' tag and the idea that we called more than other clubs on local talent was something that grew out of the late 1950s.

Hammers supporters were singing long before other teams took it up. But we always sang, and a tune like *Bubbles*! The area made people tough. The crushing poverty of the General Strike – the East End was at the very centre of this – was followed by the Depression and the Blitz, again the district took more than its share of punishment. We produced champion boxers and hardened criminals. But somehow it fits. West Ham is a place for dreamers, even if few dreams come true. The song reflects the need to lace irony with humour, and this alleviates some of the hardships. *Bubbles* demonstrates our attitude to life.

So that's a hundred years. A life. It's not just been about supporting a football team. West Ham have been part of the background to my life, they are not the most important thing, but they are related to all the most important things ...and people. West Ham is just people after all. Not directors, that's for sure, not managers either, not even players. They are part of the ephemeral, the dream. The reality lies only in the minds of the supporters and the spirit they share. One perspective Ron Greenwood and I share is that:

*It is a game; but it can be more than a game. It is what we choose to make it.*

I lost a brother in a war. I was one of those who won and lost a revolution. I fought fascists in Spain, fell in love and was left by that love. I found a son who is now trapped by another war. Another brother died. My niece is widowed. My nephew is back in jail. Sounds sad. But I have a very happy granddaughter who has found love, after having love snatched away from her before she knew it.

Things go round and round and at the centre is West Ham. There, through it all. Last night I dreamt that Chengsei took me by the hand and took me back to meet her ancestors. I walked along the line and shook the hands of venerable Chinese people, traders, artisans in beautiful clothes. But I came to one man who was smiling at me. I saw that he was European looking, pale and lean. He was smart, wearing a tidy suit and stiff collar. "How'd yer do," he said in the broad, rolling Cockney I remember from my youth. "I see the Irons are still keeping us on our toes." I nodded or something. "Don't you wanna be worrying, they'll stay up." I got lost in sleep after this. Dreams sometimes come true you see.

I am standing again at Wembley. It is a bright day. The West Ham team are playing all the rest. The side looks a bit unbalanced, but impressive:

**Gregory**
**Walker, Dicks, Bonds, Martin**
**Moore**
**Peters, Brooking**
**Shea, Hurst, Watson**
**Subs: Hufton, Puddefoot, Ruffell, Watson.**

We start as all Wembley Cup Finals start. In 1923 it was for the veterans. In 1940 it was for those who would die. In 1946, for those crushed at Burnden Park. 1964, the hope for peace. 1975, Moorgate and Cambodia. 1980, hostages in Iran, the Gdansk shipbuilders and the Alexander Kielland. 1985, those killed by fire at Valley Parade. 1986, Heysel. 1989, Hillsborough. Now, in this timeless place, it is for me.

> *Abide with me; fast falls the eventide;*
> *The darkness deepens; Lord with me abide!*
> *When other helpers fail, and comforts flee,*
> *Help of the helpless, O abide with me.*
> *Swift to its close ebbs out life's little day;*
> *Earth's joys grow dim, its glories pass away;*
> *Change and decay in all around I see;*
> *O thou who changest not, abide with me.*
> *I fear no foe with thee at hand to bless;*
> *Ills have no weight, and tears no bitterness.*
> *Where is death's sting? where, grave, thy victory,*
> *I triumph still, if thou abide with me.*
> *Hold thou thy Cross before my closing eyes;*
> *Shine through the gloom, and point me to the skies:*
> *Heaven's morning breaks, and earth's vain shadows flee;*
> *In life, in death, O Lord, abide with me!*

# 2095 – They Fly So High

# Chapter Fourteen

**T**WO HUNDRED years of football! The West Ham bicentenary. Our first game against New Wapping was worth the trip, although I hate the shuttle. Nearly 30 hours cramped up with 150 others, half of whom are guaranteed to be spacesick at some point — and we only have two toilets — is not my idea of fun, but who can afford to go light speed?

It was a good match, boding well for the coming season. Wapping are a decent enough side. Promoted last year, they might do all right in the M & M's Solar System League. But they were up against the champions today. Gz, the lad from Jupiter, did well in goal, pulling off half-a-dozen great saves in the first half. There's a lot of people who are very sceptical about bringing in players from other planets, but the odd one seems to be a good idea (and Gz is very odd!). Most of our team are local, though. But I don't think we'll see another team like our 2086 championship side, one that can win a major trophy just with people from Earth.

Rosty Oask played a captain's role today. Not only did she marshal the midfield, but she scored a magnificent goal. Following the early pressure from Wapping, Tadcalf broke through the centre, his inch-perfect pass to Margie Bliff just beating the offside. Young Marg beat three defenders, including that nutter Lump. The Bull from Moon they call him (he's a bull from the Moon see), before laying back for Oask. Rosty flicked it up and then belted it on the volley. Gradshaw, the Wapping 'keeper, didn't stand a chance. To their credit they came back at us, though. Plob went close and Yazmri Condyke brought out a magnificent save from Gz, but at half-time we were well in control.

We came out for the second half a new team, well practically, Rolo Ferdinand had used seven of the 12 substitutes. Rolo is a real club man. His great-grandfather, his grandad, and Mum, like him, played for and eventually managed West Ham. What a family. All great internationals too. The old man, Rio, got 153 caps when they used to play for countries. Roko got 65 Continental caps and Rolo's Mum, Reno, played for the Earth no less than 12 times, once as skipper, (against Neptune).

Kracker, the Gorgon, banged in our second with ten minutes of the second half gone. One of his 50-yard specials. Straight as a laser. Soon afterwards he got into a terrible fight with Lump and both were sent off for an early cleanse.

The game then got a bit bogged down in a midfield chess match. Tablet did hit the virtual post near the end, but for the most part West Ham were coasting.

I was glad to get home, though. Even if it meant straight into work. It's not the easiest of lives in the docks. You can find yourself stuck in for up to two hours if a big shipment is going out. Most of the traffic in the Carling is Moon stuff, but about once a week we'll have a freighter going out to Pluto or Uranus. Their big galluts, and even with jet loaders can take 30 minutes to fill.

But I'm already thinking about next week's 'derby' game. Away to Wimbledon. I've booked my place on the club transport. Forty minutes in the sky and I'll be landing right outside the 'Hammam'. The best stadium in the cosmos. It's a magnificent ground, surrounded by 'Disney Land Tashkent'. Wimbledon moved there just two years ago from their old ground, 'The Vinney', in Alaska. Last season they were our main rivals in the League. Indeed, we needed to win the last match of the term against them, in Tashkent, to retain our quadruple Cup, League, Earth Vase and Inter-Toto Shield. We needed all five points to snatch the League from them for our tenth straight title.

The atmosphere was incredible. 200,000 fanatical Wimbledon fans almost filled the Kinnear End. As always we outnumbered them, but they really wanted to break our run and be the first side in a decade to stop West Ham taking the title. The first 20 minutes were fast and furious. Both sides were going for it, but most of the attacks petered out before anyone could come close. Then, on the half-hour, Halooo, the Wimbledon winger, broke infield from the left. He darted passed Bloink and shot, low and hard, just outside the first penalty area. Our goalie, Porlor, made a terrific three-handed save, but in the process knocked the ball out to the incoming Shifty, who lobbed it over the fallen 'keeper. The Dons' fans and players went ecstatic. It was the first goal scored against us that season.

As the players came out for the second half, we noticed that Rolo had brought on the Spanner sextuplets, Ted, Ned, Fred, Jed, Red, and Mon-Kee. Oask moved out of midfield to lead the attack. West Ham meant business. We really lashed their goal and had the big Saturnian, Nnvgtx, diving all over the place. First Ted and Mon-Kee combined well to get the ball to Oask. She sent in a cross that caught Fred Spanner on the rise. His header cannoned against the bar. Next, Red sent in a delicate chip to loft the ball over the defenders for Rosty, who feigned with her right and then smacked in a left-footed drive from close range. It hit Nnvgtx on the legs as he threw himself the wrong way. It was all Wimbledon could do to keep up with play. Every time they got possession, a Spanner was on them, hustling the ball back and making a charge for goal.

With time floating by we were caught on the break. Dob went galloping through the gap. Porlor came off his line and Dob committed himself. The ball hit the inside of the left post and scuttled the length of the goal-line. As it trickled towards the right post we knew that if it struck it would be deflected in, and we would have as good as lost the title. Porlor and Dob were up and racing towards to the ball. Dob just had the advantage. From nowhere Oask screeched into the goal, got behind the ball and booted it off the line for a throw. That was the turning point. Less than a minute later Rosty scored a great solo goal. Winning the ball from the Sciv following the throw-in, she made directly for Nnvgtx, jiggling past four defenders on the way. She rounded the 'keeper, stood for a second with her foot on the ball, waving to us with both hands, before tapping the ball in and taking a bow. This gave Nnvgtx the hump and he pushed the gutsy little East Ender. To our delight she laid the nut on him and he fell to the ground. Ms Hititic ran to the scene as blood poured from Nnvgtx's nose. She could do nothing but send Rosty off. Wimbledon brought on a substitute 'keeper and the game was restarted. But it made little difference. Mon-Kee took over as skipper and immediately moved the midfield forward, keeping the back four tight. Wimbledon were confused. They wanted to come forward but were being kept busy holding us off. The Hammers were not letting one pass reach its mark and when Wimbledon did have possession, they were harried without mercy. They started to go for the draw, which would be enough for them. This was their downfall. Allowing attacks to come in meant that it was only a matter of time before one paid off. But we were running out of time. Hititic was looking at her watch when Jed picked up full-back Martin Klub's long pass. Speeding down the right, he signalled for a general charge. He slowed in space, looked up and played the ball square to Bilge. With a Wimbledon defender coming at him, he quickly passed it back to Jed who, in one touch, centred the ball. Meanwhile, wily old Mon-Kee shuffled in on the blind side of the Wimbledon defence. He drifted in to meet the ball with a powerful diving header. We were 2-1 up. The Spanner family had only just finished celebrating when the referee blew full-time. Champions again! *Bubbles* rang around the Hammam. The Wimbledon fans stood to applaud us. They knew history had been made.

So, we go into another hundred years. What will it bring? It could be even more glory for the Hammers. But who knows? When I look at our history it seems anything can happen. For example, our first Cup game this season is against little Manchester United. Football is a funny game. The minnows will have their day. Even junt from the lowly English Premiership can come up trumps once in a green comet. But I don't think so. We've got to go to their place, New Traffic or something its called. They're sponsored by Walls, the condom people. Well they'll need some protection. I've got my new shirt for the game. I got all the shirts last season, home and away. I don't know how they think up the designs. I mean, there were over a hundred games last season. I quite like this one. Round neck. Mostly all light blue with two claret hoops around the centre. The Dagenham Intergalactic Transport logo is quite discrete. They went back to sponsoring the shirt this season. I suppose the left sock promotion wasn't as successful. Haagen-Dazs has got that this year, Casio sponsors the right one. The shorts have been taken by Paddy's Curry Houses and both boots have gone to Nissen. Apparently if gloves or hats are worn at any point TyPhoo Lasers will be advantaged. *The Sun* has a hand in the sports bras and jock straps (of course).

Well, I look the part, now I'm off down to Upton Park for the Bicentennial bash. The Boleyn is an 'all-stander' now, no more of those uncomfortable seats and that lack of atmosphere. One of the advantages of modern stadiums is that you can do a rollicking good knees-up with no obstacles. All the 200-strong squad will be there and Gretty Norm, interplanetary superstar and local boy done good. They will be performing a new version of *Bubbles* — *Bubbles, blowing*. See you at the Tricentenary.

## Or …2047 — They Fade and Die?

Last game of the season, the last-ever dog fight against relegation. The end of the world, Ibrox Park. It's them or us. The loser today is out of the British League Division Six, and must fold. There was a core of ardent fans who made the trip. We don't have many who can make the journey, but with 20 million out of work, it's amazing the few who cheered the lads on made it. The fan base has really eroded. The virtual game has taken over and you can be who you like, where you like. Why would you go outside and breath the fumes in order to go to Upton Park? Of course, the big boys, Torquay, Brighton and the rest, get the fans along, but then they have air fumigation at most of the big indoor venues.

I will not describe the match. It is enough to say that we lost. It was a nasty game played in anxiety and fear. Now there is no more West Ham. We are marched back to the trucks to the *Thunderbirds* march, the awful anthem of the League, by the mili-police for the long, torturous journey back to London. Perhaps it will be less than the 40 hours it took to get here, but I hear the traffic is solid from Manchester on. The Devonshire Monastic Militia have blown up the MA1 again.

I have watched West Ham crash through the divisions over the last 20 years. Lack of investment – there's only so much room at the top. I think the beginning of the end was so long ago. At the turn of the century we watched as Fulham and Orient were bought by big investors. We stayed small. The board were mean and the rot set in.

What will we do now? It is impossible for someone like me just to take up with another club. It's not just the money, but how do I support Brentford or Orient? They are great sides, but they are not mine. I have to do what my play wife tells me, to get in touch with reality. But that's none too attractive. When I was on a past trip once I saw galleries full of pictures, of landscapes and people and animals. There were places where people could go and watch other people act out other lives and there were tablets full of words that people would look at and think about their lives and the lives of others. Dad used to tell me about this stuff, but I put it down to his madness. If these things still existed, then I'd be all right. But now the dreams are no more.

Maybe it is all for the best. Perhaps it was always 'Just a game', 'Twenty-two idiots running round after a ball'. Maybe it's all too creative. As the mega-party says, "Creativity is more subversive than destruction." And this can only lead to a lack of rest. 'Rest' is all important. You see the big sides don't encourage creativity, they do it all for you, your support is irrelevant, that's why it's so quiet at the big grounds. It doesn't matter if you're there or not. Oh dear, my buzzer is going. They've detected my thinking. Now I'm for it...

# Epilogue

WE ALL ARE the result of our dreams. What in this book has been real? All the characters are products of your mind, be they players or supporters. The grounds are habitats of the sentient. We make these things. Who knew Bobby Moore, or Danny or Willow? They are all '*us*', they are our projections and, as such, our creations. West Ham will be what people want it to be, one day villainous, the next glorious. They will be entertaining or boring. People will devote a small part, a great deal or nothing at all of their lives to watching, talking and thinking about them. They can carry our hopes or act as a depository of our resentment. To this extent they are useful. That is why, I believe, that while we are human we will have West Ham, or a version of West Ham. This is why they will never *fade and die.* They will be resurrected wherever there is a need for colour, hope and dreams.

Paint me desire in claret and blue. Draw me a line in my mind that makes it mine. Give me players who will energise my wishes, who will dance the poetry of glory and swiftly pass a ball of light down every channel of humanity. Make this picture a thing that can be perceived by all peoples. Make it a language that can be understood in Africa, Japan or East London. Turn and twist and rive, jive, dive. Let it not be separated by gods, or politics, wars or disasters. May it make people stronger, in solidarity, community, fraternity and let it be done … gently.

Then you would have made something. You would have evolved an idea in action. The strange hybrid of competition, that gives rise to co-operation. In the words of Big Jock of Celtic, 'a kind of socialism'.

Whisper that we are people before we are anything else; man, woman, black, white, gay, straight. Send the message along the rivers of the mind and each passage of the soul. Let everyone know that it is more than a game. Celebrate not the sport but the sup-port of what is 'us', 'we', our light and dark togetherness. Each different in a supportive whole. And it will rain bubbles of light and we will move across the pitch and will experience what it is to be one, with many. The voice of the crowd. The sway and thunder of desire. The movement of eternity and being. The deep, deep potential of dreams.

> *Our matches now are ended*
> *These our players*
> *As I foretold you, were all hammers and*
> *Are melted into bubbles, into pretty bubbles in the air:*
> *And, like the baseless fabric of the television,*
> *The twin towers, the gorgeous stadiums,*
> *The solemn League headquarters, the great Boleyn itself,*
> *Yes, all which it inherit shall dissolve*
> *And like the insubstantial Irons fade,*
> *Leave not a ball behind. We are such stuff,*
> *As dreams are made on, and our little life*
> *Is rounded with a game.*

# Glossary

Aussie: Australian

Alakeefic: Couldn't care less

Bent: Dishonest

Billy B: Billy Bonds

Bint: Tart/loose woman/girl of low repute

Blades: Sheffield United FC

Blues and Whites: Blackburn Rovers FC

Bloke: Man

Bob: A shilling, 12 old pennies

Bonce: Head

Bonk: Hit

Bonny: Bonfire

Bonzo: Billy Bonds

Boomer: Old Kangaroo

Bosch: German armed forces

Bottle: Courage

Brass Razzoo: Very small amount of money (next to nothing)

Brook, The: Trevor Brooking

Budgie: Johnny Byrne

Bung: Bribe

Chicken Run: Original stand replaced by the East stand. Torn down in 1968

Clocked: Seen/notice

Conga: Parade dance

Cotters: Tony Cottee

Cottagers: Fulham FC

Corker: Well/good/fine

Crooked: Broken/messed up

Crocked: Injured

Deep sea trader: Big ship

Dev: Alan Devonshire

Dilk: Mentally deranged person

Din: Noise

Dairy: Goodness/edge

Dollar: Five shillings (25p)

Dosh: Money

Dough: Money

Drongo: Fool

Drop: Deal

Ducker and Diver: Wheeler-dealer

Dunnage: Timber on which cargo was stowed

Fergie: Fergus Hunt

Flea Pit: Cinema

Flick: Film, Cinema show

Flog: Sell

Gallar: Idiot

Gallut: Monster

Gated: Relegated

Gooner: Arsenal supporter

Grass: Informer

Grog: Beer

Gunners: Arsenal FC

Haddicks: Charlton Athletic FC

Hammers: West Ham United FC

Huffling: Working a barge by means of an oar

Humdinger: Good

Hun: German armed forces

Irons: West Ham United FC

Job and finish: Work until ship is empty

Job Shop: Unemployment Office

John Thomas: Penis

Junt: Rubbish

Kip: Sleep

Knocking shop: Brothel

Like no one's business: Indescribable.

Magpies: Newcastle United FC

Marleesh: It doesn't matter

Man on the beach: Quay Foreman

Mike Yarwood: An impressionist

Med: Mediterranean

Maestro: Trevor Brooking

Minces: Mince pies (eyes)

Mucker: Friend

Muggo: Tea break

Mushroom: Bollard that held mooring ropes of the ships

Nabbed: Arrested

Nancy: Effeminate man

Nick: Prison

Napper: Head

Noggin: Head

Nut, out of: Mad

Okca: Crude person

Old Bill: Police

On the Block: A simple job.

On the Cobbles: Waiting to be recruited for work

On the Pencil: Tallying

On the Stand: see 'On the cobbles' above

'Oppo: Companion/friend

O's, The: Leyton Orient FC

Peelers: Police

Peg: Leg

Pen: Place where dockers would gather if they did not get work

Peterman: Safe cracker

Philadelphia Lawyer: Someone who has all the answers

Piko: Pike

Pilgrims: Plymouth Argyle FC

Pinched: Stolen
Pompey: Portsmouth FC
Pongo: Soldier
Psycho: Billy Bonds
Quack: Doctor (derogatory)
Quid: Pound (money)
Puddy: Syd Puddefoot
Prossies: Prostitutes
Railwaymen: Swindon Town FC
Rams: Derby County FC
Ricket: Mistake
Ripper: Good
Robins: Swindon Town FC and Wrexham FC
Sack: Bed
Saints: Southampton FC
Seagulls: Brighton and Hove Albion FC
Shakers: Bury FC
Sky Blues: Coventry City FC
Slope: Sneak
Smoke, The: London
Soapy/Soapo: Ingratiating person
Sock: Hit/strike
Spiffing: Good
Spliced: Married
Sparrow: Alan Taylor
Sprasey: Six old pennies
Sprog: Child
Sussed: Understood
Sweaty: Sweaty Sock: Jock: Scottish person
Syph: Syphilis
T.C.: Tony Cottee/Top Cat
T & G: Transport and General Workers Union
Tanner: Six old pennies
Tea leaf: Thief
Terminator: Julian Dicks

Thames Borley Men: Men catching shrimps on the Thames
Ticker: Ronnie Boyce
Toke: Food
Topped: Killed
Trotters: Bolton Wanderers FC
Tucker: Food
Tuppence: Two old pennies
Twerp: Fool
WEA: Workers Education Association

# Chronology

**June 1895:** Creation of the Thames Ironworks Football Club.

**1896:** Seven matches played under electric lights mounted on poles at Hermit Road ground.

**September 1897:** First match at the Memorial Grounds.

**September 1898:** Thames Ironworks join the Southern League.

**June 1899:** Arnold F.Hills (owner of Thames Ironworks) condemns the football club for being professional.

**July 1900:** Formation of West Ham United Football Club Ltd.

**September 1901:** E.S.(Syd) King is appointed secretary of the club.

**May 1904:** West Ham United move the Boleyn Ground.

**February 1911:** West Ham defeat Manchester United in the FA Cup.

**August 1912:** Charlie Paynter appointed trainer and coach of the first team.

**April 1917:** West Ham win the London Combination War League.

**April 1918:** West Ham are runners-up in the London Combination War League.

**April 1919:** West Ham finish third in the London Combination War League.

**August 1919:** West Ham joins the Football League Second Division.

**1921:** First game on the continent v Madrid (won 4-0).

**December 1921:** First home game against foreign opposition v Harlem of Holland (won 4-2).

**February 1922:** Syd Puddefoot is transferred to Falkirk for £5,000 — a record fee for an English player to a Scottish club.

**March 1923:** Benefit match for the Docklands Settlement is played with the Duke of York attending.

**April 1923:** West Ham defeated 2-0 by Bolton Wanderers in the first FA Cup

Final to be played at Wembley — the 'White Horse Final'. West Ham are runners-up in the Second Division and are promoted to the First Division for the first time.

**May 1923:** West Ham become the first English club to visit Germany since the end of the First World War.

**August 1923:** West Ham play their first match in the First Division (v Sunderland, 0-0) and their first home match in the First Division (v Arsenal; West Ham win 1-0).

**October 1925:** King Faisal of Iraq is among the near-30,000 crowd who watch West Ham beat Notts County.

**February 1929:** Vic Watson establishes the club record for goals scored by an individual in one game by scoring six goals at home to Leeds.

**April 1930:** Vic Watson scores his 50th goal of the season, completing a hat-trick at home to Aston Villa. This is a record for a West Ham player in one season.

**April 1932:** West Ham relegated to the Second Division.

**November 1932:** Charlie Paynter is appointed manager.

**January 1933:** Syd King is dismissed and commits suicide.

**March 1933:** West Ham reach the semi-final of the FA Cup (v Everton, West Ham lose 2-1).

**December 1934:** Vic Watson scores his final goal for the club, at home against Bury. He holds the club record as a goalscorer with 326 in all competitions.

**April 1936:** Director A. C. Davis suggests that West Ham may be better off staying in the Second Division.

**June 1940:** West Ham win Football League War Cup (v Blackburn Rovers, 1-0).

**August 1944:** Boleyn Ground struck by flying bomb.

**August 1945:** Len Goulden transferred to Chelsea for £4,500. The FA Cup competition is resumed. West Ham in the Football League (South).

**August 1946:** The Football League proper resumes. West Ham play in the Second Division.

**July 1950:** Charlie Paynter retires. Ted Fenton takes over as manager.

**February 1951:** Malcolm Allison is transferred from Charlton for £7,000.

**16 April 1953:** First floodlit match at Upton Park v Spurs (won 2-1).

**22 March 1955:** First live televised match from Upton Park v Holland Sports (0-0).

**19 March 1956:** First League game under floodlights v Bury (won 3-2).

**May 1957:** Youth Cup Final v Manchester United (lost 8-2 on aggregate).

**April 1958:** West Ham win the Second Division championship and are promoted to Division One.

**October 1958:** First League match for Bobby Moore.

**November 1958:** Supporters Club officially recognised.

**May 1959:** West Ham buy the Boleyn Ground for £30,000.

**March 1961:** Ted Fenton resigns.

**April 1961:** Ron Greenwood becomes manager.

**March 1962:** Johnny Byrne is transferred from Crystal Palace for £65,000, a record fee between English clubs.

**April 1963:** Youth Cup Final v Liverpool (West Ham win 6-5 on aggregate after extra-time).

**February 1964:** West Ham reach the semi-final of the League Cup (v Leicester; West Ham lose 6-3 on aggregate).

**May 1964:** West Ham win the FA Cup (v Preston North End, 3-2).

**September 1964:** First West Ham match in a European competition (v La Gantoise in the Cup-winners' Cup).

**May 1965:** West Ham win the European Cup-winners' Cup (v TSV Munich, 2-0).

**August 1965:** West Ham's Peter Bennett becomes the club's first-ever substitute in the Football League (v Leeds at Upton Park — West Ham win 2-1).

**March 1966:** West Ham reach the Final of the League Cup (v WBA, West Ham lose 5-3 on aggregate).

**April 1966:** West Ham reach the semi-final of the European Cup-winners' Cup (v Borussia Dortmund, West Ham lose 5-2 on aggregate).

**July 1966:** England win the World Cup. Bobby Moore, Martin Peters and Geoff Hurst, all West Ham players, take part. Hurst scores three and Peters one in the 4-2 win for England. Moore captains the side.

**January/February 1967:** West Ham reach the semi-final of the League Cup (v WBA, West Ham lose 6-2 on aggregate).

**May 1967:** Bobby Ferguson is transferred from Kilmarnock for £65,000. A world record fee for a goalkeeper.

**October 1968:** Geoff Hurst scores six goals against Sunderland, equalling Vic

Watson's record for the most goals scored by an individual in one match.

**December 1971/January 1972:** West Ham reach the semi-final of the League Cup. (v Stoke). After two legs and three replays West Ham are defeated 3-2.

**March 1975:** John Lyall is appointed team manager.

**May 1975:** West Ham win the FA Cup (v Fulham, 2-0).

**May 1976:** West Ham reach the Final of the European Cup-winners' Cup (v Anderlecht, West Ham lose 4-2).

**May 1977:** First all-ticket match at Upton Park since before the Second World War (v Manchester United. West Ham win 4-2).

**December 1977:** John Lyall appointed manager following Ron Greenwood taking up the job as England manager.

**May 1978:** West Ham finish 20th out of 22 and are relegated to the Second Division.

**May 1980:** West Ham win the FA Cup (v Arsenal 1-0).

**August 1980:** Paul Goddard is transferred from QPR for £800,000.

**October 1980:** Second leg of the Cup-winners' Cup tie v Castilla is played at Upton Park behind closed doors. Spectators were banned by UEFA.

**April 1981:** West Ham draw with Liverpool in the League Cup Final (1-1). Liverpool win the replay (2-1).

**May 1981:** West Ham win the Second Division championship and are promoted to Division One.

**21 April 1986:** West Ham beat Newcastle United 8-1. Captain Alvin Martin scores a hat-trick against three different goalkeepers.

**May 1986:** West Ham finish third in the First Division, the highest final placing achieved in the history of the club.

**9 May 1987:** Billy Bonds wins Hammer of the Year award at the age of 40.

**July 1988:** Tony Cottee is transferred to Everton for £2.2m, a British record.

**February/March 1989:** West Ham reach the semi-final of the League Cup (v Luton, West Ham lose 5-0 on aggregate).

**May 1989:** West Ham finish 19th out of 20 and are relegated to the Second Division.

**July 1989:** John Lyall sacked.

**July 1989:** Lou Macari appointed manager.

**February 1990:** Lou Macari resigns.

**February 1990:** Billy Bonds appointed manager.

**February/March 1990:** West Ham reach the semi-final of the League Cup (v Oldham, West Ham lose 6-3 on aggregate).

**April 1991:** West Ham reach the semi-final of the FA Cup (v Nottingham Forest, West Ham lose 4-0).

**May 1991:** West Ham are runners-up in Division Two and are promoted to Division One.

**November 1991:** Bond scheme launched.

**May 1992:** West Ham finish bottom of Division One and are relegated – to Division One.

**February 1993:** Bobby Moore dies.

**March 1993:** Bond scheme collapses due to supporters' action.

**May 1993:** West Ham are promoted from the new Division One to the Premier League.

**August 1994:** Billy Bonds sacked.

**August 1994:** Harry Redknapp appointed manager.

## All 'first-class' competitive matches in 100 years:

| | P | W | D | L | F | A |
|---|---|---|---|---|---|---|
| **Total** | 4,343 | 1,793 | 1,039 | 1,511 | 7,120 | 6,300 |

We win by 820 goals or about 5-4 (good game!).

# Bibliography

Allison,M. *Colours of My Life* — Everest 1975

Banks,R. *An Irrational Hatred of Luton* — Independent 1995

Boyle,J. *A Sense of Freedom* — Pan 1977

Barber,D. *We Won the Cup* — Pan 1981

Barrett,N. *The Daily Telegraph Football Chronicle* — Carlton 1994

Beilenson,J.P. *The Gift of Hope* — Peter Pauper 1994

Berrigan,F. *Animation Projects in the UK* — Leicester 1976

Blows,K. *Terminator* — Polar 1996

Branson,N. *Poplarism* — Lawrence and Wishart 1984

Brooking,T. *Trevor Brooking* — Granada 1982

Butler,B. *The Official History of The Football Association* — Queen Anne 1991

Campbell,D.& Shields,A. *Soccer City* — Mandarin 1993

Churchill,R.C. *English League Football* — Sportsmans 1962

Cook,C. and Stevenson,J. *Modern British History* — Longman 1988

Cottee,T.& McDonald,T. *Claret & Blues* — Independent 1995

Cunningham,V. *Spanish Front* — Oxford University Press 1986

Durkheim,E. *The Elementary Forms of The Religious Life*. — Allen & Unwin 1976

Edman,I. *John Dewet* — Greenwood 1968

Fenimore Cooper, J. *The Last of the Mohicans* – Penguin 1996

Fleming,J.& Honour,H. *A World History of Art* — Laurence King 1995

Foucault,M. *Discipline and Punish* — Penguin 1977

Francis,D. *West Ham United Official 1996-97 Handbook* — Independent 1996

Gambaccini,P., Rice, J.& Rice,T. *Top 40 Charts* — Guinness 1997

Gilbert,A (ed). *The Desert War* — Sidgwick and Jackson 1992

Green,G. *Soccer in the Fifties* — Ian Allan 1974

Greenwood,R. *Yours Sincerely Ron Greenwood* — Collins Willow 1984

Heatley,M.& Ford,D. *British Football Grounds Then and Now* — Dial 1994

Hirst,P. *Associative Democracy* — Polity 1994

Hopcraft,A. *The Football Man* — Collins 1970

HMSO *People in Prison* — HMSO 1971

Hogg,T. and McDonald,T. *Who's Who of West Ham United* — Independent UK Sports 1996

Humphries,S. *Hooligans or Rebels?* — Blackwell 1995

Inglish,F. *The Name of the Game* — Heinemann 1977

Joyce,M. *It's Only a Game* — George Williams YMCA College 1997

Kelly,S.F. *A Game of Two Halves* — Mandarin 1992

Korr,C. *West Ham United* — Duckworth 1986

Leech,M. *The Prisoners' Handbook 1995* — Oxford University Press 1995

Lyall,J. *Just Like My Dreams* — Penguin 1989

McDonald,T.& Baskcomb,J. *West Ham United Official 1991-92 Handbook* — Colour Print 1991

McDonald,T.& Blowers,S. *West Ham United Official 1994-95 Handbook* — Independent 1994

Maclean,N. *A River Runs Through It* — Pan 1990

Mason,T. *Association Football and English Society 1863-1915* -Harvester 1980

Masters,J. *Fourteen Eighteen* — Corgi 1970

Melville,H. *Moby Dick* — Oxford University Press 1992

Moore,G.(ed.) *Robert Frost* — Clarkson, N.Potter 1994

Northcutt,J. & Shoesmith,R. *West Ham United: A Complete Record* — Breedon 1993

Oxford University *The English Hymnal* — Oxford University Press 1994

Pallot,J.(ed) *The Virgin Film Guide* — Virgin 1996

Palmer,A.W. *Modern History* — Penguin 1978

Parker,N. *Parkhurst Tales* — Smith Gryphon 1994

Pearson,G. *Hooligan. A History of Respectable Fears* — Macmillan 1993

Preston,P. *The Spanish Civil War* — Weidenfeld & Nicholson 1986

Pickering,D. *The Cassell Soccer Companion* — Cassell 1994

Powell,J. *Bobby Moore* — Robson 1993

Preston,P. *The Spanish Civil War* — Weidenfeld and Nicholson 1986

Prole,D. *Football in London* — Hale 1964

Rollin,G.*Rothmans Football Yearbook* — Headline 1996

Simpson,W.O. *Changing Horizons. Britain 1914-80* — Stanley Thornes 1986

Stern,V. *Bricks of Shame. Britain's Prisons* — Penguin 1989

Stevenson,R.L. *Treasure Island* — Wordsworth 1993

Taylor,R.& Ward,A. *Kicking and Screaming* — Robson 1995

Tuan,Y. *Space and Place* — Edward Arnold 1977

Vaughan,C.(ed.) *Quintessential Pleasures* — Thames and Hudson 1994

Wagg,S. *Giving the Game Away* — Leicester University Press 1995

Wenborn,N. *The 20th Century* — Hamlyn 1989

West,W.J.(ed) *George Orwell. The War Broadcasts* — Penguin 1987

Whitfield,D.(ed) *The State of the Prisons — 200 Years On.* — Routledge 1991

Woolf & Tumin,S. *Prison Disturbances April 1990* — HMSO 1991

Young,M.B. *The Vietnam Wars* — Harper Perennial 1991

Young,P.M. *A History of British Football* — Arrow 1968